MANAGING WORKER SAFETY AND HEALTH FOR EXCELLENCE

MANAGING WORKER SAFETY AND HEALTH FOR EXCELLENCE

MARGARET R. RICHARDSON

VAN NOSTRAND REINHOLD
I(T)P® A Division of International Thomson Publishing Inc.

New York • Albany • Bonn • Boston • Detroit • London • Madrid • Melbourne
Mexico City • Paris • San Francisco • Singapore • Tokyo • Toronto

Cover design: Greg Simpson

I ⓣ P®   An International Thomson Publishing Company
         The ITP logo is a registered trademark used herein under license

Printed in the United States of America

For more information, contact:

Van Nostrand Reinhold   Chapman & Hall GmbH
115 Fifth Avenue   Pappelallee 3
New York, NY 10003   69469 Weinheim
                                         Germany
Chapman & Hall
2-6 Boundary Row   International Thomson Publishing Asia
London   221 Henderson Road #05-10
SE1 8HN   Henderson Building
United Kingdom   Singapore 0315

Thomas Nelson Australia   International Thomson Publishing Japan
102 Dodds Street   Hirakawacho Kyowa Building, 3F
South Melbourne, 3205   2-2-1 Hirakawacho
Victoria, Australia   Chiyoda-ku, 102 Tokyo
                                         Japan
Nelson Canada
1120 Birchmount Road   International Thomson Editores
Scarborough, Ontario   Seneca 53
Canada M1K 5G4   Col. Polanco
                                         11560 Mexico D.F. Mexico

1 2 3 4 5 6 7 8 9 10 MP 01 00 99 98 97

Library of Congress Cataloging-in-Publication Data

Richardson, Margaret R.
    Managing worker safety and health for excellence/Margaret R. Richardson.
        p. cm.
    Includes bibliographical references and index.
    ISBN 0–442–02393–6 (hc)
    1. Industrial safety. 2. Industrial hygiene. I. Title.
T55.R49 1997
658.3'82—dc21   97–9095
                                                         CIP

http://www.vnr.com
product discounts · free email newsletters
software demos · online resources

email:info@vnr.com

A service of I ⓣ P®

To those who pioneered the Voluntary Protection Programs, both in government and private industry. Their faith, trust, pride, and relentless quest for excellence will resonate for years to come.

Contents

Preface   xv

PART 1. Introduction   1

1. The Voluntary Protection Programs (VPP)
   and Excellence   3

   Background   5
   Benefits from the VPP   17
   The VPP Participants' Association   20
   The Future of VPP   21
   References   22

PART 2. **Closing the Management Loop:
A Structure for Zero-Defect
Management of Safety and Health**   25

2. Introduction to the Management Loop   27

The Voluntary Guidelines   28
Zero-Defect Management   29
The Management Loop   31
References   33

3. Providing an Effective Policy   35

The Purpose of the Safety and Health Policy   35
The Length of Written Policy Statements   36
Communicating the Written Policy   38
Communicating the Safety and Health Attitude   39
*Developing or Revising the Written Safety
    and Health Policy*   40
Key Points   40
References   41

4. Establishing an Overall Goal for the Safety
   and Health Program   43

Purpose of the Goal   44
Descriptive versus Numerical Goals   44
Communicating the Goal   47
Setting or Revising the Goal   48
Key Points   48
References   49

5. Setting Objectives for the Safety and Health
   Program   51

Establishing a Baseline   52
Types of Objectives   54
Ensuring Clear, Measurable Short-term Objectives   58
Communicating Objectives   60
Key Points   61
References   62

6. Assigning Safety and Health Responsibilities   63

   Basic Ongoing Responsibilities   65
   Short-Term Responsibilities   72
   Ensuring Appropriate Authority and Resources   73
   Communicating Responsibility   76
   Key Points   76
   References   77

7. Making Accountability Work for Safety
   and Health   79

   Foundations for Accountability   80
   Accountability Systems   81
   Key Points   87
   Reference   87

8. Evaluating Safety and Health
   Program Effectiveness   89

   Getting Evaluation Right   93
   Scope of Evaluation   97
   Choosing the Evaluators   97
   Information-Gathering Tools   99
   Evaluation Judgments   103
   Written Evaluations   106
   Use of the Evaluation   106
   Key Points   107
   References   108

9. The Closed Management Loop   109

PART 3. **Achieving Total Involvement
   in Worker Safety and Health**   *111*

10. Introduction to Total Involvement   113

   The Voluntary Protection Programs (VPP)   114
   The Safety and Health Program Management
     Guidelines   115
   References   116

11. Ensuring Line Employee Ownership
of the Safety and Health Program   117

The Benefits of Employee Involvement   119
Ways to Involve Workers   123
The Safety Culture   125
Legal Concerns   129
Achieving Ownership   131
Key Points   134
References   135

12. Making Sure the Top Manager's Involvement
Is Visible   137

*Top Manager's Safety and Health
    Responsibilities*   138
Methods for Visible Leadership   142
Benefits of Visible Management Leadership   153
Key Points   156
References   157

13. The Challenge for Safety and Health
Professionals   159

Maintenance of Professional Expertise   161
Establishing the Vision   166
Coaching Line Managers and Employees   167
Providing Continuous Evaluation   169
*Acting as the Conscience of the Safety
    and Health Program*   170
Key Points   171
References   172

14. Other Important Members of the Safety
and Health Team   173

Line Managers   174
Other Staff Professionals   180
Contractors and Their Employees   184

Key Points	*185*
References	*186*

15. The Totally Involved Workplace — *187*

Reference — *188*

PART 4. Systems Approaches to Analyzing and Preventing or Controlling Hazards — *189*

16. Introduction to Systems Approaches to Hazards — *191*

The VPP	*191*
OSHA Voluntary Guidelines for Safety and Health Program Management	*192*
References	*194*

17. The Hazard Inventory — *195*

Comprehensive Surveys	*197*
Change Analysis	*201*
Job Safety Analysis (JSA)	*206*
Process Hazard Analysis (PHA)	*207*
Phase Hazard Analysis	*210*
Key Points	*212*
References	*214*

18. Basic Tools of Hazard Prevention and Control — *215*

Engineering the Control	*216*
Work Practices	*218*
Personal Protective Equipment (PPE)	*221*
Administrative Controls	*223*
The Role of Accountability Systems in Supporting Controls	*224*
Key Points	*233*
References	*234*

19. Supplemental Tools for Hazard Control   237

    Hazard Correction Tracking   237
    Preventive Maintenance   239
    Unplanned Event Preparedness   241
    Medical Program   248
    Key Points   250
    References   252

20. When Hazards Get Away from Their Controls   253

    Routine General Inspections   254
    Employee Reports of Hazards   257
    Accident/Incident Investigations   264
    Trend Analysis   269
    Key Points   271
    References   273

21. Systematically Approached Hazards   275

PART 5. **Learning to Own Safety and Health**   277

22. Introduction to Learning Ownership   279

    The Role of Training in the VPP Requirements   280
    The Role of Training in the OSHA Voluntary
       Guidelines   280
    References   281

23. Methods to Ensure Learning   283

    Determining Training Objectives   284
    How People Learn   286
    Providing Stimulating Learning Experiences   288
    Evaluating the Learning Achieved   301
    Key Points   303
    References   304

24. Learning for Ownership   307

    Safety and Health Training in Orientation to the Job 308
    Ongoing Safety and Health Courses   311

Drills 312
Safety Meetings 323
Training Supplements 325
Key Points 326
References 328

25. Learned Ownership 329

Author's Afterword: The Future of Excellence 331

Appendixes **335**

Appendix 1. The Voluntary Protection Programs
(VPP) Process 337

Appendix 2. Further Description of a Safety
and Health Program Assessment 343

Appendix 3. Hazard Analysis Flow Charts 363

Appendix 4. Walking the Fine Line 367

Index **373**

Preface

In writing this book, I set out to reflect what has been learned by OSHA and by me, personally, from the excellent worksites and companies that have been recognized by OSHA, and more recently by the Department of Energy (DOE), for outstanding protection of their workers' safety and health. I have also learned from the fine companies and DOE contractor firms that have consulted with me in their pursuit of excellence. I have used written materials from OSHA about the management of worker safety and health protection as a starting point, because these companies and worksites are using the systems that are described. Whether OSHA learned from the companies or vice versa—and I believe that it is some of both—is irrelevant, since whoever had the ideas, they work.

Although I have used quotes from traditional safety and health experts, this is not a compilation of traditional experts' wisdom. I believe that it is one of the qualities that makes the book fresh.

There is very little technical safety or health to be found in this book. A novice safety and health professional would not be able to construct a safety program using only the information in this book because the focus here is management systems for safety and health.

Managing Worker Safety and Health for Excellence is aimed at those who want to learn everything they can about achieving excellence in an area that is a major workplace value—worker safety and health. It is intended for safety and health professionals who wish to step back and look at how the overall safety and health program is managed and where that management could be improved. It is also for those managers seeking excellent protection for their workers, who need to know how familiar management techniques can be used to help achieve this goal. In fact, it can be used by teams of managers, hourly or non-exempt workers, and safety and health professionals to assess their own management systems and guide their improvement.

Although there is much information that would "prove" the benefits of safety and health excellence contained in this book, it is not organized to make such a case.

Nor is the book a "how to" on getting into the OSHA, state, or DOE Voluntary Protection Programs. It is my personal belief that there is much to gain by applying and participating in the VPP, but the "how to" will have to await another book. Chapter 1 is an introduction to the VPP for those who have not yet experienced it. Appendix 1 describes the VPP application process briefly.

Although the book takes its information mostly from worksites and companies in the VPP, it is not necessary to join the VPP to use these systems to keep workers safe and to achieve excellence. Certainly, constructing a safety and health program based on this book will make attaining VPP approval relatively easy.

The reader will note that I have used a lot of material from an unpublished manual prepared by OSHA staff. There is some question about whether that manual will ever be published and, if that is the case, why I would want to quote it. The answer is twofold. First, the unpublished manual contains much good material that was gleaned from the VPP experience that should not be allowed to go to waste. Second, over the years since 1990, when the major substance of the manual—as opposed to editing revisions—was completed, OSHA and the VPP Participants' Association have given out several thousands of draft copies. So that regardless of whether the report is ever published, it probably can be considered to be in circulation.

I would like to acknowledge the assistance I received from my husband, Bill Richardson, and Peter G. W. Keen, both of whom read every word and advised me on changes; Robert J. Brant, who read many parts of the book and always had good suggestions for additions; and Cathy Oliver, who was particularly helpful with information for Chapter 1, "About the VPP," and Appendix 1, "The Voluntary Protection Programs (VPP) Process."

Part **1**

Introduction

1

The Voluntary Protection Programs (VPP) and Excellence

The concepts of and the experience from the three OSHA Voluntary Protection Programs (VPP), State, Merit, and Demonstration, are the basis of this book. The VPP were sources of some profound changes in regulatory attitudes towards the importance of management systems in achieving worker safety and health protection. The VPP also resulted in a movement away from "command-and-control" regulation. Additionally, there was a movement in industry away from its own, in-house "command and control" as a means of achieving a safe workplace. These changes have not been completed. In fact, they may still be in their infancy.

What is most important for this book, however, is that the worksites that met VPP criteria based on methods to manage safety and health were so successful in preventing injuries. Since 1985, when combined measurements

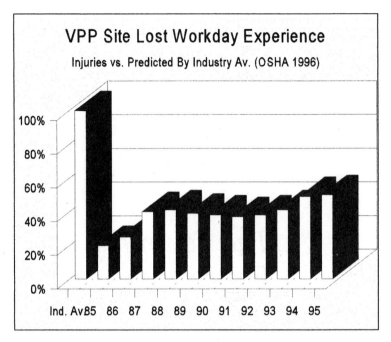

Figure 1-1. VPP site lost workday experience. *Source:* "Federal and State VPP Facts," Office of Cooperative Programs, OSHA, 7/31/96.

were first used to aggregate the VPP results in terms of individual industry averages, lost workday case rates have stayed more than 50 percent below the industry averages as a group[1] (see Figure 1-1) (OSHA 1996a). Additionally, looking at the most successful of the VPP sites over the period of time since 1982, when the VPP began,

---

[1]OSHA analysts arrive at their combined figure for worksites in many different industries with different average injury rates by calculating the number of injuries each site would have if it had injuries equal to its industry average. These numbers are then added together to make up the overall "predicted" or "expected" number of injuries. That "expected" number is then divided into the number of actual injuries at all the VPP sites to derive the percent of "predicted" injuries that actually occurred.

provides solid information about how excellence in protecting both workers' safety and their health is achieved.

BACKGROUND

The impetus of the Occupational Safety and Health Act of 1970, which created OSHA, was to provide a federal mechanism for setting technical rules to protect worker safety and health and a strong enforcement arm to ensure that these rules were followed. The Act also contained some attempts to mitigate the harshness of these goals by allowing individual states to operate their own miniature OSHAs with 50 percent funding from the federal government, and with a short list of methods to achieve the goals of the Act that included:

- Encouraging employers and employees in their efforts to reduce hazards
- Stimulating employers and employees to institute new and to perfect existing programs for providing safe and healthful working conditions
- Building upon advances already made through employer and employee initiatives
- Encouraging labor-management efforts to reduce injuries and disease arising out of employment (PL 91-596)

From its inception in 1972 until 1982 when the VPP were initiated, the agency's only activities in addition to standards setting and enforcement were those aimed at helping employers understand what the standards required them to do. Consultation could be provided over the phone by enforcement personnel or in person by state employees through the federally funded state consultation program. Training in classroom settings was also provided on a space-available basis for courses designed for agency compliance personnel. (Classroom training for private sector employers was greatly expanded in the late 1980s and 1990s.)

When the VPP were implemented to "seek out and recognize exemplary safety and health programs as a means of expanding worker protection" (OSHA 1982, 29025), they were the first OSHA steps to acknowledge that employers might be able to protect their employees beyond the requirements of the mandatory standards, and that they might want to do so for reasons other than fear of OSHA enforcement.

While it was a first step, it was not a giant step by any means. The VPP were practically a secret for ten years during which they grew very slowly. By 1992, there were still only 104 worksites approved and participating. Most applicants heard about the availability of the VPP from companies with worksites already participating in the VPP. A major push from the Clinton administration resulted in a doubling of sites (to 208) in two years (see Figure 1-2). This increase was achieved mainly by adding resources to speed the process of application review and approval for those who had already applied or decided to apply rather than by actively seeking new applicants. By July 1996, the number of federal OSHA VPP sites stood at 240 (OSHA 1996b).

Lack of resources at OSHA was not the only reason for the slow growth. During the first ten years of the VPP a great deal of misunderstanding existed among unions, employers, and even the OSHA mainstream about what VPP approval involved. The VPP require trust between a regulatory agency and employers. Many employers are wary of inviting a regulatory agency into their places of business.

Employees and their representatives also expressed trust concerns about the "inspection exemption" con-

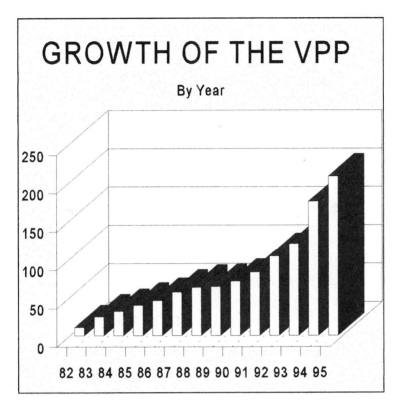

Figure 1-2. Growth of the VPP by year. *Source:* "Federal and State VPP Facts," Office of Cooperative Programs, OSHA, 7/31/96.

ferred on VPP sites. This was true as well in the mainstream of OSHA, where compliance personnel had similar concerns about trusting employers. Since the program was very small, few compliance-oriented OSHA employees had the opportunity to experience firsthand what the VPP meant.

The "inspection exemption" that caused so much concern was only an exemption from computer-generated, random inspections that were based on the average incidence rates of entire industries. No worksites were ever exempt from inspections resulting from anything that specifically occurred at that worksite, such as employee complaints or fatalities/catastrophes. VPP approvals can only follow a site visit in which OSHA employees determine whether the site met the requirements for at least one of the three VPP, including the requirement for meeting and exceeding OSHA standards.

It was only practical to rule out any inspection based solely on industry-wide injury and illness rates that might otherwise occur. This was particularly true since VPP teams returned to each approved site every year or every three years depending on the program to which each was approved.

Purpose of the VPP

OSHA has been consistent in stating that one reason for the VPP is that compliance with standards may not be enough to provide excellent protection to worker safety and health. It also clearly defined three purposes for the VPP in the 1985 *Federal Register* notice announcing changes to the VPP that remain through the current notice of requirements. These purposes are to:

- Emphasize the importance of site-specific, employer-provided occupational safety and health programs.
- Encourage improvement of those programs.
- Recognize excellence in those programs (OSHA 1982).

Another unstated purpose that has evolved is the use of the excellent programs recognized at VPP sites, particularly Star sites, as models for others to emulate. This purpose stemmed from the enthusiastic response of worksites and their employees to achieving the honor of approval, realizing the benefits, and desiring to share what they knew.

The Concepts of the VPP

The concepts of the VPP include a view of what is necessary for excellence and the respective responsibilities of the worksite and OSHA in this voluntary relationship.

Excellence

"VPP may not be the only recipe for excellence in worker safety and health protection, but it is the only one that has been successfully demonstrated in large and small worksites, union or non-union, and in every industry where it has been tried" (Oliver 1996). Through the VPP, OSHA is saying that excellent protection of worker safety and health requires a systematic approach by the employer and employees rather than solely attempting to meet the technical requirements of the mandatory standards. This does not mean that meeting the standards is not important, just that a program of systems will also ensure the meeting of standards as it goes beyond them to strive for complete protection.

The VPP also provide for quite a bit of flexibility, demonstrating an understanding that excellence cannot be mandated. For example, by permitting the worksites to come up with ways to provide "active and meaningful" participation for employees, as long as it involved both hazard identification and resolution, OSHA discovered that employees could be involved in all facets of their safety and health, including planning, oversight, and evaluation of the safety and health program itself, and that such involvement was key to higher levels of excellence. It might never have happened if OSHA had attempted to specifically mandate the employee participation methods that it knew of at the time it set the requirements for the VPP.

By requiring employee participation at all worksites, whether unionized or not, and setting safety and health program roles for line managers, OSHA also made it clear that excellence could only be achieved by full participation in safety and health programs by everyone at every worksite.

Worksite Responsibilities

The VPP were the first government statement of the (unmandated) responsibility of the worksite to find all hazards and either prevent or control them. The VPP requirement to "begin with a thorough understanding of all potentially hazardous situations and the ability to recognize and correct all existing hazards as they arise" (OSHA 1988, 26343) went beyond the Section 5 (a) (1) of the Act, which mandates that the employer shall provide employment and a place of work that are free from recognized hazards that are *likely to cause death or serious harm* to employees (PL 91-596).

For itself in the VPP, OSHA took on only the responsibility of evaluating the success of the worksite program and helping the site understand any flaws that might be found in the program. In their onsite reviews for the approval decision and again when they return, OSHA teams are looking at how well the site program of systems is being implemented and whether what is meant to be implemented is appropriate for the achievement of excellence. OSHA does not attempt to discover whether the whole site is free of standard violations, but whether their review shows that the site systems can keep workers from being exposed to hazards in violation or any other kind, understanding that if the site systems operate successfully, standard violations will be found and corrected without the need for OSHA.

The Three Programs of the VPP

The VPP is made up of three programs: Star, Merit, and Demonstration. The core program of the VPP has always been the Star program, which is intended to recognize the truly excellent protectors of worker safety and health. All other programs in the VPP are meant to lead towards Star. Merit and Demonstration, however, do not line up as second and third best. They are different approaches to Star, based on different needs.

Star

Star is meant to be limited to outstanding protectors of worker safety and health. The quantitative requirements for Star state that the average incidence rates for total OSHA recordables and lost workday cases *combined for the last three complete calendar years* be at or below the rates most recently published by the Bureau of Labor Statistics for the specific industry (at the three or four digit level, where published) (OSHA, 1988, p. 26343).

The programmatic or systems requirements of Star are basically the requirements of the VPP; however, for Star they must have been met at a high level of quality for at least twelve months preceding approval (OSHA 1988, 26343). These requirements are similar to the elements discussed in the following chapters.

Under requirements current in early 1997, once a worksite is approved for Star, OSHA returns only every three years to evaluate the program and its results, unless there is some indication of a problem. If such an indication does occur, it is usually resolved with telephone calls or a brief onsite assistance visit (OSHA 1988, 26347). OSHA's main concern is that the site understands the problem and how to resolve it, and that they will resolve it.

Proposed changes to the requirements would set a range of time between OSHA onsite visits to Star sites—

within 30 to 42 months after the initial approval and within 60 months after continued approval—that could allow periods of up to five years with no OSHA visits for Star sites after the first three years (Oliver, 1996).

Over the years of the VPP, OSHA teams have come to expect not only program maintenance but improvements from one evaluation to the next.

Merit

The Merit program is meant to recognize good protectors of worker safety and health that have demonstrated the ability and desire to be excellent. Merit sites may not have had all parts of the requirements in place for at least twelve months, and/or some parts of the program may not yet be at a level of excellence. Merit sites do not have to meet the rate requirements of Star, but they do have to show, either through a diminishing trend or through the institution of an improved program, that they will be able to meet the rate requirements within the time of their Merit approval. They are given specific goals to meet. When they meet these goals (and as long as they continue to meet the requirements they met before Merit approval) they are eligible for Star (OSHA 1988, 26345).

Merit sites are approved for specific time periods. Historically, these time periods have never been longer than five years. In early 1997, OSHA was proposing to change the requirements to limit the time for Merit approvals to five years. At or before the end of the approval period, the Merit site must be able to meet Star qualifications. They do not have to serve out the whole period of Merit approval if they can qualify for Star before that.

Under requirements current in early 1996, OSHA returns each year to Merit sites to evaluate their progress towards their Merit goals and to make sure they continue to meet Star qualifications in the other aspects

(OSHA 1988, 26348). Proposed evaluation requirements call for an agreed-upon schedule for evaluation visits with the first visit within 24 months of the approval date. Eighteen months is recommended as the best timing. The proposal still allowed for earlier evaluations when the Merit participant requests the earlier evaluation for the purpose of demonstrating that Star requirements have already been met (Oliver 1996).

Demonstration

This is the least used and least understood of the VPP. It is meant to be used to gather information about Star-level qualifications in situations or industries where OSHA does not have enough experience to know precisely what Star-level protection would entail or when some other unusual aspect of the application is involved (OSHA 1988, 26345).

For example, the Stanton Energy Center construction site was the first Demonstration program. At this construction site, 15 percent of the crafts were nonunion. Since construction VPP approval requires joint labor-management committees, OSHA needed to find out how such a committee would function where unions do not represent all hourly employees. Having volunteers from the crafts not represented by a collective bargaining agent join the union-selected craft representatives on the joint committee was the experimental aspect. There was also contract language that bound all subcontractors to maintaining effective safety and health programs and to complying with applicable safety and health rules and regulations. After one year of demonstration, the requirements for construction sites were changed to allow for this variation (OSHA 1987, 7337).

In 1996, OSHA had two Demonstration sites that were resident contractors to Star-approved sites in the chemical industry. They are testing what the qualifications for

Star would be where the applicant employer is not in complete control of the workplace. Control of the worksite has traditionally been considered to be necessary for excellence in protecting workers.

Demonstration programs have also been discussed for such situations as two regulatory agencies having jurisdiction—such as the Nuclear Regulatory Agency and OSHA for the nuclear power industry—and for industries where employees spend much of their working time in environments over which the employer has no control, such as electrical power or telephone linemen.

Demonstration sites must meet the same rate qualifications as Star sites. They must be able to demonstrate Star quality in their programs and offer alternatives, if any, that show promise for meeting the overall objective of the requirements, even if they do not meet the exact letter of them. Demonstration approvals could be considered more difficult to achieve than Star approvals, because the approved worksites are teaching OSHA what excellence is in their special circumstances (OSHA 1988, 26346).

Demonstration program approvals may last no longer than five years (OSHA 1988, 26346). Demonstration sites are currently evaluated every year. OSHA proposes to evaluate within 24 months of the last onsite visit (OSHA 1996a, VII-4).

DOE and the 18(b) States

In addition to the VPP offered by federal OSHA, the Department of Energy (DOE) offers the DOE VPP (DOE 1994) to its sites that are not under the jurisdiction of OSHA because of nuclear implications. Under agreement with OSHA, DOE may also grant VPP status to DOE non-nuclear sites under OSHA jurisdiction to save

OSHA VPP resources. OSHA has agreed to honor the DOE approvals. DOE had approved two sites for Star in 1996. Other applications, including at least one from a fossil fuel reserve, were pending. The DOE VPP requirements are similar to those of OSHA (Eimer 1996).

OSHA has delegated jurisdiction, under section 18(b) of the Act, for full OSHA programs to twenty-one states and two jurisdictions.[2] For worksites in these states and jurisdictions, the federal OSHA VPP are not available. Of these, as of July 1996, six had active VPP-like programs and had made twenty-nine site approvals. Other states were in various stages of development or consideration (OSHA 1996b).

State VPP programs may have somewhat different rate requirements. Several only offer the Star program. Otherwise, they are very similar to the federal OSHA programs. When the state and DOE approvals are added to the federal OSHA approvals, the total of VPP sites rises to 271 as of July 1996.

The VPP Participants

Figure 1-3 shows the breakdown of participants among the three VPP for federal OSHA, the states, and DOE as of July 1996. The Star program consistently has the most participants, since both Merit and Demonstration are "up or out" approvals. Some Star sites have successfully been through multiple reevaluations. In 1996, the AB Air Preheater site in Wellesville, New York had the distinction of having the longest running Star approval, continuous (no one-year conditionals) since October 1982.

---

[2] Puerto Rico and the U.S. Virgin Islands.

Numbers of Sites Per Program
(Fed, State, DOE)

As of 7/31/96

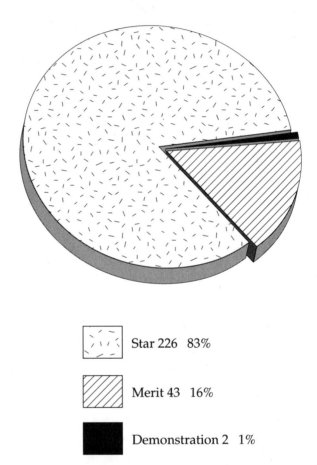

Star 226   83%

Merit 43   16%

Demonstration 2   1%

Figure 1-3. Numbers of sites per program (federal, state, DOE) as of 7/31/96. *Source:* "Federal and State VPP Facts," Office of Cooperative Programs, OSHA, 7/31/96.

The makeup of the participants in terms of the types of industry is quite varied. As of mid-1996, the chemical industry, with 74 approved sites, had more participants than any other in federal OSHA's VPP. A general category of manufacturing was the next largest, but other industries were also well represented. Figure 1-4 shows a representation of the proportion of industries in federal OSHA's VPP.

The makeup of the VPP sites in terms of collective bargaining agreements is somewhat more non-union than union. Union sites, however, tend to be the larger ones with more employees. In mid-1996, union sites were only 31 percent of all federal OSHA VPP sites, but employees at union sites made up 43 percent of all employees at all federal OSHA VPP sites (OSHA 1996b).

BENEFITS FROM THE VPP

It is clear from looking at Figure 1-1 that the comprehensive program required by the VPP does result in considerably better than average safety performance. Some VPP sites may have had to make little adjustment in order to prepare for approval to the Star program. Others may have worked hard for more than a year, or even several years, to prepare for application. Some made preparations, but were willing to work within the Merit program towards Star.

The most dramatic impact of the VPP is seen with the Merit sites that achieve Star approval. For example, Thrall Car, a maker of railroad cars, had 17.9 lost workday cases per hundred workers per year before it came into the Merit program in 1992. By 1995, it had been approved to the Star program for two years and had reduced its lost workday case rate to 1.0, a reduction of 94 percent (Catanzaro 1995).

VPP Industry Make-up (Fed. Only)

As of 7/31/96

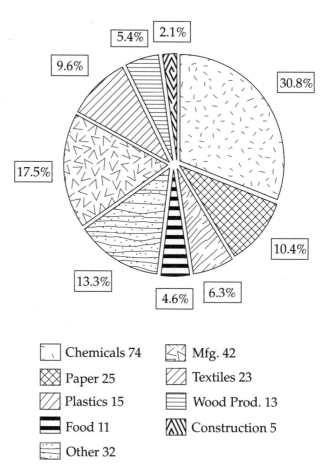

Figure 1-4. VPP industry makeup (federal only) as of 7/31/96. *Source:* "Federal and State VPP Facts," Office of Cooperative Programs, OSHA, 7/31/96.

But even sites directly approved for Star sometimes have dramatic results. For example, see Figure 12–1, concerning Mobil's Joliet, Illinois refinery.

The total involvement encouraged by the VPP has a very positive impact on the morale of employees. The most dramatic demonstrations of this are the presentations made by hourly and salaried non-exempt workers at the VPP Participants' Association (VPPPA) conferences, where the atmosphere of enthusiasm is contagious but hard to describe—it really should be experienced.

A key benefit to VPP participants is the chance to work with and learn from each other through the VPPPA. Through their contacts at conferences and committee work, VPP participants can get access to programs, policies, and procedures used by other excellent companies and worksites. They can also exchange visits to see program implementation for themselves.

The benefits to OSHA have included a slow but steady improvement in agency understanding of the importance of the way that safety and health protection is managed. By early 1996, work was well underway at OSHA on a proposal to mandate safety and health programs (Pfeffer 1996), and compliance officers had been taught the rudiments of evaluating safety and health program implementation (Oliver 1996). The establishment of safety and health programs similar to VPP requirements was the centerpiece for most of OSHA's new initiatives in 1996, whether they were compliance or cooperatively oriented.

In a more informal impact, OSHA compliance officers who did temporary assignments as members of VPP teams learned what could be accomplished by highly motivated members of worksites and could pass the information along to employers involved in OSHA compliance inspections.

The VPP Participants' Association

In 1985, under the leadership of Ron Amerson, then construction safety coordinator for Georgia Power, several representatives of participating VPP sites got together and decided to form an association to assist OSHA with publicizing the VPP. Mr. Amerson became the first chairperson of the new association.

Every year since 1985, the VPPPA has presented a conference and invited all interested parties. The 1996 conference attracted approximately 1400 attendees. The conferences feature speakers and workshops concerning OSHA, DOE, and EPA initiatives; explanations of VPP requirements; and presentations by the VPP participants about the programs and achievements at their sites. This also occurs more locally around the country as regional chapters of the VPPPA also host annual conferences.

In addition, the VPPPA also cosponsors with OSHA and DOE a mentoring program whereby an approved VPP worksite becomes the mentor for an aspiring applicant site. These sites exchange visits with safety and health professionals, hourly workers, and managers. The Oklahoma AT&T Network Systems site achieved brief fame as a mentor when its mentoring team arrived at the Oklahoma City airport to discover that their flight to Kansas City to assist Allied Signal's Kansas City Division had been canceled due to fog. Allied Signal had understood their difficulty and had given up on the visit when the AT&T crew arrived by rented van, having driven nearly 400 miles (Fitzpatrick 1995).

The VPPPA has assisted OSHA by meeting with 18(b) state plan states to help convince them to develop VPP-like programs and by educating members of Congress about the advantages of the VPP and the kind of management systems that the participating sites use. It also provided assistance and encouragement to DOE in the development of its own VPP and to EPA in the development of the Environmental Leadership Program.[3]

THE FUTURE OF VPP

The VPP ideas had generated a great deal of momentum by 1996. Budget difficulties slowed the ability of OSHA to review applications and make onsite visits, but they did continue and applications continued to arrive. The idea of VPP was becoming more firmly established. Congressional conferees put language into the OSHA budget conference report, emphasizing their support for cooperative programs and specifically the VPP. "It is the intent of the conferees that the Occupational Safety and Health Administration give high priority to effective voluntary cooperative efforts such as the Voluntary Protection Program" (House-Senate Conferees, 1996).

Both the National Safety Council (NSC) and the American Society of Safety Engineers (ASSE) gave support for the continuation and expansion of the VPP, although ASSE's was much stronger than the NSC's (ASSE 1996, 16, Scannel 1996, 7). The point of view of participating companies is well summed up by Ken De Costa of the Dexter Corporation, "VPP is a process and must be included in the overall business strategy of a company in order to be a world-class organization" (VPPPA 1996).

Even if OSHA were to find it necessary to discontinue its involvement in the VPP, some companies have indicated that they would want to keep VPP going even without OSHA. That might possibly be accomplished

---

[3]For more information about the VPPPA call (703) 761-1146 or see the Web page http://www.fiesta.com/VPPPA.

through OSHA-approved third parties or by a mechanism of the companies themselves, such as hospitals have for accreditation.

By 1996, OSHA was looking for methods to cope with the demand for VPP that would not dilute the program or its credibility but was not considering its discontinuation (Oliver 1996). The future looks very good for the VPP, and we can expect to find that VPP sites continue to evolve the concept of excellence for years to come.[4]

REFERENCES

ASSE. 1996. "ASSE Testifies to the Senate." *Professional Safety* 41, no. 3 Catanzaro, Gerry. 1995. OSHA VPP staff member, personal conversation.

DOE. 1994. *Voluntary Protection Program, Part 1: Program Elements.* Washington, DC: Office of Safety and Quality Assurance, Office of Occupational Safety.

Eimer, Ron. 1996. DOE VPP Team Leader, personal conversation.

Fitzpatrick, Don. 1995. Allied Signal, Kansas City Division contact person for VPP, personal conversation.

House-Senate Conferees. 1996. *Congressional Record* (April 25): H-3954.

Oliver, Cathy. 1996. Chief of the Division of Voluntary Programs, OSHA, personal conversation.

OSHA. 1982. *Federal Register* 47, no. 128 (July 2): 29025–29032.

OSHA. 1987. *Federal Register* 52, no. 46 (March 10): 7337–7345.

OSHA. 1988. *Federal Register* 53, no. 133 (July 12): 26339–26348.

OSHA. 1996a. TED 8.1a, *VPP Policies and Procedures Manual,* Office of Cooperative Programs, Division of Voluntary Programs.

OSHA. 1996b. Unpublished charts provided by the Division of Voluntary Programs.

Pfeffer, Ric. 1996. Department of Labor attorney assigned to the development of the safety and health program standard, personal conversation.

---

[4]For more information on the VPP call OSHA at 202 219-7266 or DOE at 301-903-2927.

Public Law 91-596. 91st Congress, 1970. "The Occupational Safety and Health Act of 1970," Sections 2 (b) and 5(a) (1).

Scannel, Gerard F. 1996. "Meet the Challenge of Compliance," *Safety + Health*, 153, no. 4.

VPPPA. 1996. "New Approvals: Dexter Corporation Steps up to Star." *National News* (Spring): 22.

Part 2

Closing the Management Loop: A Structure for Zero-Defect Management of Safety and Health

2

Introduction to the Management Loop

The phenomenal success demonstrated by the VPP participants, as described in Chapter 1, makes it clear that good management is as important as good technical safety and industrial hygiene (IH) knowledge and skills. The concept of the management loop provides an easily grasped structure that can be applied to any aspect of an organization. Its main principles are stating a clear policy, setting an overall goal and supporting objectives, assigning responsibility and holding those responsible accountable, and evaluating the results against the goal and objectives.

The management loop is certainly not a new concept—it has been integral in the efforts to achieve total quality in products and services. Yet, it is rarely seriously used in setting up or managing ongoing occupational safety and health programs. As Peterson points out,

"Management officials have not effectively used the tools of communication, responsibility, authority, accountability; rather they have chosen committees, safety posters, literature, contests, gimmicks and a raft of other things that they would not consider using in quality, cost, or production control" (1988, 12).

The VPP require management systems to locate and correct all existing and potential hazards. Although the requirements for the most prestigious of the VPP, the Star program, are that the applicant worksite's injury rates be at or below its industry average (OSHA, 1988, 28343), the VPP participants from all three programs and in widely different industries, taken as a whole, greatly exceed that requirement. As Figure 1-1 in the preceding chapter indicates, worksites participating in this prestigious program have lost workday case rates that average between 50 and 80 percent *below* their industry averages. And, these rates are not just self-reported, they are checked by OSHA for accuracy.

THE VOLUNTARY GUIDELINES

In 1989, seven years after the VPP were first implemented, OSHA published voluntary guidelines for safety and health program management that it based on their experience with the VPP. In the notice that announced these guidelines, OSHA explained:

> The Occupational Safety and Health Administration (OSHA) has concluded that effective safety and health management of worker safety and health protection is a decisive factor in reducing the extent and severity of work-related injuries and illnesses. Effective management addresses all work-related hazards, including those potential hazards which could result

from a change in worksite conditions or practices. It addresses hazards whether or not they are regulated by government standards.

OSHA has reached this conclusion in the course of its evaluation of worksites in its enforcement program, its State-operated consultation program, and its Voluntary Protection Programs.

These evaluations have revealed a basic relationship between effective management of worker safety and health protection and a low incidence and severity of employee injuries. Such management also correlates with the elimination or adequate control of employee exposure to toxic substances and other unhealthful conditions. (OSHA 1989, 3908)

The concepts discussed in Part 2 are also found in the first of the four major elements in the OSHA guidelines, "Management Commitment and Employee Involvement." In the guidelines, OSHA introduces this element as follows:

Management commitment provides the motivating force and the resources for organizing and controlling activities within an organization. In an effective program, management regards worker safety and health as a fundamental value of the organization and applies commitment to safety and health protection with as much vigor as to other organizational purposes. (OSHA 1989, 3909)

ZERO-DEFECT MANAGEMENT

Threats to the well-being of workers result from defects in the management systems set up to protect them. As Larry Hansen, Loss Control Service Manager for Wausau

Insurance Cos. in Syracuse, New York, said, "True accident causes rarely lie on the production room floor; symptoms do. Real causes are found in corporate offices and planning rooms, places not frequented by safety directors" (Hansen 1995, 28). As the National Safety Council says, "Practically every incident is the result of inadequate management action, worker and supervisor training, procedures and work conditions and/or safety rules and policy enforcement. These are management failures" (NSC 1995, 2).

This is not to say that managers should be blamed personally for every injury or occupational illness. However, it is the responsibility of management to understand potential hazards to workers' health and safety, just as it is to understand threats to efficient production and product quality and to plan for prevention or control of those threats.

In fact, the three values—productivity, quality, and safety—are closely interrelated. One case in point is the Ford New Holland plant in Grand Island, Nebraska, which during its early years in the VPP (1985 to 1988) cut its workers compensation costs in half, increased productivity by 13 percent, and had a 16 percent decrease in scrapped product (OSHA undated, 1-15).

At Wainwright Industries, a 1994 Malcolm Baldrige Award winner located in Missouri, a decision to place safety above all other concerns led not only to an 86 percent drop in workers compensation costs but also to increased customer satisfaction and profits. Mike Simms, the plant manager, believes that every aspect of the business has benefited from the priority given to safety (Smith 1995, 33).

After the first responsibility to understand all potential hazards to workers, management must then prevent those hazards or control them to reduce potential exposure. Since most hazards cannot be totally eliminated, most require engineering and/or administrative controls. Even when hazard controls can be built into a job through engineering design, there are likely to be certain instances in which the designed controls of hazards are disabled, such as during maintenance. Other management systems must then take over. A safety and health program is a complex combination of many systems that are designed to control hazards and to catch hazards that escape their controls.

One example of an escaped hazard is a pinch point on machinery that is guarded. Once the guard is removed, for whatever reason, the hazard has escaped that control and others, such as lock-out, tag-out procedures, must now take over. Another example of an escaped hazard involves a safe work procedure that protects the worker from hazard exposure. A shortcut taken by the worker bypasses the safe procedure and the hazard has escaped the control.

These escapes are defects of management. How serious they become depends upon systems that are set up to catch those hazards quickly before someone is hurt or exposed to health hazards that may take years to show resultant symptoms.

The goal, then, of the safety and health program is to allow zero defects that permit exposure to health or safety hazards.

THE MANAGEMENT LOOP

The parts of the management loop that will be described below are all included in the recommended action items for this element in the OSHA guidelines described previously. The management loop includes:

- Safety and health policy
- Overall goal for the safety and health program

- Ongoing and annual objectives
- Assignment of responsibility with adequate authority and resources
- Holding those responsible accountable
- Evaluation of program achievements

Figure 2-1 gives a visual sense of the management loop when it is completely closed. The closing of the loop occurs when the program has been evaluated and recommendations are made that result in new objectives and sometimes revised policy and overall goal for the program as well. An effective evaluation cannot occur, however, if the initial steps of the management loop have not been completed effectively. In fact, each of these steps is heavily dependent upon those that precede it.

Safety and health policy provides a statement of the attitude of the worksite toward the safety and health of its workers. The *overall goal* of the safety and health program establishes the desired result of the combined systems and activities of the safety and health program. The *objectives,* whether ongoing or set annually, allow for corrections in those programs and systems and provide the route to the goal. These three together set the stage and begin the management loop.

Assignment of responsibility follows directly upon the goal and objectives by designating who will perform what tasks to achieve the objectives. *Ensuring adequate authority and resources* are provided to those who have responsibility allows the assigned tasks to be completed. *Accountability* for those tasks emphasizes the importance of the responsibilities and ensures that the objectives will be met. *Evaluation* reviews the accomplishments of the safety and health program systems and activities and measures them against the objectives and the overall goal. Determination of needed improvements leads back to new objectives and perhaps revision of policy or goal.

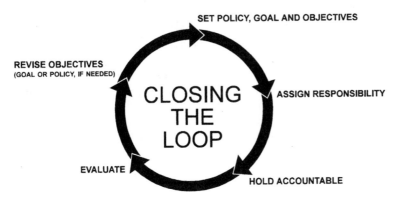

SAFETY AND HEALTH PROGRAM EVALUATION LOOP

Figure 2-1. Safety and health program evaluation loop.

By completing each step effectively, the management loop remains closed and the program running smoothly. The problem with completing these steps effectively is that they have come to be taken for granted and too often are completed without much thought. As a result, one or more steps of the loop may be ineffective. Since each step affects the others, the whole loop is weakened and less effective. In Part 2 we will examine the techniques to ensure that each step can be taken effectively so that the whole loop works to provide an excellent safety and health program.

REFERENCES

Hansen, Larry L. 1995. "Re-Braining Corporate Safety and Health: It's Time to Think Again!" *Professional Safety* (October).

OSHA. 1988. *Federal Register* 53, no. 133 (July 12): 26339–26348.

OSHA. 1989. *Federal Register* 54, no. 16 (January 26): 3904–3916.

OSHA. Undated. Unpublished manual, *Managing Worker Safety and Health*, Chapter 1, "Introducing OSHA's Safety and Health

Program Management Guidelines." Washington, DC: Office of Cooperative Programs.

National Safety Council. 1995. "In Safety, Half-truths Hide the Whole Story." *Retail Trades and Services Section Newsletter* (November/December): 2–3. National Safety Council: Itasca, IL.

Petersen, Dan. 1986. *Safety Management: A Human Approach.* Goshen, NY: Aloray.

Smith, S. L. 1995. "How a Baldrige Winner Manages Safety." *Occupational Hazards* 57, no. 2: 33–35. Cleveland: Penton Publishing.

3

Providing an Effective Policy

The concept of having a written safety and health policy for corporations and worksites is well established, and a good deal has been written about the subject. As a result of all this well-meaning attention, safety and health policy statements have become longer and longer, incorporating assignments of responsibility and even some concepts of accountability. It is possible that such statements have been refined to the point of no longer achieving their purpose.

THE PURPOSE OF THE SAFETY AND HEALTH POLICY

The purpose of the safety and health policy is simply to communicate the attitude toward the priority of protecting worker safety and health. "A safety policy is management's expression of the direction to be followed" is the way that Dan Petersen puts it. "The only important thing is whether or not management's interest is accurately communicated" (1988, 44).

In the OSHA voluntary guidelines, the action item concerning the safety and health policy is also clear on the concept of communication:

> State clearly a worksite policy on safe and healthful work and working conditions, so that all personnel with responsibility at the site and personnel at other locations with responsibility for the site understand the priority of safety and health protection in relation to other organizational goals. (OSHA 1989, 3909)

In its unpublished manual, OSHA makes a statement that warrants some thought: "Keep in mind that this written statement is not the policy. It is simply one way of communicating the policy. The real policy is your attitude toward your employees' safety and health. You demonstrate this attitude by your actions" (OSHA undated, 2-2).

THE LENGTH OF WRITTEN POLICY STATEMENTS

If the point of a policy is to reflect an attitude and if the intent of a written statement is to communicate that attitude effectively to all employees, shorter statements may achieve that result better than the paragraphs and pages we have come to expect. In the early 1990s many companies began to print their quality policy on the backs of their employees' business cards. These consisted of one or two concise sentences. By using such concise statements about their attitude towards quality, these companies were providing easy access for communication purposes. These statements were easy to read, understand, and remember.

The communication of safety policy would also be easier with a short, concise statement in one or two sentences. OSHA's draft manual gives four examples:

> "People are our most important resource. Our company's principal responsibility is the safety and health of our employees."
> "Every employee is entitled to a safe and healthful place in which to work."
> "No job is so important it can't be done in a safe and healthful manner."
> "If it is not safe and healthful, we will not do it." (OSHA undated, 2-2)

Although OSHA has not indicated where these examples come from, at least one is recognizable as close to, if not exactly, Dow Chemical Company's policy. It is also similar to Bell Atlantic's "No job is so important and no service is so urgent that we cannot take time to perform our work safely" (Lawson 1996, 38).

All of the above examples achieve a statement of priority of worker safety and health. In fact, they specifically make worker safety and health the first priority. This placement at the top of priorities was even more direct at Mobil Chemical Company's Flexible Packaging Plant in Temple, Texas. Workers interviewed at that plant in 1992 unanimously and without hesitation said that their company policy was that "safety, quality, and production are important, but safety comes first and quality comes second." Each employee said this in his or her own words, but they all conveyed the same concept of priority.

COMMUNICATING THE WRITTEN POLICY

To communicate effectively, the concepts must first be provided to those with whom communication is to occur, then understanding must be ensured, and, finally, understanding must be reinforced.

Getting the Policy to the Workers

Once a policy is written, it serves no purpose unless it is accessible to all employees of the worksite. Employee handbooks and/or posters on the bulletin board are traditional ways to communicate policy. Transmittal of personal memos or letters to all employees is another method.

Helping Ensure Understanding

However, just getting the policy to the workers does not mean that it will necessarily be absorbed. Every employee should have an opportunity to discuss the new policy and ask questions. Discussions about the new policy and what it means would make a good topic for weekly tool box talks or monthly employee safety meetings/training. Asking members of the safety and health committee to talk with the members of their work teams is another technique. A discussion of the new policy would also make a good opening lead-off topic for a meeting between the site manager and employees, particularly in view of the fact that policy is supposed to reflect attitude. Employees could provide an interesting discussion from their perspective about how well the written policy and the actual attitude match.

Reinforcing Understanding

A game of asking employees what the policy is and awarding a small prize such as a ticket for coffee or a soft drink from the company canteen for correct answers (or just publishing names of those employees giving the correct answer in the worksite newsletter) can help reinforce the learning process. Reinforcement does not even have to be that formal. If the top manager or any other manager visits production or service areas and randomly selects employees to query about the safety policy and then either expresses disappointment or pleasure with the responses, the results may be just as effective.

The best reinforcement is attitude conveyed through actions. If the safety policy is that nothing that is not safe will be done, seeing managers, supervisors, and other employees making sure of safety before proceeding and stopping activity in the face of hazard exposure will reinforce understanding of the policy much more forcefully than any other mechanism.

COMMUNICATING THE SAFETY AND HEALTH ATTITUDE

Crafting a policy statement that puts worker safety and health first in the order of priorities is all well and good but useless unless it *does* reflect the attitude of the site management. And this is only the beginning. Attitude towards safety, which is articulated by the written policy, must also be communicated by the actions taken by each and every employee at the site, starting with management and first-line supervisors. The example set by managers and supervisors speaks very loudly, communicating very clearly what the real priorities are to the workers who see and hear what management says and does.

DEVELOPING OR REVISING THE WRITTEN SAFETY AND HEALTH POLICY

If your written statement of policy is too long for ease of communication and does not clearly reflect the attitude of the worksite's members about the priority that worker safety and health has, or what you are determined it will have, it may be time to revise or redevelop that policy. Involving workers or their representatives in deciding the statement of policy is a good idea. This worker involvement in the written safety development achieves two purposes: First, worker involvement will either help assure the most representative statement of policy as it reflects the attitude toward safety and health at your worksite or help institute a more desirable attitude; second, involvement will provide the first step in making employees aware of the statement of policy.

KEY POINTS

- The real policy is the attitude about worker safety and health.
- Working with employees from all levels of your worksite to decide what the attitude of your worksite about worker safety and health should be will help get the old attitude changed.
- The purpose of the written policy is to communicate the attitude of the worksite leadership toward worker safety and health to every member of the organization.

- Communication of the policy is easier if the policy is concisely written in one or two sentences.
- Communication requires that all employees have the written policy, that they have a chance to discuss it or at least ask questions, and that some method of reinforcement of the communication occurs.
- While the written policy statement is very important, even greater communication is achieved through the examples that managers and supervisors set for the employees.

A policy statement, no matter how well communicated, by itself cannot carry the management of the safety and health program. It is but the beginning of the management loop. However, as with all beginnings, it is important. The statement of management attitude toward safety and health goes far toward setting the stage for the rest of the management loop.

References

Lawson, Connie S. 1996. "Bell Atlantic Calls on 'Safety Diligence.' " *Occupational Hazards* 58, no. 7: 38–40. Penton Publishing: Cleveland.

OSHA. 1989. *Federal Register* 54, no. 16 (January 26): 3904–3916.

OSHA. Undated. Unpublished manual, *Managing Worker Safety and Health*, Chapter 2, "Determining the Direction of Your Program." Washington, DC: Office of Cooperative Programs.

Petersen, Dan. 1988. *Safety Management: A Human Approach*. Goshen, NY: Aloray.

4

Establishing an Overall Goal for the Safety and Health Program

      The concept of a single overall goal for the safety and health program is still fairly new. While it is not clear that OSHA created the concept in the development of the voluntary guidelines, there is little, if any, reference to this concept before the publication of the guidelines in 1989. In fact, one usually sees or hears "goals" used interchangeably with "objectives." But, by clearly differentiating between the singular "goal" and the plural "objectives," OSHA has provided us with a useful concept for thinking about what we expect from the programs we put in place and a useful tool in the effective management of safety and health.

PURPOSE OF THE GOAL

In the guidelines, OSHA introduces the goal by saying, "Establish and communicate a clear goal for the safety and health program and objectives for meeting that goal, so that all members of the organization understand the results desired and the measures planned for achieving them" (OSHA 1989, 3909).

The notice containing the guidelines also has a section that provides commentary on each part of the guidelines. In the commentary on the action item concerning the goal, OSHA adds, "A goal, and implementing objectives, make the safety and health program more specific. Communicating them ensures that all in the organization understand the direction it is taking" (OSHA 1989, 3912).

It seems clear that OSHA intends that the objectives be used to achieve the goal. In its draft manual, *Managing Worker Safety and Health*, OSHA provides the analogy of a journey, saying that the policy is the reason for the trip, the goal is the destination of the trip, and the objectives provide the travel route. That analogy strengthens the concept that the goal refers to the overall result and the objectives to the means of achieving that result (OSHA undated).

Diane Whittier, Manager of Government Occupational Safety and Health Programs at Westinghouse Electric Corporation, in her remarks before a workshop audience gathered to learn about the Department of Energy (DOE) VPP, seems to have defined it exactly when she spoke of the OSHA concept of a goal as a vision of where the safety and health program should be (1994).

DESCRIPTIVE VERSUS NUMERICAL GOALS

There is, of course, more than one way to establish a vision of the overall desired result. It can be described qualitatively or specified as one or more numerical goals.

Numerical Goals

Much of the business literature in the last half of this century has emphasized the need for quantitative measurement. This is especially true of the Total Quality Management (TQM) movement. It is not surprising, therefore, to find that most seriously minded companies approach safety in a quantitative manner, such as setting annual objectives for decreasing certain numbers or rates of injuries. There are several problems with injury rate goals or objectives:

- Injuries are only half of what should be the concern of a safety and health program.
- Injuries are the end result of defects of management, but are not themselves the defects.
- Limitation of injuries is a negative goal, rather than a positive goal or objective.
- The only acceptable goal for injuries should be zero, which, as a short-term annual goal, may not be realistic.

Injuries are only half of the issue, because illnesses, which also harm workers, are frequently disregarded in numerical goals. Even if an annual numerical goal for illness were to be set, it would have to be based solely on those manifestations of illness that are easily ascertained, ignoring the fact that most chronic illnesses do not manifest themselves until long after the defect that allows exposure occurs. Setting feasible and helpful annual numerical goals for illness is highly unlikely.

Injuries are only the end result of defects. Good management should be addressing the defects before the injury occurs. While injuries are being counted, how many hazards are going unrecognized, unprevented, or uncontrolled?

By planning to limit the number of injuries, the negative is being emphasized rather than planning for positive action that would prevent the injuries.

Finally, by setting a goal that allows for any injuries at all, you are making a statement that injuries are acceptable. If you say, for example, that your goal is two lost workday injuries, it may be a big improvement from the ten suffered last year, but it says that two is okay when two is not okay. Only zero injuries is acceptable.

On the other hand, for many worksites, zero injuries may not be feasible in the short term. For other worksites, where by the nature of the type of work, hazards and/or the number of workers may be fewer, a goal of zero injuries may be too easily attained too frequently, at least in the short run, without achieving real excellence.

Descriptive Goal

In its draft manual, OSHA urges a goal that is broadly inclusive and attainable. In fact, the manual provides a goal that appears to be adaptable to most worksites—that is, to achieve "a comprehensive program that addresses all existing and known potential hazards of your worksite and prevents or controls these hazards" (OSHA undated, 2-9).

Upon analysis, OSHA's suggested goal does meet its own guidelines. The statement is broadly inclusive. It speaks of a "comprehensive program" and addressing "all existing and ... potential hazards." All ongoing and/or annual objectives should be easy enough to fit into that goal. It also speaks of either preventing or controlling those hazards. While prevention is ideal, most of the hazards addressed at the worksite will only lend themselves to control, and imperfect control at that.

OSHA's suggested goal would be attainable and yet continually challenging. It may, however, lend itself to a more narrow interpretation than OSHA probably intends. It could be improved by a slight revision and expansion to read: "A comprehensive program that addresses all existing and potential hazards of the worksite, prevents or controls those hazards, and ensures that all employees understand the hazards and their responsibilities in protecting themselves and others."

Mobil Oil Corporation uses a vision statement that the goal is "to protect the environment and the health and safety of our people and the community in which we work" (Richardson 1997).

Use of the Goal

Every part of the safety and health program should fit comfortably into the vision of the goal. If the goal has been carefully constructed, any activity conducted in the name of safety and health that does not fit into the goal probably should be discontinued. Every activity should be approached with the question in mind, Does this help us move toward the achievement of our goal? This will be discussed further in Chapter 8.

COMMUNICATING THE GOAL

Just as the safety and health policy must be provided to all employees, so should the goal. It, too, should be the subject of discussion and questions and management should make an effort to reinforce the knowledge of the goal. If the goal is a statement of the vision of the safety and health program, the desired result, then all members of the organization need to know what that is. It will help them understand the direction in which the responsibilities they are assigned as a part of that program are expected to take them and their co-workers.

SETTING OR REVISING THE GOAL

If you have not used a goal in the sense that OSHA advises you to, you will probably want to take another look at what your program attempts to achieve and set an overall goal for it. Once again, the more members of your organization, especially including the hourly workers, that can be involved in deciding what the statement of goal should be, the better.

KEY POINTS

- The goal should be a statement of the vision of the safety and health program, the overall desired result from the combination of all the systematic approaches used to help protect worker safety and health.
- The goal should not need to be changed any more often than, for example, the safety and health policy.
- The goal should be stated in a way that is understandable to every member of the organization.
- The goal should be attainable but challenging.

- The goal will serve to be the standard against which objectives and ongoing programs will be measured.
- The goal must be communicated in much the same way that the policy is.

With a policy statement that conveys the worksite attitude toward safety and health, a goal for the safety and health program that provides a healthy challenge, and both of these communicated well to all members of the organization, the management loop is well underway.

REFERENCES

OSHA. 1989. *Federal Register* 54, no. 16 (January 26): 3904–3916.

OSHA. Undated. Unpublished manual, *Managing Worker Safety and Health,* Chapter 2, "Determining the Direction of Your Program," Washington, DC: Office of Cooperative Programs.

Richardson, Margaret R. 1997. "Comprehensive Evaluations: Safety's Annual Checkup." *Occupational Hazards* 59, no. 3: 51–53. Cleveland: Penton Publishing.

Whittier, Diane. 1994. Remarks at VPPPA National Conference, Phoenix, Arizona, September 27.

5

Setting Objectives for the Safety and Health Program

There is nothing new about the use of objectives as intermediate stops along the way to the ultimate success. And yet, in practice, the setting of objectives is accomplished without relating them to an overall goal or taking care that performance against them will be measurable. The idea of objectives is also sometimes confused with quick fixes.

As noted in Chapter 4 OSHA intends that objectives be used for the purpose of achieving or implementing an overall goal for the safety and health program. To that end, they should be more short-term and more frequently revised than either the policy or the overall goal. OSHA refers to the objectives as the "travel route" for the analogy of a "journey," wherein the policy is the reason for the journey and the goal is the destination (OSHA undated, 2-1).

Establishing a Baseline

Before meaningful objectives can be set, it is necessary to have a clear idea of the status of the safety and health program in terms of measurement against the goal. If a good evaluation has already been accomplished against last year's objectives and the program goal, new objectives can be set. If not, a good and complete assessment of the program as it now exists must be made, measuring it against the goal. What is missing? What doesn't work as well as desired? What does work well?

To establish a baseline, the OSHA guidelines for safety and health management are good measures for the programs (OSHA 1989). The major elements and their action items provide a framework that can work well for any safety and health program and contain statements of what each part of the program should achieve. Figure 5-1 provides an outline of the guidelines.

Establishing a baseline is a good opportunity to get employees from all levels of the worksite involved in the safety and health program. Committee work, interviews, and surveys are just some of the means of doing this. Even in 1964, Robert K. Burns was writing about the benefits of employee participation in the setting of objectives. "Most individuals find it hard to develop a deep sense of commitment for objectives set unilaterally by others. With joint discussion and involvement, people usually accept stated objectives more readily, and become more deeply committed to their achievement" (Burns 1964).

It is also helpful to have varied perceptions and positions as measurements are made. Some of what is learned from others may come as surprises, possibly both pleasant and unpleasant. All of it will be helpful.

MANAGEMENT COMMITMENT AND EMPLOYEE INVOLVEMENT

Clear and communicated policy

Clearly established and communicated goal and objectives

Visible top management involvement

Employee involvement in the structure and operation of the safety and health program

Assigned and communicated responsibility

Adequate authority and resources

Accountability

Annual program evaluation

WORKSITE ANALYSIS

Hazard identification through:

Comprehensive surveys

Potential hazard analysis changes to the workplace

Routine hazard analysis

Regular general inspections

Employee reports of hazards

Accident and incident investigations

Analysis of trends

HAZARD PREVENTION AND CONTROL

Prevention or control of hazards using:

Engineering or substitution

Safe work procedures, training, positive reinforcement, unsafe performance correction, and, if necessary, enforcement through fair, consistent, and communicated discipline

Provision of PPE

Administrative controls

Facility and equipment maintenance

Emergency planning and preparation, including drills

Medical program

Figure 5-1. OSHA guidelines in brief.   *(continued)*

SAFETY AND HEALTH TRAINING	Analysis of work for hazards
	Maintaining physical protection
All employees understand hazards, how to protect themselves and others	Reinforcing employee training
Supervisors understand and carry out responsibilities including:	Managers understand their safety and health responsibilities

Figure 5-1. OSHA guidelines in brief (*continued*).

TYPES OF OBJECTIVES

Each part of the safety and health program must have an objective that fits into the goal. Some of these are ongoing objectives and some will be objectives to achieve over a finite period of time, usually one year. Once either a formal program evaluation or a newly developed baseline assessment is performed, objectives can be established for the short term. But there is another type of objective as well, the program objective, which provides a "goal" statement similar to that established for the overall program goal. Since these "goals" are similar to "objective points," used by the military as targets for achievement on the way to the accomplishment of an overall objective, they are called "ongoing objectives."

Ongoing Program Objectives

Every part of your safety and health program should have at least one ongoing objective that fits into the overall goal. That ongoing objective or several objectives act in much the same way as the overall program goal for the whole safety and health effort. It is a description of the end result desired from that activity.

Determining Ongoing Objectives

While the overall program goal is evaluated against the goal, each major activity should be considered in terms of what it is expected to achieve and how that fits into the overall goal. Some activities have more than one ongoing objective. If, for example, there is an employee committee or a joint management/employee committee that conducts routine general inspections for safety and health hazards, what should that activity achieve? Chances are that those committee inspections aim to achieve more than one objective. The first that might come to mind is to identify all uncontrolled hazards so that they can be controlled. Another might be to involve employees with the most intimate knowledge of the worksite in the hazard identification and control process. Still another might be to communicate to employees that hazard identification and control is important to work-site management, so that they might be encouraged to point out possible hazards to the inspection teams as they come through their areas. Regardless of what and how many they are, the objectives should be articulated and checked to see if they fit into the overall goal.

Objectives Not Related to Safety and Health

Worksite management may also have objectives for committee inspections that do not relate directly to safety and health. For example, the use of hourly employees to make safety and health inspections may also have the objective of trying out employee participation to determine whether more general employee participation at the work-site might be possible and useful. There is nothing wrong with that objective—in fact, it is valid and may very well be commendable—but it is not a safety and health objective and does not move closer to the safety and health goal. It is not, therefore, of concern in this exercise.

Activities That Do Not Fit the Goal

Some activities may be discovered that appear to have no meaningful objective in terms of achieving progress towards the overall goal. Those activities may have continued year after year simply because they have always been done. When such activities are found, one of two decisions should be made: either to discontinue the activity or to change it in such a way that it can fit into the overall goal. One note, however: If either discontinuing or changing the activity becomes uncomfortable because of the strong belief that it is valuable for protecting worker safety and health, then perhaps it is the goal that needs to be reevaluated. Does it really state what achievement is desired? Is it broad enough to include everything felt to be important?

Short-Term Objectives

When activities are evaluated against ongoing objectives, some of them may fall short. When that happens, short-term objectives are probably needed to improve program performance.

Determining Short-Term Objectives

To continue with the committee inspection example, suppose a check against the inspection objectives has been made and at least one objective is not being met. For example, the inspection team is not finding all uncontrolled hazards. Now some short-term objectives will need to be set up to help achieve that ongoing objective. What the objective will be and whether more than one objective will be necessary can be decided when it is determined why the team is not finding all uncontrolled hazards. (Making that kind of determination will be covered in Chapter 8.) Let's assume a determination that the team is not finding all uncontrolled hazards because team members do not always recognize them. In that case, an objective would be set to provide hazard recognition training to the team members, perhaps some additional or ongoing training as a follow-up, and possibly some testing or evaluation of learning.

Suppose the determination was that they were not finding all uncontrolled hazards because their procedures did not require them to enter every part of the worksite or because they are not allowed enough time to complete their inspections (or do not make them often enough). In these cases, different short-term objectives would be set to improve achievement of the ongoing objective and the overall program goal.

Short-Term Objectives versus Quick Fixes

While deciding upon short-term objectives, it is important to take care not to label quick corrections as formal objectives. If the action considered can be totally completed in less than a month, there is probably no need to set up a formal objective for that action.

Timelines for Short-Term Objectives

All short-term objectives are set with a definite time for their achievement incorporated into them. The statement of achievement time should be as specific as needed to ensure that objectives are met within the time intended. If the achievement of the objective will not be evaluated for one year but certain parts are expected to be completed before that time, the objective should provide time guidance. The formal objectives, however, do not have to specify day and month of the milestones along the way to completion of the objective. That should be left to the person or group of people who have the responsibility for the objective.

Short-Term Objective Examples

Examples of formal short-term objectives for training the inspection team might be stated as follows:

- Locate or develop and provide effective, comprehensive hazard recognition training for all inspection team members within the first quarter of the year.
- Develop and, by the second quarter, implement ongoing periodic training in hazard recognition for all inspection team members.
- Assign responsibility to a safety professional resource by the second quarter to accompany each inspection team once during the first half of the year and once during the second half, to evaluate their ability to recognize hazards, and to provide on-the-job refresher training.

The training department may then set up milestones to ensure that it meets its responsibilities for achieving the objective. The safety professional will also need to plan a schedule to make sure he or she can meet the responsibility for achieving the objective.

Ensuring Clear, Measurable Short-Term Objectives

Some of the attributes of a "well-formulated objective," according to OSHA's draft manual, are listed. The well-formulated objective

- Starts with an action verb
- Specifies a single key result to be accomplished
- Specifies a target date for its accomplishment

- Is measurable and verifiable
- Specifies what and when, avoids why and a specific how
- Is readily understandable by those who will be contributing to its attainment
- Is consistent with available or anticipated resources (OSHA undated, 2-6 to 2-8)

Starting the objective with an action verb helps guarantee that the objective will be an action that can be accomplished. Keeping each objective to a single key result helps keep the desired results clear. If, for example, the three example short-term objectives above had been combined into one objective, some of the desired results might have been overlooked.

Specifying a target date or time period helps keep the objective verifiable and measurable in the time frame you desire. If, for example, the objective for training the inspection team did not specify a time frame for providing the comprehensive training, it might not be accomplished until near the end of the year. By then, it would be too late to accomplish the other two objectives that were meant to be accomplished after the first one but before the end of the year.

Measurability and verifiability are crucial for evaluating accomplishments against the objectives. When an objective is created, the first test of it is to ask the question, How would performance be measured against it or verified as achieved? That does not mean that every objective needs to be quantifiable. Take for example our sample objective for training. "Locate or develop and provide effective, comprehensive hazard recognition training for all inspection team members within the first quarter of the year." Compare that to an objective that states only that training be "improved." Our example gives us a much clearer idea of what we are measuring our achievement against.

Limit the information in the objective to what and when. Adding the reasons for objectives or specifically how they will be achieved simply clutters them and makes them harder to communicate and be understood. The person or group developing objectives cannot be expected to be the expert on how to accomplish them. That should be left to those who have that responsibility.

Another test of any newly created objective is, Can the person who will be responsible for this or part of this understand it clearly? If not, chances are the objective will not be achieved.

Finally, if the objective is not consistent with available or anticipated resources, it is a waste of time to articulate it. For example, we might all agree that tearing down the physical plant and completely rebuilding it with state-of-the-art design would greatly improve the safety. However, if we know that we will not be provided the resources to do that, there is no point in making that an objective.

Taking time to check objectives to see how well they meet these criteria will prove worthwhile when the time comes to judge how well the objectives have been met.

COMMUNICATING OBJECTIVES

Communication of the objectives for the safety and health program is equally important but somewhat different than communicating the safety and health policy and goal. Every employee should be completely aware and completely understand the policy and goal in their entirety. Objectives, on the other hand, should be made available to all employees, who should have an opportunity to discuss them and ask questions but should not be expected to retain all of them.

Communication to those who have responsibility becomes the key. Every worker should feel some responsibility for some part of the objectives, particularly the ongoing ones. Communicating responsibility will be discussed in Chapter 7.

KEY POINTS

- Meeting objectives should take the program closer to meeting the overall goal.
- Objectives should be based on a recent comprehensive program evaluation or baseline.
- Every part of the safety and health program should have one or more ongoing objectives, which are statements of desired results.
- Short-term objectives concern specific actions needed to improve some part of the program and specify a general time frame for accomplishment, usually a month or more.
- Quick fixes, which can be accomplished in less than a month, probably do not need to be set as formal objectives.
- Objectives must be verifiable and measurable.
- Objectives must be understandable by those who will help accomplish them.
- Objectives must be communicated generally to all employees and more intensively to those who will help achieve them.

With the safety policy, goal, and objectives established, the first part of the management loop has been completed.

REFERENCES

Burns, Robert K. 1964. "Management—A Systems Approach." *ASSE Journal* (December).

OSHA. 1989. *Federal Register* 54, no. 16 (January 26): 3904–3916.

OSHA. Undated. Unpublished manual, *Managing Worker Safety and Health*, Chapter 2, "Determining the Direction of Your Program." Washington, DC: Office of Cooperative Programs.

6

Assigning Safety and Health Responsibilities

Topf and Petrino tell a story of asking employees at a small parts plant who was responsible for safety. They recount that most responded that the line safety representative, the safety department, or a supervisor was responsible. A construction worker responded that the project manager was responsible for safety (Topf and Petrino 1995).

While these workers also mentioned supervisors and managers, far too often the assignment of safety and health responsibilities appears to start and stop with the professional safety and health personnel at the worksite. More and more, however, enlightened managers understand that safety and health are line rather than staff responsibilities. Those who have responsibility for the production of the product or services of the organization should also have responsibility for ensuring that the work is done in a safe and healthful manner in safe and healthful conditions. This includes not only managers and supervisors but the employees themselves.

Safety and health professionals should not have to act as police, playing "gotcha" with managers and workers, and they certainly should not be trying to keep the worksite safe and healthful by themselves. They should act as professional resources to those who have that responsibility.

As Jim Andrews, the Safety and Loss Prevention Director for Dow Chemical Company's Texas Operations, says, "Line management has responsibility for safety. The safety professional makes recommendations. Management has the right not to accept those recommendations. If they do reject them, they bear the responsibility for the success or failure. As a result, when safety professionals stress the importance of recommendations, managers usually agree" (Andrews 1994).

Making sure that safety and health responsibility is clearly and completely assigned and that it is spread to every member of the organization is key to the successful operation of the safety and health program. This is clearly OSHA's intent in the voluntary guidelines. "Assign and communicate responsibility for all aspects of the program, so that managers, supervisors, and employees in all parts of the organization know what performance is expected of them" (OSHA 1989, 3909).

In fact, the section-by-section commentary in the notice announcing the guidelines is even more direct:

> Assignment of responsibility for safety and health protection to a single staff member, or even a small group, will leave other members feeling that someone else is taking care of safety and health problems. *Everyone* in an organization has some responsibility for safety and health. A clear statement of that responsibility, as it relates both to organizational goals

and objectives and to the specific functions of individuals, is essential. If all persons in an organization do not know what is expected of them, they are unlikely to perform as desired. (OSHA 1989, 3913)

Assigning responsibility involves writing down both basic ongoing responsibilities and those that are short-term. It also involves ensuring that appropriate authority and resources are provided to accomplish the responsibilities and that assigned responsibilities are appropriately communicated to those who have the assignments.

BASIC ONGOING RESPONSIBILITIES

It is important to distinguish ongoing responsibilities from short-term responsibilities. Just as some objectives are ongoing and broad, so are the basic responsibilities for worker safety and health. But for short-term corrections or improvements to the safety and health program, short-term objectives must also be set, and some short-term responsibilities must be spelled out formally.

In all organizations—even small businesses—responsibilities must be written down to make sure that everyone understands just what they are. In its unpublished draft manual, OSHA stresses the importance of carefully thought-out, written assignments of responsibility:

OSHA believes that, with respect to safety and health responsibilities, written statements are preferable to oral assignments. Carefully written documents:

- Remove any doubt about the responsibilities and authority of each position;
- Enhance communication and coordination among jobs;

- Aid in determining whether all responsibilities have been accounted for within the organization, and whether new tasks and responsibilities should be assigned; and
- Aid in developing job performance objectives and establishing performance measurements. (OSHA undated, 5-1)

In its draft manual, when OSHA recommends that safety and health responsibilities be part of written job descriptions, the concern is obviously for basic ongoing responsibilities (OSHA undated, 5-2) Short-term responsibilities are more likely to be found in annual personal objectives.

Some organizations, most notably the federal government, have written directive systems that tend to assign a new version of responsibility each time a new directive appears. It is difficult for employees at any level to keep track of what has been assigned them in such systems. This is particularly true of line managers, since they have leadership responsibilities in almost every area of worksite activity.

While there may not be a perfect answer for where written statements of responsibility should be located, the important point is that, wherever they are located, the persons assigned responsibility should know all of them without too much difficulty.

It is important to make sure that at least five groups of employees at the worksite have specific safety and health responsibilities. These are the top manager, safety and health manager, middle managers, first-line supervisors, and hourly or non-exempt employees.

Top Manager

The responsibilities of the top manager could be characterized as "the buck stops here." It is not so much that the top manager must take a lot of specific safety and health related actions but that he or she must ensure that these actions are taken (see also Chapter 12).

- Set the priorities so that everyone is clear about how safety relates to productivity and quality.
- Assign responsibility, provide authority and resources, and encourage active involvement in prevention of hazard exposures by employees at all levels.
- Hold subordinate managers clearly accountable for ensuring the priority of safety and health and for meeting their responsibilities.
- Demonstrate to all workers at the worksite that safety and health have the same *personal* priority as the official policy claims.
- Make good use of the professional expertise offered by safety and health, medical, and other important resources to the safety and health program.

Safety and Health Manager

Here the important concept is that the person in charge of safety and health resources, whether working alone or leading a staff, should be responsible for providing the best resources possible. Safety and health professionals should not be responsible for making the worksite safe and healthful or for catching and punishing those who break rules or ignore safe work practices (see also Chapter 13). The following are their most important responsibilities.

- Maintain safety and health expertise, including knowledge of laws and standards as well as best industry practices.

- Help employees and managers establish a vision of the safety and health program.
- Provide technical assistance, coaching, and support to the top manager, middle managers, supervisors, employees, and contractor companies operating at the worksite.
- Provide continuous evaluation of the effectiveness of the safety and health program's ability to protect employees and all who earn a paycheck at the worksite.
- Act as the "eyes, ears, and conscience" of worksite leadership where safety and health is concerned.

Middle Managers

Assignment of responsibility here is much the same as the responsibilities of the top manager, except for the fact that the scope is narrower and the personal involvement in actions is greater.

- Ensure that responsibilities are assigned to subordinate managers and supervisors to achieve the goal and objectives of the safety and health program.
- Ensure that those responsible have adequate authority and resources to accomplish their responsibilities and are held strictly accountable for their accomplishment.
- Provide visible evidence of personal safety and health involvement, including taking part in the activities of the program as well as setting a good example in following rules and safe work practices and in providing a means of direct access for employees having safety and health concerns.

- Understand the hazards and potential hazards of the worksite to the extent of being able to judge the quality of the overall safety and health program in protecting those employees and contractor companies for whom the manager has responsibility.
- Make good use of the professional expertise offered by safety and health, medical, and other important resources to the safety and health program.

Supervisors

Responsibilities for first-line supervisors need to be more specific (and numerous) than those for managers.

- Know and understand the hazards and potential hazards of the work operations for which each supervisor is responsible.
- Insist on good housekeeping practices and that all areas, equipment, and tools are maintained for safe and healthful operations.
- Make sure through on-the-job training and positive reinforcement that those employees in each supervisor's area understand the hazards and potential hazards of their jobs and how to protect themselves and others, including what to do in emergencies.
- Insist on safe and healthful working practices and actively discourage short cuts, using fair and consistent enforcement when necessary.
- Provide recognition and positive feedback for employees who work safely, especially those who take initiative to protect themselves and others.

- Provide a good example and follow all safety rules and safe work procedures, stopping work when it is unsafe or unhealthful.
- Investigate accidents and near-misses thoroughly to determine root causes and how to prevent reoccurrence.
- Make good use of the professional expertise offered by safety and health, medical, and other important resources to the safety and health program.

Employees

Employee responsibilities are a combination of following the rules and taking initiative. The more sophisticated the worksite, the more taking the initiative overshadows the need to remind workers of the responsibility to follow rules and procedures.

- Make sure each employee understands safety and health information, rules, and work practices.
- Avoid taking shortcuts that bypass safety precautions.
- If any employee is not sure that proceeding is safe, he or she should check to be sure of safety beforehand rather than risking possible danger.
- Any hazard that is noticed and can be corrected by an employee should be fixed immediately.
- If any employee notices a hazard that cannot be corrected by the employee alone, or if an employee thinks of a way to improve health and safety, use the available systems to notify those who can take action.
- Each employee should make sure that he or she knows exactly what to do in any type of foreseeable

emergency, including evacuation routes and how to get help.

- Make sure that all accidents or near-miss cases are reported promptly to those with authority to investigate.
- Volunteer to be involved in the safety and health program through such activities as inspections, accident/incident investigations, job hazard analysis, training, and awareness program development and presentation.
- Support fellow employees who are actively involved in safety and health program activities.
- Make good use of the professional expertise offered by safety and health, medical, and other important resources to the safety and health program.

Each worksite's responsibility statements will be more specific about the programs and systems to be used. It is important that employees at all levels understand that they are responsible for taking initiative. The ideal safety and health program is one for which every employee feels "ownership" and does not leave responsibility to the "other guy" (see also Chapter 11).

Additional Groups with Ongoing Responsibilities

Besides these classic five groups, OSHA suggests that engineering and purchasing be given safety and health responsibility.

Engineering: Ensure that all equipment that could affect the safety and health of employees is selected, installed, and maintained in a manner that eliminates or controls potential hazards.

Purchasing: Ensure that safety and health equipment and materials are purchased in a timely manner; and that new materials, parts, and equipment are obtained in accord with all applicable safety and health requirements. (OSHA undated, 5-3)

To these could be added two others (see also Chapter 14):

Maintenance: Ensure that equipment is maintained in a timely manner to avoid costly and dangerous breakdowns and that equipment with the primary purpose of controlling potential or existing hazards is kept in smooth operating condition.

Human Resources: Ensure that performance measures and performance measurement systems require a real and analytical evaluation of performance impacting the safety and health program, and that such performance measures will be used in a system of rewards or corrections consistent with that used for other high priority organizational concerns.

SHORT-TERM RESPONSIBILITIES

In addition to these basic ongoing responsibilities, short-term objectives for the safety and health program are going to result in short-term, special emphasis responsibilities. If we consider the example short-term objectives from the discussion of objectives in the preceding chapter, we can see the responsibility needs. Our example outlined three short-term objectives concerning the inspection team that did not recognize hazards as well as desired. The example objectives were for a one-time training program for hazard recognition, ongoing refresher training to be begun sometime after the one-time training, and evaluation and on-the-job training by one or more safety and/or health professionals.

Taking just the first objective we can see at least the following responsibilities:

- Development or procurement of the one-time training
- Presentation of the one-time training
- Ensuring that every member of the team has the opportunity to receive the training
- Keeping records of who has received the training
- Evaluating the impact of the training

All of these will probably be the responsibility of the manager who has ongoing responsibility for training. If that manager has training specialists, they may be delegated parts of the overall responsibility. But certainly the safety and health professionals have some responsibility as well. Since they are the subject matter experts, they should help ensure that the training covers every aspect of hazard recognition. They are also the most likely candidates to evaluate the results of the training.

This type of short-term safety and health responsibility should also be written and formally assigned, probably through yearly performance objectives. A formal, written assignment will facilitate the next step in the management loop—accountability.

Ensuring Appropriate Authority and Resources

Responsibility is a cruel hoax unless it is accompanied by commensurate authority and resources. OSHA's guidelines follow the action item of assignment of responsibility immediately with another concerning authority and resources. "Provide adequate authority and resources to responsible parties so that assigned responsibilities can be met" (OSHA 1989, 3909). The comment section expands the idea:

> It is unreasonable to assign responsibility without providing adequate authority and resources to get the job done. For example, a person with responsibility for the safety of a piece of equipment needs the authority to shut it down and get it repaired. Needed resources may include adequately trained and equipped personnel and adequate operational and capital expenditure funds. (OSHA 1989, 3913)

Authority

As responsibility statements are developed, consideration should be given to whether the group of employees who will be assigned this responsibility will have the appropriate authority to carry it out. For example, if first-line supervisors have the responsibility to stop work that is unsafe for their workers, do they have the authority to stop work in all circumstances? If not, could it be given to them? If necessary authority cannot be given to them, the responsibility should not either.

In a weapons plant, all the workers interviewed knew they had the responsibility to stop work if they felt it might be dangerous. In some parts of the plant, however, when asked about exercising that responsibility, employees responded that they did not really stop work because they were not sure what would happen if they did so. In other words, they were unsure of their authority to stop work on their own. In such a case, the assigned responsibility becomes meaningless.

Resources

Resources are another necessary ingredient for meeting responsibilities. Resources can cover a variety of needs— budget is only one of them. Resources also include equipment, time, professional expertise, training, and more. It is important, therefore, to think carefully about what resources are necessary to meet responsibilities. If they are not now available or cannot be made available, then assigning the responsibility is useless. For example, if an employee safety committee has a responsibility to make site inspections and find all hazards, they cannot meet that responsibility without: (1) the time to make inspections, (2) knowledge of how to make an inspection, and (3) the knowledge of hazard recognition, or the training to get it.

Authority and Resource Determination

Looking at the example of our short-term responsibilities, have enough authority and resources been provided to make it possible to meet those responsibilities? Does the training manager have either the time and skill (either personally or with staff) to develop the one-time training? If not, is there enough training budget provided to allow procurement of the training?

It is important to take the time to think through everything that is needed to meet responsibilities and make sure that it can all be provided. One good way to make sure this is thoroughly explored is by involving the group of employees to whom the responsibility is being given. They will be quick to think of any reasons why the responsibility cannot be met. After all, they do not want to fail.

COMMUNICATING RESPONSIBILITY

In written statements of responsibility, the ability to communicate clearly so that those assigned responsibility will understand is of paramount importance. Communication does not stop with putting something in writing. Most employees will have only the need for a general idea about the assignment of responsibilities to other groups of people. However, it is crucial that they understand their own responsibilities clearly and completely.

Human understanding is aided by the opportunity to play a role in the development of concepts and their applications. Employees at all levels of the organization should have periodic opportunities to discuss their responsibilities and to suggest revisions to them. That does not mean that groups of employees can be allowed to refuse responsibility. If there is considerable sentiment for reduction of responsibility, that would probably be a symptom of other problems that top management should explore in more depth.

Periodic refresher training and positive reinforcement should also be used to ensure that understanding does not fade.

KEY POINTS

- Everyone at the worksite should have some assigned responsibilities for worker safety and health.
- Hourly or salaried non-exempt workers should have responsibilities that require taking initiative as well as following rules and safe work practices.
- There should be assigned responsibility for every part of the safety and health program and for each

of the formally designated short-term objectives as well.

- Responsibilities should be in writing to aid in clarity and completeness of assignments as well as to provide a clear measure for holding those responsible accountable.
- Safety and health professionals' responsibilities should be limited to a strong resource role, avoiding duties of policing.
- Authority and resources must be commensurate with the responsibility assigned.
- Ensuring understanding of responsibilities is vital to getting the responsibilities accomplished.
- Having employees take part in the development or revision of their responsibilities is a tremendous aid to understanding and can help to avoid assignment of responsibility without adequate authority or resources.

With safety and health responsibilities assigned with commensurate authority and resources, your safety and health program is underway.

REFERENCES

Andrews, James C. 1994. Presentation to representatives from the Department of Energy in Lake Charles, Texas, June 29.

OSHA. 1989. *Federal Register* 54, no. 16 (January 26): 3904–3916.

OSHA. Undated. Unpublished manual, *Managing Worker Safety and Health*, Chapter 5, "Assigning Safety and Health Responsibilities," and Appendix 5-2, "Sample Assignment of Safety and Health Responsibilities." Washington, DC: Office of Cooperative Programs.

Topf, Michael D., and Richard A. Petrino. 1995. "Change in Attitude Fosters Responsibility for Safety." *Professional Safety* 67, no. 12: 24–27. Des Plaines, IL: ASSE.

7

Making Accountability Work for Safety and Health

Having responsibility is one thing; taking it seriously is another. In today's smaller organizations, every worker at every level is being asked to do more and more with less and less. Meeting responsibilities may be a matter of priorities. Accountability reinforces priorities. In the guidelines, OSHA makes it clear that holding employees at all levels accountable is important for ensuring that desired outcomes are achieved. "Hold managers, supervisors and employees accountable for meeting their responsibilities, so that essential tasks will be performed" (OSHA 1989, 3909). This simple statement is expanded considerably by the comment section:

Stating expectations of managers, supervisors, and other employees means little if management is not serious enough to track performance, to reward it when it is competent and to correct it when it is not. Holding everyone accountable for meeting their responsibilities is at the heart of effective worker safety and health protection. If management states high expectations for such protection but pays greater attention to productivity or other values, safety and health protection will be neglected. (OSHA 1989, 3913)

Foundations for Accountability

Successful worker safety and health accountability must be built on a foundation that includes clear assignment of responsibility and an organizational culture that places a high value on worker safety and health protection.

Clear Assignment of Responsibility

Much of what is necessary for accountability occurs when responsibility is clearly assigned with adequate authority and resources. Without effective actions in these areas, accountability systems will not work well. It would be unfair and unrealistic to attempt to hold someone accountable for responsibility when he or she is unaware, or when adequate authority or resources (including time) have not been made available (see Chapter 6).

Organizational Culture

Successful accountability requires a culture that holds the safety and health of the organization's members as a high value. Where this does not yet exist, accountability will probably not work well. This condition can, however, be changed if top management really wants it to change. Cultures do not change overnight, but they can be changed more quickly than many believe.[1] This change requires asking everyone to take part in the process of remaking the culture and taking ownership of safety and health.

ACCOUNTABILITY SYSTEMS

Holding an employee at any level accountable for his or her responsibilities is a simple matter of deciding whether a responsibility has been met and prescribing something positive to "reward" for desired outcomes and "correct" for outcomes other than those desired. Accountability exists in one form or another, whether or not it is formally established.

Informal Accountability

Even where no formal system is in place, informal accountability goes on continuously and has a tremendous impact on how employees at all levels perceive their "real" responsibilities. It is a rare organization where those in charge do not care about anything their employees do. In some cases, informal accountability may be totally negative where the only reward for desired outcomes is being "ignored," while those who do not produce the

---

[1]Major positive safety culture changes have occurred at VPP applicant or participant sites in less than a year's time. Unfortunately, culture changes for the worse have also been seen just as quickly with major management philosophy changes, mostly in the early part of the program experience. Needless to say, those sites either asked to withdraw or were asked to withdraw. All of them did so.

desired outcomes are subject to negative attention. In other cases, employees will be praised and find themselves in better position to get raises or promotions to more desirable jobs when they produce desired outcomes, while those who do not may be the ones who are ignored. In either case, an accountability system is working to show employees where the organization's priorities are and where to put their best efforts.

Negating Formal Accountability

Informal accountability can completely negate the intention of a formal accountability system if the formal system is not taken seriously. An organization can make the pronouncement that safety and quality come before production, but if the informal accountability system is rewarding those who put productivity first and possibly even providing negative response to those who attempt to put safety or quality before production, the formal pronouncement means nothing.

For example, an organization has a formal policy to encourage and reward hourly employees who identify and notify the safety department of safety hazards. Individual supervisors, however, manage to give the most unpleasant work assignments to and find fault with any employees who do report hazards. Soon those supervisors will have no hourly employees who are willing to report hazards. The formal policy has been defeated.

No Accountability

Informal accountability may also take the form of no accountability. An example with relationship to safety occurred in a chemical plant. The responsibility for preventive maintenance was moved from a central maintenance organization to area superintendents, whose reports were to go directly to the plant manager. Since it did not take long for the area superintendents to discover that the reports were not being read and no questions were being asked, they stopped making the reports and sending them to the plant manager. As a result, eventually it was impossible to find any documentation of preventive maintenance, and thus to determine whether it had even been done.

Countering Negative Informal Accountability

Informal accountability systems may be difficult to catch in action but the results of those systems are not. In the case of the employee reports of hazards, the remedy is for the managers over the supervisors to hold them accountable for actively encouraging and getting employees to report hazards. In the case of the maintenance reports to the plant manager, a good program evaluation, which will be discussed in the next section, would have found the accountability problem with preventive maintenance.

Positive Informal Accountability

Informal accountability does not have to be negative. In an organization where the culture places a high value on safe and healthful work practices and employees at all levels feel ownership for a safe and healthful workplace, informal accountability can strengthen formal systems stressing the importance of safety and health. In a magnesium extrusion plant run by a major chemical company, hourly employees took informal responsibility to call attention to safety rules and safe work practices to each other and especially new or contract temporary employees. At a plastics manufacturing plant in Georgia, hourly workers did not hesitate to point out to a visiting videotaping crew that safety shoes must be worn if certain lines painted around manufacturing equipment were crossed. These informal gestures are taken without resorting to enforcement or disciplinary systems, but they act to support those systems.

Formal Accountability Systems

The best way to overcome informal accountability systems that run counter to the organization's formally decided desired outcomes is to provide workable formal systems and insist that they be followed.

Performance Evaluation

Every employee should have a written statement detailing what are the most important desired outcomes for assigned work. That statement should be used in evaluating the performance of the employee. These statements should be changed at least annually to reflect changing responsibilities and priorities. They will probably contain a mixture of ongoing responsibilities and short-term responsibilities.

Care must be taken in the construction of the statements, no matter what they are called. For simplicity's sake, let's call them "annual personal objectives." They should carefully reflect the priority for each person's time spent working. They should also be verifiable and/or measurable in some fashion. It is, for example, very difficult to decide what it takes to have met the responsibility to "improve the safety of the work."

On the other hand, some very measurable quantitative standards may not really measure what is desired. If a numerical goal such as "no more than one lost time accident and five OSHA recordables" is set, there could be a situation where at least one of the actual injuries incurred may not have been totally under the control of the person being evaluated. It is best to state safety and health personal objectives in terms of positive actions that can be totally controlled by the person to be evaluated. (There is more discussion about setting objectives in previous chapters on objectives and responsibility.)

Once set up, the annual personal objectives must be taken seriously and accountability applied consistently and fairly. OSHA further expands upon this in its commentary on accountability in the guidelines:

> To be effective, a system of accountability must be applied to everyone, from senior management to hourly employees. If some are held firmly to expected performance and others are not, the system will lose its credibility. Those held to expectations will be resentful; those allowed to neglect expectations may increase their neglect. Consequently, the chance of injury and illness will increase. (OSHA 1989, 3913)

There must also be a direct relationship between the achievement of the personal objectives and either immediate monetary reward or widely understood improved standing in the organization. Otherwise, the formal accountability system is futile and informal accountability will take over.

Disciplinary Systems

Although enforcement of rules is also a key component of hazard prevention and control, it plays a natural role in accountability. In fact, enforcement is a system of holding personnel accountable for following rules and work practices. Having a fair and consistent system of discipline to emphasize the importance of following rules and work practices is an important part of a program to protect worker safety and health. But "fair" and "consistent" are sometimes the missing aspects of discipline. To many hourly workers, the word "discipline" means punishment for hourly workers and nothing else. A disciplinary system that is really fair and consistent will be applied to every employee, no matter what level, in the same manner as OSHA recommends the accountability system work. The disciplinary system should be also completely understood by each employee. In fact, employees should have the opportunity to help construct the system or to revise it. The best disciplinary systems are those that are well understood by all employees but seldom needed because everyone knows the importance of following rules and practices.

Positive Reinforcement

The complementary program concept to enforcement and discipline is positive reinforcement. It, too, is an important part of hazard prevention and control. A program to recognize and reward workers at all levels who work and interact safely and healthfully can be a positive method of holding employees accountable. Rewards do not need to be expensive or extensive. Cards giving the bearer a free coffee or soft drink in the canteen for working safely are inexpensive rewards. Having the top manager stop at a worker's station to compliment him or her on safe working techniques will brighten up that worker's day at no cost but time.

Positive reinforcement can come as recognition to groups as well as individuals. One method might be a rotating trophy for good housekeeping. The rewards of a positive reinforcement program should not be such that workers react to the materialism of a prize rather than the recognition. Recognition should be the most important prize in itself.

One cautionary note about positive reinforcement: It is not wise to set up a system of awards for having no injuries or for limiting injuries. If the cultural value of protecting workers' safety and health is not high, this may lead to underreporting of accidents and incidents. It is better to base recognition and/or awards on positive steps employees have taken (see the discussion of the role of accountability in hazard control in Chapter 18).

KEY POINTS

- Accountability means deciding whether a responsibility has been met and prescribing some sort of positive reward or corrective action.
- Accountability reinforces priorities among competing organizational values.
- Successful accountability systems to help protect worker safety and health require clearly assigned responsibilities and an organizational culture that places high value on protecting worker safety and health.
- Informal accountability occurs even where no formal system is in place and will reflect the organization's *existing cultural values* rather than idealized policy.
- Formal accountability systems include some form of performance evaluation, disciplinary systems, and positive reinforcement programs.
- Formal accountability systems must be fair and consistent and be taken very seriously or they will be defeated by informal accountability systems.

Once good formal accountability systems are added to clear policy, goal, objectives, and responsibility, the management loop is moving towards closure.

REFERENCE

OSHA. 1989. *Federal Register* 54, no. 16 (January 26): 3904–3916.

8

Evaluating Safety and Health Program Effectiveness

Closure of the management loop occurs when the outcomes of the safety and health program are measured against ongoing and short-term objectives and the goal of the program. The action of evaluating the program for its effectiveness leads to program revision and new objectives, starting the loop again. As OSHA advises in the voluntary guidelines for safety and health program management:

Review program operations at least annually to evaluate their success in meeting the goal and objectives, so that deficiencies can be identified and the program and/or the objectives can be revised when they do not meet the goal of effective safety and health protection. (OSHA 1989, 3909)

OSHA's VPP have a requirement for annual program evaluation:

Safety and Health Program Evaluation. The applicant must have a system for evaluating the operation of the safety and health program annually to determine what changes are needed to improve worker safety and health protection.

1. The system must provide for written narrative reports with recommendations for improvements and documentation of follow-up action.

2. In particular, the effectiveness of the operation of the self-inspection system, the employee hazard notification system, accident investigations, employee participation, safety and health training, the enforcement of safety and health rules, and the coverage of health aspects, including personal protective equipment and routine monitoring and sampling, should be used to improve the implementation of the company's written safety and health program. (OSHA 1988, 26345)

This requirement is one of the most frequently unmet by VPP applicants at the level required for Star approval, the highest category of the three programs (Sherrill 1994). There are many reasons for this. Sometimes the evaluation does not cover all the required program elements and subelements, such as employee participation or the system for employees to report hazards. Sometimes the applicant has confused program evaluation with comprehensive inspections or audits of procedures. Even where the applicant's evaluation focus is the program and the right aspects of the program are covered, analysis of effectiveness and judgments as to value in the achievement of the overall goal of the program are likely to be flawed or totally missing.

While there are some misunderstandings about every step of the management loop as it impacts worker safety and health protection, the evaluation step is probably the least understood and therefore the least effectively used. A request to OSHA's VPP staff in early 1995 for examples of good program evaluations from Star participants brought only a few the staff considered worthy of being called "good." If the best safety and health programs in the country are not producing excellent evaluation reports, how are others supposed to do it?

The problem may be threefold: first, not understanding the full benefits of a good evaluation; second, the time demands on those who are responsible for the evaluation; and third, the skills of those who are assigned the responsibility.

It is not surprising that the benefits of excellent evaluation are so little understood. If very few companies know how to do an excellent evaluation, only those few will have experienced the benefits. Sloppy evaluations, particularly ones that do not ask real evaluative questions (and get answers), may very well be a waste of time. This is because the frequent result is a series of descriptions of routine activities rather than judgment as to the effectiveness of those activities in meeting the objectives and the overall goal. Sometimes the recommendations—that probably existed before the formal "evaluation" was done—are not related to what is described.

But when the evaluation is done well, a better understanding of what can make the program better is sure to occur. At a 1996 workshop on evaluation, participants listed some of the major program changes that resulted from their evaluations:

- Revamping the contractor safety and health program
- Establishing hourly employee review of proposed procedure changes
- Hiring an industrial nurse
- Developing more visible management involvement in safety and health (Richardson 1997)

A Mobil refinery in Illinois reported that careful evaluation helped with the realization that the joint labor-management safety committee was really being run by management. They used the evaluation system to set an objective to move to a worker run committee over a period of years (Richardson 1997). Many of the examples in this book are the results of evaluations that found management problems in safety and health programs and recommended ways to improve.

To achieve the full benefit of evaluation, those who are responsible must be allowed enough time to do an excellent job. If they are not, the chance is that excellence will not be achieved. What frequently happens is that the safety and health manager (or the safety department) is given responsibility for the evaluation and no relief is provided from other demanding duties to allow the care that should go into an excellent evaluation.

The most likely reason that evaluations probably fall short is that those who perform them have had little real training in planning evaluations and making evaluative judgments and therefore are not skilled in evaluating an entire safety and health program and its component systems. While program evaluation may come naturally to some safety and health professionals, it does not necessarily get taught along with the technical skills of evaluating hazards and the methods to prevent or control hazards.

GETTING EVALUATION RIGHT

A true program evaluation asks whether the program effort is achieving what is expected of it and if it helps reach the goal. Evaluation should also actively search for potential improvements in the safety and health program. Excellence is a moving target and change is necessary to achieve continuing excellence. Roger Milliken said that insanity is "doing the same things, the same way and expecting to see a difference" (Minter 1995, 6).

In the unpublished draft manual chapter, "Evaluating Your Safety and Health Program," OSHA explains, "A safety and health evaluation looks at the systems you have created to carry out your safety and health program. It asks if these systems are working effectively and efficiently. All systems that contribute to your safety and health program should be reviewed" (OSHA undated, 12-1).

OSHA illustrates this with an example:

> ... has employee participation at safety committee meetings helped improve the worksite's safety and health program? How is the work of the safety committee helping you meet your goal? These are the kinds of issues addressed by the evaluation. (OSHA undated, 12-2).

Many people confuse "evaluation" and "audit." While there are components of auditing that are used in evaluation, auditing, as Leigh Sherrill, OSHA's instructor in program evaluation explains, "is more a question of counting things and comparing what is done to government rules or company procedures." Evaluation is determining how well activities are achieving what they were designed to accomplish (Richardson 1997).

International management expert, Peter Keen, also sees evaluation as important in planning for the future. "Audits are about control and compliance. Evaluation is about value and benefit. Audits look back. Evaluation looks ahead. Excellence demands evaluation as the link from today's to tomorrow's excellence" (Richardson 1997).

You will be aided in determining value and benefit if you have set up a good, clear goal and both ongoing and short-term objectives. With a clear goal and objectives, you will know from the start what yardstick you are using for comparison and what you expect your program activities to provide for your safety and health program.

Evaluating Short-Term Objectives

Evaluating short-term objective accomplishment is similar to an audit. Take the example from Chapter 5—the discussion of objectives concerning training the safety and health inspection team. There were three short-term goals: (1) to locate or develop and provide effective, comprehensive hazard recognition training for all inspection team members within the first quarter of the year; (2) develop and, by the second quarter, implement ongoing training in hazard recognition for all inspection team members; and, (3) assign responsibility to a safety professional resource by the second quarter to accompany each inspection team once during the first half year and once during the second half, evaluate team members' ability to recognize hazards, and provide on-the-job refresher training.

For the first of these objectives, the evaluators would check to see if training that meets the qualifiers "effective" and "comprehensive" was provided during the first quarter. Training records and interviews with team members will be the best source of information to check that the training was given on time and that the team members felt it was comprehensive and effective. Evaluators would also check with the safety resources who were involved to see what they concluded about the comprehensiveness and effectiveness. Another key to whether the training was effective will be whether the team did a better job of recognizing hazards after the training than before. That was, after all, the overall objective for this short-term objective. Evaluators would use similar techniques to determine if the other two short-term objectives were met as well.

Clear Objectives Help Evaluation

The clarity and completeness of objectives facilitates good evaluation. Suppose that instead of coming up with these three short-term objectives, we had come up with one that said "train all team members in hazard recognition." It would be possible in this case to meet the language of the objective without necessarily meeting the ongoing objective of identifying all hazards. This briefer short-term objective does not specify anything about the scope or quality of the training, or even frequency. When evaluators discover short-term objectives that have not been fully articulated, they should take an extra step and ask if the accomplishment of the short-term objective helped achieve ongoing objectives, and, of course, the overall goal for the safety and health program.

Evaluating Ongoing Objectives

Ongoing objectives are sometimes overshadowed by the more precise short-term objectives, but the ongoing objectives are very important in evaluation. Suppose, for example, you had determined that one ongoing objective for your accident/incident investigation system was to determine root cause and to provide more than one method of preventing future occurrences. As the evaluators reviewed your accident/incident investigation reports and discussed results with employees at various levels, they would be looking for evidence that the investigators had analyzed each instance deeply enough to establish a root cause. They would also take note of recommendations for future prevention to check on the numbers of recommendations and the quality of those recommendations to see if the ongoing objective had been met.

It is clear that this ongoing objective of establishing root cause and making recommendations for future prevention should help achieve the overall goal of addressing "all existing and potential hazards of the worksite, prevent[ing] or control[ing] those hazards. . . ." But supposing the evaluators discovered that although the accident/incident investigations are excellent, nothing was done with them? Suppose that the recommendations were never acted upon. Suppose employees were never provided information about why the accident had occurred and what was being done to prevent it. How does that information fit in with the last part of the goal, "prevents or controls those hazards, and ensures that employees understand the hazards and their responsibilities in protecting themselves and others"? Does the ongoing objective need to be changed?

Perhaps it does or perhaps additional ongoing objectives for the accident/incident investigation system are needed. The evaluation team might recommend that an ongoing objective for that system be adopted that would express the intention that resulting recommendations for future prevention be reviewed and, when feasible, implemented. They might also suggest an additional ongoing objective to track accepted recommendations resulting from the system to completion. A final recommendation by the evaluation team might be that the results of accident/incident investigations be routinely provided to all employees in a forum where questions could be asked and answered and suggestions made.

SCOPE OF EVALUATION

The evaluation should cover every aspect of the safety and health program. At a minimum, that should include every major element and action item that OSHA has suggested in the voluntary guidelines. Other aspects of the program that have an impact on or are related to the safety and health program, such as security, should be added as well. The way that these aspects are organized does not have to follow OSHA's organization precisely. Figure 5-1 in Chapter 5 shows a simplified outline taken from the guidelines that can be used as a reference to ensure complete coverage.

CHOOSING THE EVALUATORS

Evaluations should be performed by more than one person so that the judgments that are required can be shared by at least one other. Many worksites have evaluations done by a team. Concerning who should do the evaluation, OSHA's unpublished manual recommends outside personnel to provide a "fresh look" at the program:

> Who should conduct the evaluation? Although evaluations can be performed by worksite employees,

they are best done by people who are knowledgeable about the site's processes and about managing safety and health programs, but who **do not work at the site being evaluated.** The fresh look an outsider brings produces a more accurate and helpful evaluation. This outsider may come from corporate headquarters, another site within the company, an insurance company, or a consulting firm. (OSHA undated, 12-2)

At the Idaho Springs Monsanto plant, an outside consultant firm is used to perform the evaluation. According to Conrad Watkins, Safety Specialist, "We like the idea of bringing in fresh eyes to look at our programs. We may be too close to what we do to see it clearly" (Richardson 1997).

It is true that outsiders with appropriate qualifications may be essential ingredients in the evaluation, but worksite members may have an important role as well. When a team performs the evaluation, it is possible to have one or more members that work at the site on the team. They will bring a familiarity with the programs (and their problems) that can be quite helpful. This is particularly true of hourly or non-supervisory salaried employees.

Another aspect of the evaluation team is the expertise that they bring. While technical safety and industrial hygiene expertise is important to the team and must be included, the most important expertise is that of evaluation experience, someone who knows how to ask the difficult questions about effectiveness and relation to the objectives and goal. Team members with health and safety technical expertise may or may not have that experience. It also helps if the team has someone who enjoys writing and can document the evaluation.

When practical, the team members should include:

- An experienced and successful evaluator
- A safety professional with experience in more than one industry
- An industrial hygienist with similar industry qualifications
- Someone from the site being evaluated
- An hourly (or non-supervisory salaried, if there are no hourlies) employee
- A top-level manager from another worksite
- An occupational health professional such as an occupational physician or nurse

Each of these characteristics does not necessarily mean an additional person; one person may meet two or more of the criteria. Having team members from outside your company need not be too difficult or expensive. The Potlatch plant in Lewiston, Idaho asks other VPP plants to help with the evaluation (Richardson 1997). You may be able to work out an agreement with another noncompetitive company in your area that has a good reputation for safety and health management and swap assistance for evaluations. This process can be a good way to bring in fresh eyes at the top management level as well as the hourly employee level.

INFORMATION-GATHERING TOOLS

OSHA now has more than a decade of experience in evaluating safety and health programs for VPP approvals. The tools that it developed and still uses remain very effective for relatively quick but knowledgeable evaluations. OSHA can complete an onsite evaluation of a worksite as large as 2,000 employees in one work week, including travel and a first draft of its evaluation report. Every aspect may not be checked but enough will be sampled that both key problems and successes will be discovered (Oliver 1996).

In its unpublished manual, OSHA advises that companies use the same tools used by OSHA teams: document review, interviews, and a review of site conditions. In fact, its detailed instructions on the use of these tools have been reproduced here as Appendix 2.

OSHA's tools—document review, interviews, and site walk-through—are also helpful for accomplishing site self-evaluation of the safety and health program. Some modification of these tools to better fit into the scheme of the worksite would have more value than just simple adoption. In addition, some tools that are useful for self-evaluation are not as helpful when the evaluators come in "cold" from the outside and have only a short time to complete their effort. Some examples of these are employee surveys and ongoing evaluation input.

Documentation

Although documentation review is thought of as a tool more consistent with audits, records of safety and health program activities lend themselves to evaluation as well. For example, general inspection reports can provide clues about the ability of the site inspection program to find hazards and get them corrected, particularly when compared to what can be seen of site conditions. It is not necessary to review every single report and document from the evaluation period. Random sampling (with access to all records and the sampling system decided upon by the team) can accomplish the same thing. If the sample is too large, the documents begin to look the same after a while and nothing new is learned from sampling additional documents.

Interviews

Interviews with employees at all levels, if approached correctly, can provide a tremendous amount of information. Employees should be asked questions that require descriptive answers, such as identifying the potential hazards they work with and how they protect themselves. Managers should be asked about the hazards their workers face and how they are protected. They should also be asked to explain what their safety and health responsibilities are and how they are held accountable for them.

It is helpful also to ask employees about how they respond to hazards that they encounter in terms of getting them corrected and the appropriateness and timeliness of the response. Other areas of interest with employees are their knowledge of the employee involvement system, the disciplinary system, and roles in emergency response.

Site Conditions

Site inspection is the tool that really demands fresh eyes. While a complete inspection is not done, enough of the site should be seen by the team to get a good impression about how the program elements are implemented and the types of hazards that can be found. OSHA suggests that the team should ask what management system should have prevented any hazard that they see and also suggests using a hazard analysis flow chart, which is provided as Appendix 3 (OSHA undated, 12-5).

If members of the evaluation team are the same as those who make inspections, this might be a good time to really look back at the records and evaluate the hazards that have been found and what they mean in terms of the effectiveness of site safety and health systems for finding and controlling hazards.

Employee Surveys

At large sites, it is difficult to interview more than just a small sample of the employees, and an employee survey can expand the numbers of people involved in providing information. At a workshop on evaluation[1] in 1996, about 75 percent of the participants said that they collected information about safety in survey form. One site that has used this method effectively is the Pantex Plant in Amarillo, Texas, which has about 3,500 people working at the site. The Pantex evaluation team drew up a questionnaire for the survey in 1995 that used questions based on the characteristics that DOE expected to see at a VPP Star site (DOE 1995). They achieved about 30 percent participation, and many respondents wrote long additional notes. They then used the information as a basis to narrow the questions used in interviews to follow up on the issues raised in the survey.

Ongoing Evaluation

OSHA does not have the same opportunity as those at a worksite every day, year-round, to provide a continuous

---

[1]The workshop was one held as part of the VPPPA Annual Conference in Orlando in September 1996. It was interactive in nature and consisted of members of VPP sites discussing various aspects of program evaluation.

evaluation of the effectiveness of the program and its activities. It may only be the safety and health professionals who collect information about effectiveness informally, or information collection may actually be built into some formal activities. A worksite in Texas has built some evaluative questions into its monthly inspection checklists, such as the quality of employee involvement in different parts of the plant. It is possible to include the interviewing as part of a monthly or weekly inspection and to check written documentation as well.

When continuous evaluation is being used, the information is collected once each year for the formal evaluation report. Safety and health professionals may simply think about the year past, or a collection of written documents such as that used for the combination inspection/evaluation done at the Texas plant may be used. It is important to take care that evaluation is not confused with inspections for hazards. Evaluation should always be focused on the effectiveness of systems rather than technical controls.

EVALUATION JUDGMENTS

As was indicated in the discussion above about what constitutes an evaluation, the key to evaluation judgment is asking tough effectiveness questions and determining the answers. As OSHA recommends in its unpublished manual:

> Insist that the evaluator determine the program's bottom line profitability, its real benefit. In other words, which activities contribute to the safety and health goal, and which do not? Judgments and decisions made by evaluators should be driven by this quest for profitability, by which we mean

improvement in safety and health protection. Do not accept a narrative that only describes the program. Insist that the hard questions about effectiveness be addressed. (OSHA undated, 12-10)

Popular and Long-Standing Activities

Sometimes activities that are supposed to be part of the safety and health program go unquestioned because "they have always been done" and "everyone likes them." Take, for example, "Safety Day." If the work is shut down for a day each year and families are brought in for Safety Day, there should be at least one objective for that day that fits into the overall goal of the safety and health program. Evaluation should be able to determine if that objective was met and if it helped move toward the goal.

Suppose the objective is to teach worker families about safety and health. If that is the case, then the overall goal should include something about family understanding of how to protect themselves and others. If it doesn't, then the goal should be rethought. A decision should be made about whether family safety and health understanding should be part of the overall goal. If it is not, then this objective is not helping reach the goal. If it is part of the goal, then the evaluators should determine whether the activities of Safety Day are achieving the objective set for it. To do that, the evaluation team would need to have information about whether families did learn something about protecting themselves and others. If no data has been gathered that allows them to determine that, then perhaps a short-term goal for the next year should be to gather that data during or following Safety Day. Whatever the situation, the hard questions must be asked.

Activities Taken for Granted

Sometimes, activities are so completely accepted in the safety and health community that it seems a waste of time to ask many questions about them. For example, everyone knows that accidents must be investigated and that certainly accident investigations should help achieve the goal. In theory, that should be true, but some systems of accident investigation may even place obstacles in the way of achieving any meaningful safety and health goal.

At one chemical plant, a committee of employees had been designated as an "accident investigation committee." Its duties consisted of reading supervisors' first reports of injuries and preparing its own report. This committee operated for a year or so before it was evaluated as part of an overall safety and health program evaluation. The evaluators discovered that the committee reports were almost the same, word for word, as the supervisor's report. The evaluators noted that no time, training, or equipment had been devoted to enable the committee's performance of a real investigation. The committee, therefore, could add no value to the achievement of any meaningful safety and health objective and actually placed an obstacle in the way of the employee participation objectives by wasting employees' time and perhaps convincing them that they had nothing to offer accident investigation.

After the evaluation asked hard questions about the committee, it was disbanded and reconstituted with volunteers who were given investigation training, time to do good investigations, and equipment for taking photographs and measurements. The quality of accident investigations improved dramatically within two months.

A good evaluation will ask hard questions about even the most popular activities and the ones we take for granted.

WRITTEN EVALUATIONS

While it is possible to do a useful evaluation using a checklist, such a system provides an opportunity to gloss over the hard questions and decisions of effectiveness that must be made. Even though being required to write out narrative descriptions of the evidence found of effectiveness (or the lack of effectiveness) may also result in glossing over the evaluation, at least the record will not hide the depth of the analysis.

In 1995, OSHA made a decision to collect the annual evaluations required for the VPP, and discussed the possibility of basing its schedule of onsite program evaluations on the quality of evaluation being done of the participating sites (Edmondson 1995; Sherrill 1996). In other words, where they could see that the hard questions were being asked and answered satisfactorily, OSHA would not feel the need to perform its own evaluation with the same frequency as it would where the written reports did not include evidence of a careful evaluation. That OSHA would consider this indicates the perception of the VPP staff members that they could tell the quality of analysis by reading the written reports. If checklists were the only records of evaluation, the sole method of ascertaining the quality would be to perform another evaluation and compare results.

Managers who wish to have excellent safety and health programs should insist on having the evaluation team write a narrative report and then read it carefully.

USE OF THE EVALUATION

Clearly, the point of evaluation is to improve the safety and health program. Each evaluation should begin with a review of the recommendations from the last evaluation and how those that were accepted for implementation were handled. When an evaluation is completed, the report usually goes to another group for decisions about the actions to take in response to the recommendations. If a thoughtful evaluation and equally thoughtful recommendations have been prepared, most recommendations should result in actions.

The most likely result from evaluation recommendations is the generation of short-term objectives. They could also result in some quick fixes that do not require formal objectives to be set. They might also result in new or revised ongoing objectives. Sometimes they result in a revised goal or policy.

KEY POINTS

- Evaluation is more than an audit, it asks hard effectiveness questions about safety and health program activities in terms of the goal and objectives.
- Evaluation should cover at least every element and action item of the voluntary OSHA guidelines.
- The evaluation team should include some "outsiders" and at least one "insider."
- The evaluation team should have an experienced and successful program evaluator as a member, probably as the leader.
- Evaluation tools include reviewing documents and records of program activities, interviewing employees at all levels, a brief site conditions review, employee surveys, and the results of continuous evaluation.
- The evaluation should determine the "bottom line" usefulness of each part of the safety and health

program in terms of short-term objectives, ongoing objectives, and the program goal.

- The evaluation should also determine the usefulness of objectives in meeting the goal.
- Sometimes the evaluation will result in a recommendation that the goal be revised or at least reconsidered.
- A narrative evaluation report provides the best record of evaluation and the progress made by the safety and health program.

The completion of a successful evaluation is the start of a new cycle of the management loop.

REFERENCES

DOE. 1995. *Voluntary Protection Program Part IV: Onsite Review Handbook,* "Appendix A, DOE VPP Onsite Review Criteria."

Edmonson, Adella. 1995. OSHA VPP staff member, personal conversation.

Minter, Stephen G. 1995. "Practicing Sane Safety." *Occupational Hazards* (June): 6. Cleveland: Penton Publishing.

Oliver, Cathy. 1996. OSHA Chief. Division of Voluntary Programs, personal conversation.

OSHA. 1988. *Federal Register* 53, no. 133 (July 12): 26339–26348.

OSHA. 1989. *Federal Register* 54, no. 16 (January 26): 3904–3916.

OSHA. Undated. Unpublished manual, *Managing Worker Safety and Health,* Chapter 12, "Evaluating Your Safety and Health Program." Washington, DC: Office of Cooperative Programs.

Richardson, Margaret R. 1997. "Comprehensive Evaluations: Safety's Annual Checkup." *Occupational Hazards* 59, no. 3: 51–53. Cleveland: Penton Publishing.

Sherrill, Leigh. 1994. OSHA VPP staff member, personal conversation.

Sherrill, Leigh. 1996. Announcement at Workshop #30, Advanced Annual Program Evaluation, September 18.

9

The Closed Management Loop

The complete and effective program evaluation closes but does not finish the management loop. The loop is ongoing and continuous, never completed. Each part leads to the next. Each part depends upon all the other parts. By effectively implementing each part of the loop, zero-defect management of safety and health can be achieved. Zero-defect management, however, does not mean that no hazard will ever escape its controls. What it does mean is that when a hazard escapes its controls, another system, another type of control will take over and get the hazard back under control before the hazard becomes an exposure or actually injures (or causes illness in) one or more workers.

The management loop only provides the structure for zero-defect management of worker safety and health. To provide a complete and effective safety and health program requires total involvement from everyone who earns a paycheck at the site, a comprehensive set of systems to assess and prevent or control potential hazards, and an effective program to provide training to managers, supervisors, and line employees for occupational safety and health. None of these, however, is more important than the structure of the management loop. Worksites that take the management loop seriously and work to keep it operating continuously will have a much better understanding of their safety and health program than others and will be able to keep it functioning effectively.

Part 3

Achieving Total Involvement in Worker Safety and Health

10

Introduction to Total Involvement

The days when worker safety and health were the provinces of professionals who exhorted and inspected and wrote up violations are passing. Industry leaders have learned that with worker safety and health, just as with quality, everyone has to be involved if excellence is to be achieved.

But where many make mistakes is in assuming that "everybody" just means all hourly or non-exempt salaried employees working in production. These workers are probably the most important component of the workforce when it comes to maintaining an effective safety and health program. But they are not the only ones. Top-level managers have a crucial role to play. Middle managers and supervisors are integral to the systems that keep the safety and health program working.

Professional staff of varied expertise also make contributions. In addition, at worksites where some of the work is contracted to other companies, true excellence cannot be achieved without involving those contract companies and their employees.

Finally, when safety and health responsibilities are shifted, as they should be, to everyone working at the worksite, the safety and health professionals have exciting new roles to play as guides, conscience, and support for the overall safety and health program as it is implemented by employees at all levels.

The Voluntary Protection Programs (VPP)

A good understanding of who should be involved in safety and health, and how, has been provided by OSHA's experience with the VPP. This group of three programs provide the Agency with the opportunity to identify good safety and health programs, to recognize them, and to encourage the improvement of safety and health programs (OSHA 1988).

When the VPP were originally implemented by OSHA in July 1982, the involvement concept centered on joint labor-management committees in unionized worksites. Non-union worksites were allowed to apply for the programs but were not expected to have any employee involvement. Instead, they were expected to demonstrate stronger management controls than the union worksites (OSHA 1982).

After a few years of experience, OSHA decided that truly excellent safety and health programs required both strong management and employee involvement. This determination was based upon observance that the best results came from VPP participants using both employee involvement and strong management control, even though only one or the other was required for the VPP approval at that time.

Starting in 1985, VPP applicants in industries other than construction were allowed to use other employee participation methods than joint committees. This was true even for non-union sites, as long as they could demonstrate that the participation was active and meaningful and involved problem resolution as well as problem identification. The employee involvement requirements for construction remained the classic form of labor-management committees (OSHA 1985, 43814).

In addition to employee involvement, management involvement in "worker safety and health concerns" is also required by the VPP, "including clear lines of communication with employees and setting an example of safe and healthful behavior" (OSHA 1988, 26343).

THE SAFETY AND HEALTH PROGRAM MANAGEMENT GUIDELINES

When OSHA published the voluntary guidelines for safety and health programs in 1989, it based these guidelines, in large part, on its experience with the VPP. The guidelines were meant to be used on a voluntary basis by any and all employers, not just those who wished to be recognized for outstanding worker protection.

The guidelines linked employee participation and management commitment into one of four major elements. This first element was called "Management Leadership and Employee Involvement." The concept of "visible" management involvement is articulated in the guidelines along with a broad concept of the involvement of employees (OSHA 1989).

In Part 3 we will describe methods to implement these ideas and also explore the ways those middle managers, supervisors, contract company workers, and staff professional resources can be fully and effectively involved in creating and maintaining an excellent safety and health program.

References

OSHA 1982. *Federal Register* 47, no. 128 (July 2): 29025–29032.
OSHA 1985. *Federal Register* 50, no. 209 (October 29): 43804–43817.
OSHA 1988. *Federal Register* 53, no. 133 (July 12): 26339–26348.
OSHA 1989. *Federal Register* 54, no. 16 (January 26): 3904–3916.

11

Ensuring Line Employee Ownership of the Safety and Health Program

Jon Grice, Executive Vice President of EBI Companies, a workers compensation insurance company, says that increasing employee job satisfaction is as important for reducing injury and illness compensation claims as eliminating physical hazards (*Occupational Hazards* 1996). The beauty of involving line workers in safety and health is that it accomplishes both increased job satisfaction and direct, as well as indirect, reduction of physical hazards.

Since the early 1980s, enough change has occurred in the amount of line employee involvement in occupational safety and health to qualify it as a revolution. Part of this is due to changes in employer attitudes toward quality and the need to get the production line employees involved in ensuring quality products and services. The number of union contracts specifying safety committees also increased. The encouragement given to employee involvement by OSHA played a role as well. Whatever the reason, by the mid-1990s, no worksite without employee involvement in safety and health could be considered to have a good safety and health program, let alone an excellent one.

OSHA's view on worker involvement is clear, as both their VPP requirements and their guidelines demonstrate. Since 1985, OSHA's employee participation requirement for the Star program has been that construction worksites must have joint labor management safety committees and that general industry worksites must have "an active and meaningful way to participate in safety and health problem identification and resolution" (OSHA 1985). The guidelines go even further:

> Provide for and encourage employee involvement in the structure and operation of the safety and health program and in decisions that effect their safety and health, so that they will commit their insight and energy to achieving the safety and health program's goal and objectives. (OSHA 1989, 3909)

The use of "structure and operation" takes the guidelines a step beyond the VPP requirement for "active and meaningful" participation. Used together, the terms "structure" and "operation" carry with them the concept that employees will be involved in the design, revision, and oversight of the safety and health program, as well as identifying safety hazards and problems and correcting or resolving them.

In the comment section of the notice that announced the guidelines, OSHA expanded on its employee involvement concepts generally:

Since an effective program depends on commitment by employees as well as managers, it is important that their concerns be reflected in it. An effective program includes all personnel in the organization—managers, supervisors, and others—in policy development, planning, and operations. (OSHA 1989, 3912)

OSHA was careful, however, to emphasize that overall responsibility still rests with management:

This does not mean transfer of responsibility to employees. The Occupational Safety and Health Act of 1970 clearly places responsibility for safety and health protection on the employer. However, employees' intimate knowledge of the jobs they perform and the special concerns they bring to the job give them a unique perspective which can be used to make the program more effective. (OSHA 1989, 3912)

THE BENEFITS OF EMPLOYEE INVOLVEMENT

The benefits of employee involvement derive from the position employees are in and their importance in the success of any processes and programs attempted in the workplace: (1) They are in the closest contact with hazards and potential hazards; (2) they have proven their worth in helping to solve workplace problems of all kinds; (3) they need a positive outlet for expression of power; (4) the more they take part, the more they feel ownership and responsibility; and (5) their involvement in safety and health has a positive impact on other values of the workplace.

Close Contact

Line workers are the ones closest to hazard exposures and potential exposures. Since they live with these possible dangers nearly every day, they are in a position to know them better than anyone else. They are also in a position to know how effective the controls for those hazards and potential hazards are. The engineer that designs equipment controls and the manager who decrees work procedures may walk away and go on to other matters. The line employees, however, must work intimately with whatever is decided and can see problems that others might not be in a position to notice. They can be, therefore, the most knowledgeable about what is wrong and how to fix it.

Problem Solvers

In 1991, at ICF Kaiser Hanford, a contract engineering and construction operation at a large worksite in the state of Washington, there was a rash of injuries and near-misses in their drilling operations. The operations were completely shut down and every line manager, employee, and the site safety officer worked to develop a start-up plan. The key element of the plan they came up with was that employees would identify problems, develop solutions including drill rig design and process modifications, and help management make the necessary changes happen. Almost immediately injuries and near-misses dropped by 70 percent (Palmer 1996).

In recent years line workers have proven themselves to be excellent problem solvers wherever they are given opportunity, training, and encouragement. They have improved productivity, quality, and the safety and environmental soundness of millions of tasks and processes.

It has also become clearer in the last decade that, although individual decisions may be fast, groups make better decisions. That has brought about the team concept's heavy use in high technology industries that must make good decisions to remain competitive in a rapidly changing market environment. In this regard, the line production worker's close contact provides a unique perspective for the decision-making process.

Expression of Power

Human beings do not want to feel powerless, with no control over what happens to them. In the workplace controlled in an authoritarian manner, the power for positive action on the part of the line production or service worker is stifled. What sometimes results is a negative expression of power—since the need to express power is so strong.

As stated in the "Law of Subordinate Superpower"—the paraphrase of the laws of physics that every action has an equal and opposite action—as explained by Hansen, "for every manipulative management action, there is an employee reaction, which will definitely be opposite but will never be equal" (Hansen 1995).

In one factory, workers had been given the right of way when their paths crossed those of the various fork-lift and other small industrial trucks that moved around the plant floor. This right of way was given for their safety, but some workers deliberately stayed in front of the trucks and moved very slowly. They had found a way to express their power in a workplace where they had no say in decisions. Negative expressions such as these may be small matters that never become concerns, but they can also be the source of serious and costly problems. At some worksites, negative expression of power can result in sabotage of processes and products. Unfortunately, negative expressions of the need for power result in no positive gains for anyone.

Where workers are provided opportunities, training, and encouragement to express their power needs positively, everyone benefits.

Sense of Ownership

People are more likely to support ideas, practices, policies, and procedures if they have a chance to help with their development. Many once-unpopular and nearly unenforceable safety and health rules have become better understood and better followed when workers had a chance to understand the problem and help find a resolution. Examples of these are no-smoking policies, no facial hair for those wearing respirators that must fit closely to the face, and rules about food or tobacco products.

Impact on Other Organizational Values

Experience with the VPP and other worksites using worker involvement effectively demonstrates that workers who are respected by management for their ideas and abilities to help with decisions of all kinds enjoy their work and perform it more effectively. They use fewer sick days and are more productive while at work. They take more pride in their work and the quality of their products. Organizations where workers are involved in decisions have lower costs and higher production. Examples of this are found among the VPP site experiences. At the Weyerhaeuser plant in Valiant, Oklahoma, production rose by 23 percent, while injuries dropped 90 percent during the period 1984–1995[1] (Strain 1995).

In Chapter 2 we noted that the experience of Ford New Holland plant in Grand Island, Nebraska, showed that workers compensation costs were cut in half during the same three-year period where productivity rose by 13 percent while the amount of scrapped product that had to be reworked was cut by 16 percent (OSHA undated, 1-15).

In fact, Mark Huselid, a professor at Rutgers, studied the link between progressive human resource management techniques (also known as high performance work practices) and company financial results. These practices include involving employees in corporate decision making and job improvements. Huselid found that significant improvement in management practices resulted in $27,044 more in sales; $3,814 in profits; and $18,641 in market value per employee (Collingwood 1996).

While Huselid's study covered more topics than just safety, the same concept of involvement applies. In fact, employees are much more willing to get involved in matters of their own safety and health than they are in matters of quality and productivity, although all three can be accomplished. These factors obviously add up to better profits and a better future in a highly competitive world market.

WAYS TO INVOLVE WORKERS

Just a few years ago a section with this heading might only have listed routine, general inspections and accident

---

[1]This was also a period of increased employee participation. The Valiant plant was approved for the Merit Program in 1992 and Star in 1994.

investigations along with membership on a safety committee. Going a little farther back, to the early 1980s, all that would be discussed would be classic joint labor-management committees. Today, the number of ways that workers can be involved is limited only by what can be done in the workplace and the imaginations of those who decide what workers will be involved in.

As demonstrated by the VPP experience, workers can, with resources of time, training, access to expertise and budget; authority commensurate to their responsibilities; opportunity and encouragement, do just about anything, including:

- Inspect equipment and facilities
- Provide routine industrial hygiene (IH) monitoring
- Analyze jobs, equipment, facilities, and processes to identify possible hazards (including ergonomic hazards) and develop methods or help improve designs to prevent or control those hazards
- Write standard operating procedures
- Develop and provide training for each other and for new employees
- Investigate accidents, incidents, and unplanned events
- Help with trend analysis of accident/incidents and hazards discovered by various means
- Make benchmarking visits to other worksites
- Evaluate the safety and health program and plan changes
- Plan and provide safety and health outreach to their communities and/or family safety programs
- Act as "hosts" to OSHA, presenting information on their safety and health programs, accompanying Agency representatives, noting any needed problem resolutions, and making sure they are accomplished.

This list is long and certainly not complete. But it is the unusual workplace that can achieve employee involvement in all of these areas very quickly. Most of the workplaces with this wide use of employees have been evolving and expanding employee involvement for long periods of time.

When planning to expand the involvement of employees at a worksite, it is best to move gradually and involve employees or their authorized representatives every step of the way in deciding how and when employees will be involved.

THE SAFETY CULTURE

Sometimes managers say that employees do not want to be involved in decisions, that they want to just do their jobs and go home. On the surface, that is probably true for those worksites. Employee involvement is not like a faucet that can just be turned on. An organizational culture that does not encourage employees to make decisions at work is sometimes very difficult to overcome. If the existing culture has emphasized the differences between management and hourly (or non-exempt salaried workers), learning to work together will not come easily.

Everyone who can hold down a job probably has experience in making "management" decisions. Running a home and family requires it. As one worker at Mobil Chemical Company's Temple, Texas plant described her feelings about being fully involved in safety and health, "I don't have to check my brain at the time clock any more."

It is true that the safety culture of an organization relies on more than just employee involvement. At the same time, getting the line employees to take ownership for good safety and health protection is a major part of that accomplishment. The safety culture for employee involvement can be improved by providing a good foundation and appropriate atmosphere.

Providing the Foundation for Employee Involvement

Employee involvement does not arrive in a vacuum. It is only part of what is required for an excellent safety and health program. Employee involvement works best where there is a sincere desire to provide excellent protection for worker safety and health. Setting a goal for the program that expresses where you expect that program to take you, objectives to meet that goal, clearly stated and communicated assignment of safety and health responsibilities throughout the organization, a system for holding people accountable for meeting those responsibilities, and a system for evaluating the effectiveness of what has been done against the goal and objectives provide a good foundation for the safety and health program (see Part 2 for more information).

Providing the Atmosphere for Employee Involvement

The workplace will be more hospitable to employee involvement if that involvement is part of the job and accomplished on company time, if management's expectations are serious and clearly stated, if employees are given the resources and authority to accomplish what they are asked to do, if management is willing to try any reasonable suggestion or recommendation, and if employee successes are communicated to the workforce as a whole.

Part of the Job

Safety and health responsibilities given to hourly or line employees must be considered to be *part* of their jobs—not something that takes them *away* from their jobs. The clearest expression of this is to make it part of the job description even if it is just a general statement.

Supervisors must also be enlisted to help ensure that this work is considered part of the job. The way that supervisors look at time spent on safety and health duties will have a major impact on the willingness of workers to be involved. It helps if supervisors are held accountable for how well they do this.

On Company Time

If workers are expected to provide safety and health duties on their own time or part of their own time, it tells them that safety and health are not part of their jobs. This can be a particular problem when a worksite is running shifts around the clock and a meeting between workers on different shifts is needed. The usual practice is to ask the night shift employees to come in during the day. This takes either their family, their recreational, or their rest time. Making sure they are adequately remunerated for that time is important.

Expectations Are Serious and Clearly Stated

There is an adage that "you get what you expect." In employee involvement this is frequently true. If management is "just going through the motions" of encouraging employee participation, it is unlikely that the participation will succeed. Employees need to know what is expected of them. At one company, the safety director complained that the employee safety committee wasted its time on cafeteria, restroom, and parking lot matters. That can only occur when the committee believes that is all that is expected from them. If serious problems are brought to them for resolution, they will work on those serious matters. In the beginning, management must insist upon meaningful involvement. Later, once the committee or team has experience working on and resolving tough problems, it will come naturally.

Resources and Authority

It is unfair and unreasonable to expect that employees will provide useful results if they do not have the necessary resources and authority for the responsibilities they are given. An example is the plant committee described earlier that was formed to "investigate" accidents. They were given no training, no equipment, and no authority to interview witnesses. As a result, they simply rewrote the supervisor's first report of the accident and wasted their time and the company's money. Once the resources were provided, they began to do real investigations and provided the company with injury and cost saving solutions (see resource discussion under "Achieving Ownership").

Try Any Reasonable Suggestion or Recommendation

When employee committees or teams begin to provide recommendations, those who make the decisions must listen with open minds, ready to try anything that may be feasible—even if they suspect that it won't work. Sometimes employees need to learn for themselves how much more difficult it is to find workable solutions than they may have thought. If their suggestion does not work, they will learn much more from finding out themselves than if someone simply tells them that it will not.

At one company, management was sure that necessary budget increases could not be obtained from their corporation to implement the employee committee solution to a problem, but when they attempted to explain that to committee members, employees were dubious of the plant management's commitment to the idea. Employees were allowed to be involved personally in the negotiations to obtain the increases. As it turned out, they did not obtain the money, but went back to their tasks with a better understanding of the reality of limitations on decision making. Before long, they had come up with another less costly solution that could be implemented.

On the other hand, management may be surprised to discover that something they think will not work actually might. As long as the proposed solution is feasible and does not put anyone in danger (including the company), it should be attempted. If, after enough time has passed to truly test it, it becomes clear that the solution has not worked, it should be taken back to the employees for another idea.

Communicate Successes

People enjoy success stories. In an organization where employee involvement is in early stages and not all employees have accepted the idea of being involved, it is also important that those employees hear about the successes of those who *are* involved. The plant newsletter, monthly or weekly safety meetings, or meetings between the plant management and employees are good ways to spread the good news. Once employees get the idea that management is serious, that employees can make a difference, and that it is part of the job, attitudes will begin to change.

Legal Concerns

In the early 1990s, decisions by the National Labor Relations Board involving joint labor-management committees raised the specter of ending the use of such committees for safety and health matters. Once consideration was given to the decisions and the additional guidance provided by the Board, most attorneys writing about this subject agreed that careful construction and implementation of employee involvement would avoid violating the National Labor Relations Act and/or the rights meant to be protected by the law.

The key concepts appear to be whether the group of non-exempt employees is "dealing" with management and whether employees are acting as "representatives." According to labor-law attorney Horace Thompson, unionized worksites must be sure to have the union's full assent in any employee participation method. Non-union worksites are a little more complicated. Mr. Thompson says that employee groups such as task forces that have full authority to study and resolve assigned safety issues will avoid "dealing" with management. He gives an example of a safety committee made up mostly of employees, which makes decisions by majority rule (or by consensus where managers do not participate in the consensus) (Thompson 1994).

Others point out that some forms of employee involvement—that is, self-managed work teams, suggestion boxes, and brainstorming sessions—are clearly legal. It helps if committee members are volunteers rather than selected by management. Nor should management hold elections of "representatives." Employee members of committees should represent themselves only. The best selection arrangement is rotating membership and making sure everyone eventually takes part.

Each company will want to discuss this issue with its own legal experts. Clearly, however, the more widespread the involvement, the more it is a part of the employee's job; the more employees who make decisions themselves rather than "negotiate" with management, the less risk there is of violating the law.

ACHIEVING OWNERSHIP

When employees are fully empowered and have "ownership," they have all the authority and resources needed to effectively carry out their responsibilities. Resources include effective training, time, budget, and professional expertise.

Training

Training is key to being able to channel line employees' special knowledge into decisions and actions that will improve safety and health. If employees are making inspections, they need to know how to recognize the hazards and potential routine hazards. If they are going to do accident investigations, they need to know how to recognize and preserve evidence, how to interview effectively, and much more. If they are going to analyze jobs, tasks, and processes to find the hidden hazards and potential hazards, they need to understand how to break down tasks and processes into the smallest possible steps and analyze even the most unlikely possible hazards. If they are going to provide routine IH monitoring and sampling, they will need training in routine calibration of instruments and understanding of nationally recognized protocols for these activities.

It is not necessary, however, to make them "experts." Training should cover what is likely to be routine. Access to experts should be provided for those occasions when broader or more in-depth knowledge is needed.

Time

No matter how well trained employees are, if they are expected to complete an inspection of a large plant in an hour, they will miss hazards. If they are expected to complete an accident investigation in one day, they may miss important pieces of evidence. They may need some time as well, probably not frequently, to consult with professional expertise of one kind or another (see discussion below). Time is a key resource, particularly when downsizing has left everyone short of time.

Remember, however, that providing time to carry out safety- and health-related duties is not carte blanche to waste time or neglect the rest of the duties that comprise each worker's job. With empowerment, employees take on the responsibility to use time wisely.

Budget

Employees will not be truly empowered until they have a budget that is under their control and for which they have responsibility. It does not have to be a large budget, but big enough to enable reasonable decisions without having to go to management for "permission." Even some small companies such as J. A. Wright, in Keene, New Hampshire, a maker of silver and jewelry polishes, provide a budget amount for employees to buy safety and health training materials and videos. With the budget also comes responsibility. It is reasonable to expect that committees will have procedures to follow in deciding to spend the money that is budgeted for them.

Professional Expertise

It is not necessary to turn line employees into safety and health professionals, although in many unionized work-sites where employee representatives have worked for years in the field of safety and health, some hourly workers have become experts. It may work better to have most of your employees knowledgeable but not expert. They will need, however, access to expertise on occasion.

Professional experts may include safety professionals, industrial hygienists, occupational health professionals such as nurses and physicians, engineers, training professionals, personnel specialists, and others. In fact, employees who are empowered to oversee and redesign safety and health programs should have access to the same kind of professional expertise as is usually provided to management. "Access" does not mean that employees will have these experts working for them, or even that the experts must be employed at the worksite. The ability to have access to contract experts may work out better in some cases.

Signs of Ownership

You will know when the hourly and/or salaried non-exempt workers have assumed ownership of the safety and health program. Because they are empowered to act and decide, they will not speak of "them" (management) as being unresponsive. They will know they have the power and authority to make things happen within limits that they understand and accept.

They will speak with pride of their accomplishments and the excellence achieved in protecting themselves and other workers. They will prefer that any workers who do not wish to take responsibility for safety and health protection find jobs elsewhere. They know that their lives and well-being are better protected by fellow employees who are willing to take ownership.

KEY POINTS

- Nonexempt line workers have the closest and most frequent contact with potential hazards and the methods used to control them.
- Workers have proven themselves to be excellent problem solvers.
- Positive involvement in safety and health fills a basic human need.
- Feelings of ownership, resulting from involvement, make it easier for employees to follow rules and required work practices.
- Employee involvement has a positive impact on employee morale, product/service quality, and productivity.
- Line workers can do just about anything asked of them as long as they are given adequate authority, resources, and training.
- Good or improving safety cultures provide an excellent environment for employee participation.
- Involvement should be on company time and clearly considered part of the job.
- Expectations should be stated clearly and employees should be held accountable for meeting them.
- Management should be willing to try any reasonable idea for problem resolution or hazard correction/control.
- Employee involvement successes should be well-publicized among all employees.

- Making involvement part of the employees' jobs, involving most employees, and empowering them to make decisions will help steer clear of violations of the National Labor Relations Law.

When hourly and non-exempt employees are truly involved, the most important part of getting everyone involved has occurred and can attract others to involvement as well.

References

Collingwood, Harris. 1996. "Trendicators: How Better People Management Adds to the Bottom Line." *Working Woman* (March): 18.

Hansen, Larry. 1995. "Re-braining Corporate Safety and Health: It's Time to Think Again!" *Professional Safety* 40, no. 10. Des Plaines, IL: ASSE.

OSHA. 1985. *Federal Register* 50, no. 209 (October 29): 43804–43817.

OSHA. 1989 *Federal Register* 54, no. 16 (January 26): 3904–3916.

OSHA. Undated. Unpublished manual, *Managing Worker Safety and Health*, Chapter 1, "Introducing OSHA's Safety and Health Program Management Guidelines." Washington, DC: Office of Cooperative Programs.

Palmer, Daniel S. 1990. Industrial Safety and Health, ICF Kaiser Hanford, personal conversation with the author, August.

Strain, Roger. 1995. Safety and Health Manager, Valiant Plant, material provided to the author in November.

Thompson, Horace. 1994. "VPP Employee Involvement Alive and Well (and Likely to Stay That Way)." *National News Report*, VPPPA (Spring).

"Workers Comp Update: Job Satisfaction Helps Reduce Claims." *Occupational Hazards* 58, no. 2 (1996): 69.

12

Making Sure the Top Manager's Involvement Is Visible

One special factor about the involvement of the worksite's top manager in the worker safety and health program is that it not only has to be real, it also has to be visible to everyone who earns a paycheck at that site. As OSHA says in its voluntary guidelines for safety and health program management: "Provide visible management involvement in implementing the program, so that all will understand that management's commitment is serious" (OSHA 1989, 3909).

In the comment section of the notice, OSHA expanded on this:

Actions speak louder than words. If top management gives high priority to safety and health protection *in practice*, others will see and follow. If not, a written or spoken policy of high priority for safety and health will have little credibility, and others will not follow it. Plant managers who wear required personal protective equipment in work areas, perform periodic "housekeeping" inspections, and personally track performance in safety and health protection demonstrate such involvement. (OSHA 1989, 3912)

In the excellent workplace, responsibility for safety and health, just as for quality and production, lies squarely with the line managers. The top manager must set the example for the subordinate managers and first-line supervisors to make safety and health protection effective.

TOP MANAGER'S SAFETY AND HEALTH RESPONSIBILITIES

The top manager's responsibilities for worker safety and health can be summarized as follows (see also Chapter 6):

- Set the priorities so that everyone is clear about how safety relates to productivity and quality.
- Assign responsibility, provide authority and resources, and encourage active involvement in prevention of hazard exposures by employees at all levels.
- Hold subordinate managers clearly accountable for ensuring the priority of safety and health and for meeting their responsibilities.
- Demonstrate to all workers at the worksite that safety and health have the same *personal* priority as the official policy claims.
- Make good use of professional expertise.

Setting Priorities

The top manager needs to be clear in his or her own mind just where safety and health protection fits into the competing values of the organization. In those organizations where safety and health have clearly been set as the highest priority or shared the highest priority with the protection of the environment, managers found that quality and productivity improved as well.[1] When appropriate attention is paid to how safely and healthfully work can be done, the same level of attention seems to naturally flow over into all concerns about how work is accomplished. But a manager cannot just make a pronouncement that safety is the "top priority" and then forget about it. Everyone looks to the top manager for evidence that the formal priorities are the "real" ones.

Assigning Responsibility with Adequate Authority and Resources

When the priority for safety and health has been set, the next step is to ensure that every subordinate manager has a clear assignment of responsibility for safety and health similar to that of the top manager. Along with that responsibility must come authority to carry it out.

The top manager must also understand the resources that each subordinate manager controls and the competing priorities those managers face and ensure that each subordinate manager has enough resources of time, budget, personnel, training, and so on, to meet the responsibilities

---

[1]See examples cited in Chapter 2, "Introduction to the Management Loop" and Chapter 11, "Ensuring Line Employee Ownership of the Safety and Health Program."

and objectives that are assigned. If safety responsibilities are simply added to an already burdensome load, subordinate managers will only be able to add safety by dropping something else for which he or she has been assigned responsibility and for which accountability also plays a role.

It is also important to ensure that middle managers and supervisors are not shut out of the process. The safety and health program should belong to them as well as to the hourly workers (see the discussion on the role of line managers in Chapter 14.).

Holding Subordinate Managers Accountable

Once the top manager has clearly decided that safety and health will come first, the subordinate managers must be convinced as well. If they have difficulty putting productivity behind any other value, it will not change easily. The top manager can move the change along much more rapidly if he or she makes it clear that both formal and informal accountability systems will focus on how well each manager performs proactively in the pursuit of a safe and healthful environment for all employees under his or her charge.

To encourage proactive safety and health actions, the top manager must be careful not to overemphasize the importance of the numbers of injuries or illnesses, because that encourages reaction rather than action. The focus should be on how well each subordinate manager has encouraged and achieved the personal involvement of all the employees in his or her charge and any contractor companies for which he or she has oversight. It should also be on the ability of the employees under that manager's charge to prevent hazard exposure (for more on accountability, see Chapter 7).

Demonstration of Personal Priority

As OSHA indicated in the guidelines (1989), "visible" management involvement is the tangible evidence of commitment. To provide that visible commitment, top managers have to be seen from time to time by the workers at their worksites. And when they are seen, they should be demonstrating their interest in worker safety and health (see discussion below under "Methods for Visible Leadership").

Making Good Use of Professional Expertise

As line managers and employees take on more and more responsibilities for safety and health, it is important that managers understand when they need professional expertise for safety and health matters. This includes safety and health professionals, medical personnel, security, and employee assistance personnel.

For safety and health professionals, professional expertise includes assistance with the vision of the safety and health program and the setting of the safety and health program goal. The top manager should also ensure that safety and health professionals are providing comprehensive surveys of safety and health hazards and are routinely a major part of any analysis of change to the workplace, including personnel and human resource changes (see Chapter 17). The top manager should also look to the top safety and health manager to remind him or her when other values—such as productivity—begin to overshadow the priority of safety and health and, finally, to provide a continuous evaluation of the effectiveness of the safety and health program.

METHODS FOR VISIBLE LEADERSHIP

In its unpublished manual, OSHA lists four techniques for showing visible involvement: "getting out where you can be seen, being accessible, being an example, and taking charge" (OSHA undated, 3-1). These categories cover the techniques used most often by site managers at worksites with excellent safety and health protection. For the purposes of this book, we have reorganized some of the ideas and renamed some of the categories to fit better with what is now being demonstrated by the most outstanding protectors of worker safety and health.

For the manager who is not now using these techniques, the best part about them is that they are quite good for showing appropriate leadership in other areas than just safety and health. As used in this book they include active safety and health intervention, accessibility, setting an example, and ensuring safety and health protection for the whole worksite.

Active Safety and Health Intervention

When the top manager goes into the areas of operation for his or her organization and takes time to "intervene" in the activity to help ensure better protection of worker safety and health, he or she is showing interest and concern. This can be done formally or informally.

Informal Active Intervention

This is simply a matter of the manager going into the areas where the work of the organization is occurring and taking an interest in the work and the well-being of the workers. This technique succeeds in keeping in touch with quality and productivity as well as safety and health.

To be effective, the manager needs to have some training in the areas of interest, such as training in the types of potential and existing hazards of the worksite and generally what is supposed to be done to prevent or control those hazards (see Chapter 24).

In the informal intervention, the manager moves through the areas where people are working and keeps his or her eyes open. Where something is occurring that looks like a problem, the manager stops and asks some questions. Even when a manager is sure that something unsafe is being done, the "why this is happening" is much more important than the "who is to blame." If, after asking questions of employees, the manager is still not certain whether a problem exists, the supervisor should be called over and asked about the situation. If the issue is still unclear, the safety and/or health professional should be contacted. All of this should be couched in terms of the manager's concern for the well-being of the workers and the work's progress. The first few times the manager attempts this sort of informal intervention, he or she may be more comfortable having a safety and/or health professional come along.

This informal approach is broader than an "inspection," as the manager should also be getting to know the employees and making them comfortable. The manager wants to encourage employees to bring up anything that concerns them when they see him or her in their areas.[2]

---

[2]Whenever a top manager bypasses the hierarchy, great care must be taken to keep the bypassed managers and supervisors feeling part of the team. OSHA's draft manual has an appendix, called "Walking the Fine Line," in which this is discussed. It has been reproduced in part as Appendix 4 in this book.

Formal Active Intervention

The formal mechanism of active intervention for safety and health is a routine inspection of work areas for housekeeping and/or routine safety and health problems. The manager may accompany other inspector(s) or perform an inspection alone. If the manager goes along with other inspectors, he or she needs to balance carefully the need to be visibly involved with the other inspectors' need to be actively involved in decision making.

While making the inspection, the manager should make sure that he or she stops to talk to some of the employees in the various areas being inspected. Talking to the employees serves at least two purposes. First, it allows the manager to find out from employees if there are any conditions or practices that are of concern in terms of possible hazard exposures. That information will improve the manager's ability to make a thorough inspection. Second, by talking to employees while making the inspection, the manager will ensure that the employees know who the manager is and realize that he or she is concerned about worker well-being.

When the manager performs formal inspections, he or she should be trained to recognize routine housekeeping and other routine safety and health problems just as any other nonprofessional inspector should be.

Neither the informal intervention nor the formal inspection requires that the manager become a safety or health professional, only that the manager be able to recognize possible problems.

While many worksite managers perform regular housekeeping inspections, it is not necessary that the top manager be involved with every inspection to provide a means of formal intervention. On the other hand, the manager should be in the worksite at least monthly to provide visible involvement.

Accessibility

While top managers may not have the time to be accessible every minute of the day to their employees, accessibility can result in important information to a top manager who otherwise may only receive the information that those surrounding him or her wish to provide. Highly successful top managers, including some corporate CEOs, make sure they are out where the work is being done periodically. As an example, it is reported that Paul Kahn, who built AT&T's Universal Bank Card into the world's largest issuer of MasterCard in four years, immediately took steps to increase his accessibility when he took over a new company. He spent about one-third of his time at planned lunches and breakfasts, meeting with employees. Symbolically, he propped open the door to the executive wing with a notebook. His chief operating officer also spent about 40 percent of his time just walking around talking to people (Austin 1995).

Nor is Kahn all that unusual. One of the twelve rules of success articulated by Bill Marriott, chairman and CEO of Marriott International, Inc., is: "See and be seen. Get out of your office and make yourself visible." Marriott is on the road one week out of each month visiting hotels around the world. "If [the workers] can see me, it helps them personalize the company. And in the end, good morale means good productivity" (Faiola 1996).

The manager of a nuclear weapons site frequently approaches employees in one of several cafeterias at midday and asks to join them for lunch. By joining different groups of employees in different cafeterias, he can get an understanding of the problems faced by the more than 3,000 employees and help to get them resolved.

Methods for accessibility include informal "instant" access, "open door" policy, "bypass" meetings, and birthday meals.

"Instant" Access

This method is similar to the informal intervention described above. It involves encouraging employees to ask questions or bring up concerns to the top manager whenever they see him or her. It requires being out where employees are working at least every other month. As the top manager goes through work areas, he or she stops and engages workers in conversation, asking about any problems that appear to interfere with getting the job done and getting it done safely. While the manager need not always focus on health and safety, he or she should be sure to bring the subject up frequently enough that workers can see that it is a personal concern that is no less important than productivity or quality.

The manager should make sure to let employees know that their concerns are being taken seriously and ensure that they get timely and appropriate responses. As OSHA points out in the unpublished manual, "In return, your employees will let you know what is troubling them" (OSHA undated, 3-3). That can be very beneficial to a manager.

"Open Door" Policy

As Paul Kahn's propped open suite door symbolically indicated, an "open door" means that the manager's door is open and employees may walk in. A modified "open door" means that employees are encouraged to make an appointment for the next open period (convenient for the employee's schedule) on the top manager's calendar, usually for the same day. When appointments are necessary, the person who makes appointments for the manager must be sensitive to the importance of these meetings.

When initiating an open door policy, be careful not to load it down with any requirements to be met before seeing the top manager. Open door means access to the top manager, not to the usual hierarchy. Allowing employees to deal with the top manager only after dealing with every supervisor and manager in between is a "chain of command" policy, not open door.[3]

It may take some reiterating of the open door invitation to find employees brave enough to try it. When someone does, it is important to make sure that everything goes smoothly. That means that no unnecessary delay is imposed on seeing the top manager and that the top manager gives his or her attention completely and is responsive to any concerns raised. It also means no unpleasant ramifications for the employees in terms of reaction from his or her supervisor or any intermediate managers. The top manager can help with this, by congratulating the managers and supervisors of the first few employees who are brave enough to try the open door. The managers and supervisors should be told that the employee's use of the open door shows confidence in them. If the top manager knows of any manager or supervisor who has actively encouraged employees to use the open door, the top manager should make it known generally how pleased he or she is.

Bypass (or Split Level) Meetings

These meetings are set up to bypass the hierarchy and allow workers at all levels to hear from and speak to the top manager. The problem to be aware of here is that large groups are intimidating for many employees. OSHA's unpublished manual recommends two hundred or less. Some people, however, will feel too intimidated by more than twenty or thirty to speak up. Others feel safer with fifty to one hundred and feel "exposed" in a

---

[3]The "chain of command" policy is a little better than cutting off all access to the top manager but not much. It can beat down all but the most determined (or fanatical) of employees.

small group. Once again, it is important to build a sense of trust and personal concern.

Many managers begin these sessions with a brief explanation of the latest concerns and problems from the point of view of management and ask for questions or comments about those subjects first before asking for additional topics. A manager might ask for a show of hands on some issue that may be expected to have employee interest. There must be enough time, however, for the employees to bring up topics of their own.[4]

Birthday Meals

The birthday meal is a more social version of the bypass or split level meeting. It is somewhat more expensive but also much more relaxed. In this version, the top manager hosts a breakfast or lunch for all employees who have had a birthday within a certain period of time, usually one month. The use of birthdays makes a nice random sample of all levels of the worksite. The food should be informal and reflect the type of food that employees enjoy. At larger worksites, there may be more than one of these birthday meals each month.

Being an Example

Albert Schweitzer once said, "Example is not the main thing in influencing others, it's the only thing" (Bridges 1991, 61). Site managers can set important examples for line employees, their supervisors, and subordinate managers by the way they are seen to behave and react. They

---

[4]Any manager who comes across an employee with a topic about which that employee would apparently be willing to speak forever while others do not seem interested will need to suggest that the employee come meet with him or her after the current meeting at a later date. It will, of course, be important to follow up and ensure that the one-on-one meeting does happen within a reasonable period of time.

must scrupulously follow safety and health rules and practices, insist that any rule or safe practice violation they notice be corrected, and be visibly involved in safety and health.

Follow Safety and Health Rules and Practices

If workers are asked to behave in certain ways and they see management officials behaving in a different way, they are unlikely to take these requirements very seriously. Managers must go out of their way to be sure that no action of theirs is likely to be seen as a rule or safe practice violation. Sometimes this means following rules that are meant for people who will be in a certain atmosphere for a whole working day, instead of a few minutes. Sometimes it means following rules meant for people who are much closer to machinery than the manager will be. By following the rules even in those situations, the manager shows respect for the rules and conveys the sense of their importance.

Insist on Rule Violation Correction

If workers, supervisors, or subordinate managers know that the top manager has seen and understood a rule or safe practice violation and ignores it, a clear signal is sent about the importance of such requirements. The top manager does not need to be concerned about blame or discipline but should simply insist that the problem be addressed immediately to remove exposed workers from hazard.

Be Visibly Involved in Safety and Health

By being visibly involved in safety and health such as discussed above, the top manager sends a signal to subordinate managers, and to others as well, that managers should make the safety and health of the line workers a primary concern.

Ensuring Safety and Health Protection for the Entire Worksite

True safety and health leadership by the top manager includes the assumption of the responsibility to ensure that any worker earning a paycheck at the site be appropriately protected from safety and health hazards. This aspect has been the subject of a revolution having almost as much impact on business today as the increasing involvement of line workers in decision making.

In the 1980s, company leadership, for the most part, believed in the importance of distancing themselves from contract operations at their worksites. There was fear that any action taken to ensure contract workers' safety would provide a basis for the contract workers to claim they were employees of the contracting company with all the benefits of employees. Additionally, there was also concern that such actions involving safety and health would make the contracting company liable for blame if one or more of those contract employees were injured or made ill by the work at the contracting company worksite.

During the late 1980s and into the 1990s, a number of catastrophic accidents in the chemical/petroleum industries involving contract workers served to call attention to the importance of ensuring good safety and health protections and practices for everyone working at a worksite. A spokesperson for one of the contractor companies involved in the Pennzoil explosion in the fall of 1995 pointed out that a lesson they had learned was that at a multi-contractor worksite "you're only as strong as the weakest safety program" (McClatchy 1995).

By the mid-1990s, it was clear that the top manager of the worksite providing excellent protection of worker safety and health was also determined that everyone who earned a paycheck at the site would be adequately protected. For most mid-size and large worksites, contractor companies are used for various tasks that require their employees to work at the worksite controlled by the contracting company. Some huge worksites, such as the Dow Chemical Freeport, Texas site, even have many vendor employees who spend their workdays and, sometimes, their work careers on the Dow worksite. Even small worksites have construction or repairs done periodically that require contracting for a whole set of contractor employees to be on the company worksite for long periods of time.

Ensuring the safety and health of these non-employee workers involves the contracting pre-bid or bid process, the contract itself, oversight of contracted activities and the authority to dismiss unsafe contract workers or whole contractor companies.

Pre-bid or Bid Process

The pre-bid or bid process provides the opportunity to review the potential contractor's history of injuries and illnesses as part of the procurement process. Sometimes the "experience modifier" (EMR) rate (set by insurance companies) is used, sometimes the OSHA 200 logs are used, and frequently both are reviewed. Comparing potential contractors' experience to the industry average, either nationally (comparing injury and illness rates to the latest Bureau of Labor Statistics' national average for that industry) or locally (the EMR) gives the contracting company a good idea how well the contractor company has protected its workers in the past.[5]

---

[5]Please note that review of safety and health experience as a consideration in the pre-bid or bidding process does not necessarily mean pre-qualification. In cases of small businesses, past history may not necessarily predict future experience. In that case, what a contractor plans to do (and does) after winning the bid may be more important.

Review of the bid also usually includes a review of the written safety and health program, although it might be called by a different name, such as "injury prevention plan." That review will provide a good idea of how well the potential contractor has prepared for possible safety and health hazards of the work in the bid. The plan or program should include provision for any needed personal protective equipment, worker training, self-inspections, and other standard safety and health protection activities. Dow Chemical Texas Operations is also requiring that their contractors provide self-evaluations of their own safety and health programs against the VPP requirements (Longino 1996).

The Contract

The language of the contract should include clear representation that the contracting company has the right to oversee safety and health practices and conditions and to make corrections if the contractor cannot or will not. It also includes the right to terminate any contract worker for repeated violations of safe work rules or practices and to terminate the contract company itself if the problems become repeated and intractable.

Oversight

Ensuring adequate safety and health protection for contractor personnel includes inspections and reviews by contracting company personnel to make sure that conditions and practices are providing the protection envisioned. This role must be assigned to individuals who have appropriate training to understand the potential hazards of the contractor work being performed as well as those that may exist due to the conditions or processes of the contracting company operations. Oversight activities that result in the discovery of hazard exposures must lead to timely actions to correct the hazards, whether by the contractor company or by the contracting company.

Dismissal

Just as in every other aspect of accountability, the ability to take action to dismiss is important as a preventive measure when dealing with the oversight of contractor companies. Frequently, when these policies are started, contractor companies do not really believe that the contracting company is serious. Sometimes, it requires some terminations before everyone understands what the rules are.

Paris Watson, Safety Superintendent at Ciba's McIntosh, Alabama chemical plant, tells a story about a contractor who had to be terminated after several violations of safety rules. As Mr. Watson walked him to the gate, the contractor said that he had read the contract but did not believe that Ciba was serious. Mr. Watson asked him why, then, he did not come back and comply, since he knew now that the company was serious. The contractor said he could not because he had not bid a high enough for the contract to cover a good safety and health program (VPPPA undated a).

BENEFITS OF VISIBLE MANAGEMENT LEADERSHIP

No aspect of a business can run well if the production or service employees do not operate well. Bill Marriott's number two rule in his twelve rules for success is: "Take good care of your employees and they'll take good care of your customers, and the customers will come back" (Faiola 1996). Excellent employees with excellent leadership produce excellent quality and productivity.

The quality of the relationship between managers and line employees is therefore a crucial and possibly deciding factor in achieving excellence. No other aspect of a manager-line employee relationship is as key as concern for the line employees' well-being. It is much easier to trust management in many areas if you already know that management cares about your well-being.

A manager who has not established a relationship with hourly or non-exempt salaried production or service workers may not yet be aware of the benefits that await the manager who has. These fall into three major categories: increased information, improved employee morale, and reduced injuries and illnesses and their resultant costs.

Increased Information

Of all the benefits of establishing the kinds of relationships described above, it is the increase in important managerial information that is most directly beneficial to the top manager as an individual. As the site manager interacts with line employees, he or she is picking up a broad source of information about the business. Employee concerns include practical production problems, quality problems, and efficiency ideas. They know more about what goes on at the points where production or service happens than anyone else.

This kind of information puts a site manager in a much better position to make managerial decisions. Employees who feel that their top manager really cares about their well-being are much more likely to share information that is helpful. The interaction, therefore, is only half of what provides the benefit. The other half is the demonstration of the manager's interest in the welfare of the line production workers, which enlists the employees' trust.

Improved Employee Morale

Hourly or non-exempt salaried workers enjoy working in an atmosphere where they can see the top manager's interest in their well-being and in what they have to say about the workplace and the work. Human beings do not enjoy feeling like cogs in a big machine. They appreciate being valued for their intelligence and special expertise. Improved morale results in improved productivity and reduced absenteeism.

Reduced Occupational Injuries and Illness

Employees who can see how important safety and health is to the top manager are much more likely to take it seriously themselves. When employees take safety and health seriously, they not only become more careful about their own well-being, they also take an interest in the safety and health of their fellow workers. As a result, the systems set up to prevent injuries and illness work much better, fewer people get hurt or become ill, and less time is spent trying to react to hazard exposures. Costs go down and profits go up. As just one example, Mobil Oil's refinery in Joliet, Illinois saw a remarkable drop in its lost workday case rates during the period 1988 to 1993 (see Figure 12-1). It also reported a decrease in workers' compensation costs of 89 percent, a decrease in absenteeism of 25 percent, improved morale and relations with contracting companies, as well as increased productivity[6]

---

[6]Tom Moeller, manager of the refinery at that period, also related in personal conversation with the author that the changes made for entry into the VPP had actually given him more time. He said that full worker involvement and good relations with contracting companies had reduced the necessity for him to spend so much time "putting out fires."

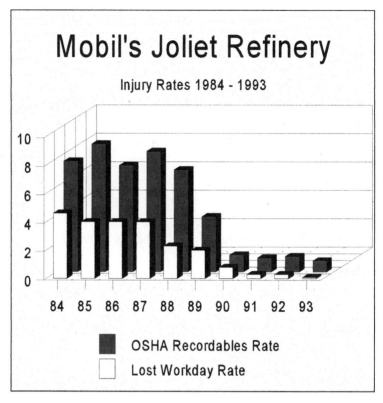

Figure 12-1. Mobil's Joliet refinery, injury rates 1984–1993.
Source: VPP Participant's Association, materials from VPP Application Workshop, undated.

(VPPPA undated b). The refinery had begun preparation for application to the VPP in 1988. It was approved for Star in 1990.

KEY POINTS

- Top managers are responsible for setting, priorities, assigning responsibilities, holding subordinate managers accountable, demonstrating their personal priority for worker safety and health, and making good use of professional expertise.

- A successful manager spends time where line employees produce products or services and takes an active interest in their concerns.
- The top manager needs general but adequate training in the types of hazards that can be found at the worksite and the expected controls for those hazards.
- A successful manager provides for access to and from line employees outside the boundaries of the hierarchy of the worksite.
- The top manager sets an example for subordinate managers, supervisors, and line employees through active and visible demonstration of concern for worker safety and health.
- The concerned top manager insists on a safe and healthful worksite for everyone who earns a paycheck at the worksite.
- The top manager who provides visible, active leadership for the pursuit of excellent worker safety and health protection earns trust and communication from employees at all levels.

With all employees and the top manager visibly involved in safety and health, total involvement has begun.

REFERENCES

Austin, Nancy. 1995. "The Skill Every Manager Must Master." *Working Woman* (May): 29–30.

Bridges, William. 1991. *Managing Transitions,* Reading, MA: Addison-Wesley Publishing Co.

Faiola, Anthony. 1996. "On the Road With a Hands-on Manager: Workers Learn . . . There's Only the Marriott Way." *Washington Post, Washington Business,* no. 258 (August 19).

Longino, Lynn. 1996. Dow Chemical Texas Operations, telephone conversation with the author, July.

McClatchy, Janet. 1995. "Pennzoil Explosion: Who's Responsible?" *Occupational Hazards* (December): 13.

OSHA. 1989. *Federal Register* 54, no. 16 (January 26): 3904–3916.

OSHA. Undated. Unpublished manual, *Managing Worker Safety and Health,* Chapter 3, "Top Management Leadership: Showing Your Commitment." Washington, DC: Office of Cooperative Programs.

VPPPA. Undated a. Interview with Paris Watson in the third segment of a ten-segment video presentation on managing worker safety and health. Falls Church, VA: VPPPA.

VPPPA. Undated b. Materials used in the VPP Application Workshops presented by the VPPPA.

13

The Challenge for Safety and Health Professionals

With top management actively and visibly involved and hourly and non-exempt workers taking over the actual implementation of the safety and health program, the question could be asked, What does the safety and/or health professional do now? This question may be more relevant for the safety professional than the IH, since line employees have not taken over much more than routine noise and contaminant monitoring or routine ergonomic analysis in the fields where IHs work. When it comes to safety, both managers and workers may feel quite knowledgeable. As Randy Barror, Safety Programs Manager for GE Plastics, notes, "Safety professionals really need to know their jobs because most of the folks on the floor know a lot about their own safety"[1] (Barror 1995). This is especially evident in the workplaces that are achieving worker safety excellence.

The role of the safety and health professional has evolved into a fascinating professional challenge that makes the job more rewarding than ever but not necessarily easier. Part of the challenge is to achieve and, even more important, maintain broad and deep knowledge about potential hazards and the means to manage their prevention or control.

It follows that the logical result of the accumulation of expertise is to provide it to those in the workplace who need it when they need it. This may either be formal or ad hoc. Formal provision of expertise is usually for major annual or biennial activities such as comprehensive surveys or planning and taking part in the annual program evaluation and planning of coming year objectives. But it may occur more frequently as formal training.

Informal or ad hoc provision of expertise comes in response to needs perceived by those who implement the various parts of the safety and health program and in coaching as the professional sees the need.

Beyond the provision of expertise, the safety and health professional is in a very good position of being able to stand back and look at the whole picture, while others are involved in program implementation. This gives the professional the opportunity to keep track of where the program is headed and to alert others when problems can be seen ahead.

Therefore, the components of this new role are maintenance of professional expertise, establishing the vision,

---

[1]Mr. Barror helped guide the Selkirk plant to Star and later was given the job of providing assistance to GE plants desiring to achieve Star approval. At time of publication, approximately eight GE plants had reached that goal.

coaching of line managers and employees, continuous evaluation, and acting as the "safety conscience."

MAINTENANCE OF PROFESSIONAL EXPERTISE

As mentioned several times, while line managers and employees need to be trained to understand and recognize routine hazards, they need not become experts. Experts are needed, however, since not everything in the workplace is going to be routine. So the experts are going to be the same people they always were, those who devote their professional careers to worker safety and health.

Being truly expert means applying much more than common sense because common sense "experts" will be around every corner in the excellent workplace. Today's safety expert needs to spend time maintaining expertise of several different types in a rapidly changing world. Not only will safety and health experts need to refresh and hone their technical knowledge and skill, but also their knowledge of management techniques and skills in group facilitation, effective listening, and persuasion. This maintenance of knowledge and skills will include continuing professional development, benchmarking for best industry practices, and tracking safety and health regulations through development to implementation.

Continuing Professional Development

Safety and health professionals will need to expand their areas of knowledge and skills to achieve two things: (1) deep knowledge of the potential hazards of their industry and how to prevent or control them; and (2) a wide area of technical knowledge that goes beyond the particular industry in which the safety or health professional is working.

Depth of knowledge allows the safety professional to understand what is known about potential hazards in his or her industry, whether or not all of the potential hazards have ever been a practical problem at that particular workplace. The breadth of knowledge beyond one particular industry will enable the professional to pick up potential hazards in unusual circumstances at the workplace.

Safety and health professionals will also need to know techniques for managing the safety and health program, even though they do not have direct responsibility to manage it, because they will be supplying ideas to and coaching those who do. Beyond that they will need to know how to facilitate group decisions about safety and health policies and programs, which requires effective listening, group dynamics, and coaching skills. There are several ways to do this and most safety and health professionals are very aware of those ways. Briefly, they include attending professional development courses and workshops, attending trade association safety and health workshops, and keeping up with the literature of their professions.

Professional Development Courses

Professional development courses offered by professional organizations as well as more standard conference workshops are the most usual way to keep professional expertise up to date in terms of both depth and breadth. The development courses are usually held in the days just before professional conferences and frequently involve an additional payment.

Local universities may also offer courses in the safety and health fields that can provide professional development. For small businesses, sometimes state OSHA Consultation Programs team up with professional organizations and VPP participant worksites to provide free courses. Information about those would be available from the individual states.

Trade Associations

Trade associations may also offer workshops on safety that can help increase depth of knowledge in potential hazards of the industry and methods to control them. These are usually held in conjunction with trade association conferences.

Literature

Keeping up with the literature is an additional help at a very low cost. Reading magazines published for the profession is less time consuming than courses and conferences but requires an ongoing commitment to small pieces of time. References in the articles will also lead to books published that can help with the maintenance of professional expertise as well.

Benchmarking for Best Industry Practices

"Benchmark" is a surveying term referring to the marks made along a survey line noting differences of level. The benchmarking done in industry today involves looking at the practices of other companies and worksites to measure the "levels" of your accomplishments against theirs. In most cases, it also means learning and following the examples of methods that get good results for those other companies and worksites.

Robert Siegel, a recent president of the National Safety Management Society, draws an analogy between modern-day industry benchmarking and what the Pilgrims at Plymouth Rock did with the Native Americans, going to them to learn best how to survive in a new land. "I am amazed, as I travel about, how many people have not gone outside their own companies to get some good safety ideas." He adds, "If we do not grow and have continuous improvement, then we are going to fall behind and our organization is going to lose. . . . While we may stand status quo with a satisfactory safety program, our competition is going to pass us with their 'world class' safety program" (Siegel 1995, 2).

What can be learned by the benchmark technique goes beyond technical knowledge of potential hazards and methods of prevention or control and includes managerial processes, programs, and concepts that are applied to protecting worker safety and health. In order to ensure learning and the possibility of improving, you will need to measure your programs and processes against the leaders. To do this well involves finding out who the industry leaders are and how to share their information.

Finding industry leaders is both harder and easier than it seems. Harder because reputations take a while to build and a while to diminish. The "grand old safety leader" in your industry (or in the country generally) may turn out be living on the laurels earned long before. A company or worksite that is trying paradigm-shifting concepts and getting great results may not yet be widely recognized. Excellence is not something that is attained to last forever. The achievements that constitute excellence provide a continuously moving target.

To find leaders in worker safety and health protection, one simple method is to attend the annual conferences of the VPP Participants' Association (VPPPA) where you know which companies have at least passed OSHA scrutiny and have been recognized for excellence by the regulatory agency. Even though some of these might disappoint from time to time, they are much more likely than any other group of companies and worksites to be on the "cutting edge" of safety and health management. The VPPPA conferences feature multiple workshops on many diverse worker safety and health protection topics and provide showcases for the programs, processes, and concepts being used at worksites recognized for excellence.[2]

It is also helpful to attend workshops on safety and health protection at your trade association meetings and conferences, as well as those of professional organizations. You may come across descriptions of new ideas that indicate a good company or worksite for benchmarking.

You can also find descriptions or references to good results or new ideas in worker safety and health literature, particularly in the magazines. Occasionally in the general press, business sections may refer to companies as having new management ideas that include worker safety and health.

Many leading-edge companies are very open to the idea of having other companies come to their worksites for benchmarking, because they then feel they can do reciprocal benchmarking of their own. Even if they are not ready for a benchmarking visit, they may be willing to provide written information about programs and processes and their results. Since OSHA encourages sharing from its VPP participants, they are usually good bets for benchmarking. Lists of participants and contact names and numbers can be obtained from the VPPPA or from OSHA.[3]

---

[2]For the phone number and website address of the VPP Participants' Association (VPPPA) see footnote 3 in Chapter 1.

[3]The telephone number for OSHA's VPP staff at the time of publication was (202) 219-7266.

Tracking Safety and Health Regulations

While government regulations usually run behind best industry practices, they can sometimes be a good source of information. The best available scientific information is collected in the process as well as information from other companies. It is helpful to follow the development of regulations from the time they are first announced. That permits catching up in any areas where the government proposal indicates it may be required.

Most trade association and professional organizations do a pretty good job of keeping safety and health professionals informed about what the government is doing and what various other people and organizations think of it. There are also publications that reprint all government announcements (*Federal Register* notices) involving worker safety and health.

ESTABLISHING THE VISION

While the vision of the results of the safety and health program is really the responsibility of the whole team, particularly managers and hourly or non-exempt employees, it usually falls to the safety and health professional to guide the group. In many cases, it is the resident safety and/or health professional who has the vision and then achieves "buy-in" from the rest of the group, because this is the person who focuses on worker safety and health and who tracks success and failure. As Roger Strain, Safety Manager for the Weyerhaeuser Valiant, Oklahoma mill, says, "Always ask yourself and others why things are the way they are and why they cannot be better" (Strain 1995).

Other safety and health team members look to the safety and health professional as the expert to provide leadership as to what they should aim for and what they can expect to accomplish in their safety and health program. As Mr. Strain advises, "Set high expectations. You get the level of performance you accept" (Strain 1995). His colleague from a competitor company, Leroy Deckelman, Safety Manager of Georgia Pacific's Crossett, Arkansas plant, agrees, "All goals must present a challenge. 'Impossible' challenges are achieved every day" (Deckelman 1995).

These gentlemen, whose worksites achieved OSHA Star status and have maintained it for years,[4] see themselves as the originators of the vision. They understand that everyone at the worksite must be involved in the agreement upon the vision, but they clearly take the lead in its establishment. Their point of view is echoed by Jeff Johnston, Manager, OSHA Resources, at Eastman Chemical Company in Longview, Texas: "Clearly define objectives with input from all workgroups" (Johnston, 1995).

COACHING LINE MANAGERS AND EMPLOYEES

The safety and health professional in the workplace where excellence is constantly sought operates much like a sports team coach, developing the game plan, helping the players hone their skills, and staying on the sidelines. There is simply no way that the safety and health professionals can achieve a safe and healthful workplace by themselves. They just cannot be everywhere at once. And in the world of occupational safety and health excellence,

---

[4]All three of the gentlemen quoted in this part have helped guide their sites through Merit approvals to OSHA's VPP, Star approvals, and Star re-approvals. The Crossett plant was approved to Merit in 1988 and Star in 1991. The Valiant plant was approved to Merit in 1992, Star in 1994. The Longview plant was approved for Merit in 1993 and Star in 1994.

the safety and health professional knows that coercion has severe limitations. As Mr. Barror says, "You can demand, you can threaten, but until you learn to coach and lead by example, you will struggle. Effective coaching requires the use of many basic management skills such as planning, employee involvement, effective listening, analysis and flexibility." For him, coaching is influencing people without the need to exercise authority (Barror 1995).

The safety and health professional as coach is on the lookout for ways to involve more people at all levels of the organization. He or she is thinking about new subjects or methods for training to increase safety and health knowledge and skills for all employees. The coach looks for opportunities to teach informally in real-life situations. Mr. Barror gives a good example of this method:

> You are walking through an area of your plant. You notice someone removing a guard with the primary source of power in plain view and not locked out. A coaching safety and health professional calmly stops the unsafe activity, asks why it is being done that way, talks through the hazards that exist, shares the case histories of accidents that were due to similar situations, covers the proper procedures and asserts confidence that the individual will, for his/her sake or for that of the family, follow the safe procedures. You can then walk away, knowing that the procedures will be followed without coercion. (Barror 1995).

The key ingredients in Mr. Barror's example are true of all good coaching, a calm approach, provision of good information, pointing out the benefits of doing what the coach suggests, and leaving the choice of action up to the individual. With members of management, the benefits pointed out could also involve direct or indirect positive impact on productivity and quality. A good safety and health coach works all the angles to persuade. The coach must also be a good listener. There may be alternative ways to reach the desirable result. It does not have to always be precisely what the coach envisions, as long as the result is achieved.

Providing Continuous Evaluation

Since the safety and health professional no longer has to try to implement the safety and health program, he or she is in a good position to stand back and take a look at how all the pieces are fitting together and to notice where some adjustment is needed to keep the overall program on track. While a major effort will be made each year by a larger group to evaluate activities and achievements against the goal and objectives for the safety and health program, the safety and health professional should provide a continuous evaluation informally. This is done both by keeping a close eye on the incidence of near misses, first aid cases, and recordable injuries and by watching how the activities of the safety and health program are being carried out.

As long as all is going well, nothing needs to be said or done. Where the professional sees signs that problems are appearing, it is time to step in and provide coaching to get things back on the track to excellence. As Mr. Strain says, "I try to stay out of the way but I audit and track to make sure we head in the right direction. I am ready to step in when we need a course correction" (Strain 1995).

Mr. Strain feels very strongly about the importance of data trending to help find patterns that need addressing.

Starting about 1988, we could see heat stress problems starting to increase. We instituted work rotation and stressed the need to drink more often. In 1992, we had the bottoms of the boilers replaced in the power house. We also hired extra people so we could rotate more workers into cooler areas more often. In 1994 and 1995, we increased ventilation and started providing special heat training each April and May. Our incidence of heat stress is now at zero. (Strain 1995)

Records of employee notices of hazards they see and of inspections made can also provide data for trending to pick up patterns that might indicate problems that are not currently being addressed satisfactorily. But there is more to continuous evaluation than records. Just walking through areas may provide information about possible areas of problems from observing conditions and practices without even making a formal inspection. Accompanying those who do make inspections or do accident investigations from time to time will help the safety and health professional understand how well those important parts of the safety and health program are being handled.

The alert safety and health professional also listens well in even casual conversations with workers to pick up any indications of possible safety and health program problems.

ACTING AS THE CONSCIENCE OF THE SAFETY AND HEALTH PROGRAM

A slightly different aspect of the safety and health professional's job is to look for slippage in the priority position of safety and health. Everyone else at the worksite is busy balancing all the competing priorities. In days of "right sizing" everyone remaining in the workplace must juggle priorities to manage the scarce resources of time, budget, and personnel. The safety and health professional is in a good position to see the impact on safety and health and remind top management as well as committees dealing with worker safety issues that safety and health must stay foremost if more than short-term productivity and quality are to be achieved. As Mr. Deckelman says, "Safety goals sometimes have to be protected from other people's priorities like production. So a safety professional must also coach managers when priorities get out of whack" (Deckelman 1995).

KEY POINTS

- In the workplace where safety and health management is excellent, safety and health professionals are no longer the implementers of the safety and health program.
- Safety and health professionals need to achieve and maintain a high level of professional expertise to supplement the routine safety and health knowledge of managers and workers.
- Safety and health professionals should always be looking for ways to improve safety and health protection and the systems to manage that protection, helping the implementers set challenging but attainable objectives.
- Safety and health professionals must be "coaches," influencing people to ensure appropriate protection rather than exercising authority.
- Safety and health professionals can provide continuous evaluation of the safety and health

program through data trending and keeping their eyes and ears open.

- Safety and health professionals act as the conscience of the program, alert to the need to protect the priority of worker safety and health.

With the top manager visibly involved in safety and health and with both hourly and salaried non-exempt workers providing most of the implementation of the safety and health program, the safety and health professionals provide their expertise and special perspective to support the achievement of total involvement.

REFERENCES

Barror, Randall. 1995. Private conversation.
Deckelman, Leroy. 1995. Private facsimile communication.
Johnston, Jeffrey. 1995. Private facsimile communication.
Siegel, Robert. 1995. *The Communique* (October/November). Weaverville, NC: National Safety Management Society.
Strain, Roger. 1995. Private facsimile communication.

14

Other Important Members of the Safety and Health Team

The key to really successful safety and health program results is *total* involvement from all members of the workplace. The need for the involvement of top managers, the workers, and the safety and health professionals is well accepted at this point. Safety and health professionals are called upon to provide their expertise and to help find best industry practices. Hourly and non-exempt salaried employees are asked to take part and assume "ownership". Everyone acknowledges that the top manager can make or break the success of the program. Frequently forgotten are three other major groups: line managers, staff professionals in fields other than safety and industrial hygiene, and contractor organizations working at the same site. These groups are very important for the success of the safety and health program.

LINE MANAGERS

When it comes to occupational safety and health, probably no other group at the workplace is more frequently blamed for lack of progress and program failures than line managers. Over and over again, a pact is arrived at by the top manager, employees, and the safety and health staff to make safety and health the "top priority." When their efforts fail or do not progress at the speed envisioned, workers and safety/health professionals quickly point to the obstacle as "line managers" or "middle managers."

Top managers, sometimes allied with their top staff members, are usually not as forthright but will indicate the problem through such phrases as "difficulty in getting the word out" or "slowness in achieving a culture change." Yet rarely do you find a situation where line managers are viewed as obstacles if they were made full partners in the effort, particularly when they are involved from the start.

Robert Brant, Mobil Chemical Company's Manager, Safety, Health and Loss Prevention, agrees that the involvement of middle-line managers and supervisors is the most frequently overlooked part of safety and health involvement planning. He adds:

> Involving line management at every level and from the start is crucial to worker safety and health excellence. Their attention to safety translates into safer working conditions and safer employee behaviors. All managers must not only have specific objectives and be held accountable for results, they must also be visibly involved. We saw reductions of injuries and improved employee morale and productivity wherever this was true.[1] (Brant 1996)

---

[1]Mr. Brant led his whole company into Star Program approval. Mobil Chemical Company was honored by the Secretary of Labor in 1987 for having all its plants

Most of what will be offered in this section has already been presented from the point of view of the top managers. Here we will review what needs to be done from the point of view of the line or middle manager. Frequently, the line manager has for years been inspected, scrutinized, and critiqued by safety and health professionals. Now with the new push for employee involvement, the only change the line manager may see is that it is hourly employees who are doing the inspecting, scrutinizing, and critiquing. He or she is still the one being judged—and probably found wanting.

The line manager is living through an ever flattening organization. First-line supervisors, if they still exist as such, are nervous that they will lose their jobs. Higher level managers are facing a future of managing large groups of people with fewer subordinate managers and supervisors to help get the product out or the services performed. They are asked to do more with fewer resources of time, budget, and personnel. They are given more priorities than they can juggle. Is it any wonder that they get a little defensive when safety and health practices and conditions in their areas are found wanting? Is it really a surprise when they are reluctant to let some of their best workers take time for safety and health committees, inspections, investigations, evaluations, and so on? On top of that, they are not quite sure that their own superior managers really mean it when they say that safety is a priority over production.

With all that, there are workplaces where all the line managers from the site manager to first line are enthusiastically and fully involved in the implementation of successful safety and health programs. The key is full

---

(at that point there were 27 of them) in Star. In the years these plants were being prepared for Star approval, Mobil reduced its losses by $8 million.

participation, top managerial support, and a good system of accountability.

Full Participation

Line managers should be involved in much the same way as the top manager and also in the same ways as line employees are. The constraints are really not so much the kind of activity in the safety and health program but the time that each individual line manager has. Obviously each line manager cannot be expected to do everything the top manager does and everything that employees do as well. But each manager should be involved in some of both types of activities during the course of a year. In any case, at least some of the activities of top managers and employees, such as routine inspections, may overlap.

Leadership Role Activities

Each line manager should provide safety and health leadership in the areas that he or she manages. The manager must make clear his or her priority for safety and health in relation to the other values of the worksite, in particular, production. The line manager must also delegate and clearly assign responsibility for safety and health tasks and activities, making sure that each responsible employee has adequate resources (time, training, budget, etc.) and authority to get the job done. Each responsible employee, whether a subordinate manager, supervisor, or non-exempt employee, with assigned safety and health responsibilities must be held accountable both formally and informally for meeting those responsibilities.

It is also important for each line manager to demonstrate his or her *personal* priority for safety and health by showing subordinate managers, supervisors, and employees his or her interest in the well-being of those who may be exposed to hazards. This demonstration can occur through the same means as advised for top managers, actively intervening for safety and health (informally or formally in inspections), making himself or herself accessible to workers for the expression of their concerns, setting an example by actions and making sure that all contract work done for the line manager is done safely and in a manner which protects not only the contract employees but also the company employees who work in or around them. (For more information about leadership role activities, see Chapter 12.)

Taking Part in Employee Participation Activities

Line managers should be considered for all of the different types of safety and health participation, but preferably not in leadership roles. Their experience and insight can be very valuable to these group activities, whether they are making routine inspections, investigating accidents, planning an awareness program, or evaluating the whole safety and health program's effectiveness. Some assistance may be necessary in the beginning to help these experienced leaders sit back and let hourly or non-exempt salaried employees take the lead. Having at least some of your line managers involved in these activities can also increase acceptance of the time that employees spend on them and understanding what is involved. As with employees, the most effective use of line managers is to rotate their participation so that all of them can have some experience working on safety and health as equal partners with line employees.

Superior Management's Support

A crucial factor in getting the line manager involved in the safety and health program is that the top manager and all superior managers provide support to each line manager for his or her involvement. This includes provision of resources and informal encouragement.

Provision of Resources

The line manager is no different from the employee with safety and health program responsibilities in terms of needing appropriate resources to get the job done. The line manager particularly needs training and time. The manager needs the same skills training as employees for specific safety and health activities. He or she may also need some training in teamwork and the understanding of group dynamics.

Time is probably the key resource. The line manager bears the brunt of too much to accomplish and not enough of anything (time, personnel, budget) to succeed. Unlike hourly workers, line managers do not get paid overtime, and an overload of responsibilities can result in a terrible erosion of personal time needed for recreation, family, and rest. It may seem like a contradiction to call for increased involvement of line management and then to lament the overload that managers already have, but it is the responsibility of the top manager and the superior managers to take everything into account and make sure the line manager can accomplish everything asked of him or her. Some additional time can be gained when more of the manager's routine duties are delegated; even more time is gained when production can run smoothly because everyone involved is prepared to ensure defect-free operation.

Encouragement

The line manager also needs informal encouragement to be involved and to encourage, in turn, the involvement of those he or she manages. Line managers who are themselves involved and whose employees are involved need informal recognition from their superiors (and from the hourly workers and subordinate managers with whom they work in partnership.)[2]

Systematic Accountability

Nothing shows the importance of actions as much as a formal accountability system that rewards those actions and provides impetus to correct the failure to act effectively. To be effective in this way, the system must hold managers accountable for positive actions for safety and health, rather than just for the negative factor of avoiding injuries. While injuries may often be a result of lack of action, it may take a while for that lack of action to actually result in a reported injury. On the other hand, some injuries that occur may not be under the control of the manager to whose employee the injury occurred.

Care should also be taken that the formal accountability system is supported by the informal accountability system. If line managers who are regularly found wanting in their safety and health responsibilities formally but are nevertheless rewarded in other ways such as with promotions, plum assignments and perquisites, or simply noticeable praise and encouragement from the top managers, the formal accountability system will have been negated.

---

[2]If a line manager has the most employees reporting hazard concerns, that manager should be praised even if the hazards are in the areas he or she is responsible for. Hazards for which controls have been designed and implemented pop up continually in workplaces. What really counts is how fast they are noticed and recontrolled. Having a workforce that is alert and responsive should reflect well on a line manager.

OTHER STAFF PROFESSIONALS

Beyond the hourly and salaried non-exempt workers, line managers, and worker safety and health professionals, there are two types of staff professionals that are important to the success of the safety and health program. The first category is staff professionals from related fields. The second category is made up of staff professionals whose expertise is necessary for some parts of the safety and health program.

Related Fields Staff Professionals

Fields that obviously are related to safety and health include occupational medicine, environment, security, and employee assistance.

Occupational Medicine
Occupational medicine has a very special relationship with industrial hygiene and safety. A worksite with occupationally trained physicians and nurses onsite or on contract should take advantage of the special expertise and perspective that these professionals can bring to hazard identification and prevention or control. Too often, this available expertise is limited to initial diagnosis and follow-up of workers compensation cases.

In its unpublished manual, OSHA devotes a whole chapter to occupational health professionals, listing the functions of the medical professionals in the safety and health program as preventing hazards, providing early recognition and treatment, and limiting the severity of injury or illness. Elsewhere in the manual, OSHA describes the use of occupational physicians or nurses in making comprehensive surveys of potential hazards (OSHA undated).

Any medical professional providing services to a worksite needs to understand the type of worksite and its potential hazards to make better diagnoses and prescribe better treatment. Periodic tours through the worksite are a good idea for that purpose. Many excellent worksites go beyond that stage to ask the medical professional to join with the industrial hygienist and safety professional for ergonomic or other surveys or analysis of potential hazards and to help with emergency response evaluation and planning.

Environment
Environmental staff professionals are frequently concerned about environmental aspects of precisely the same equipment, materials, and processes as are safety and health professionals. Working together or coordinating efforts can better utilize the time and efforts of each group. Recognizing this, many excellent worksites have combined their environmental efforts with worker safety and health at a level low enough to ensure good coordination. Some example areas for combination/cooperation are comprehensive surveys, worker committees, and worker reports of hazards and/or environmental problems.

Security
Security personnel can be of particular assistance to the safety and health program in the area of violence or terrifying threats of violence in the workplace. In one company, the security staff tracked down the source of obscene phone calls that were being made to several women on their plant telephones. The fact that the caller seemed to have a lot of personal information about them led to the discovery that a personnel booklet containing pictures and personal information about workers at the plant had been discarded in a dumpster near the printing

plant after a printing mistake was found in the first run. The security staff was able to provide information to the local police, which resulted in the arrest of the culprit. There was also a change in procedures requiring printers to shred any personnel materials not provided to the plant.

Screening of visitors to the plant (particularly when combined with metal detectors) can reduce incidence of domestic and other violent crimes on plant premises. Tracking of employees who have been released for unstable or violent behavior can reduce the chance of a return visit for violent purposes (see Chapter 19 for more on preventing workplace violence).

Employee Assistance

Employee assistance professionals can also assist in prevention of violence in the workplace. In fact, many believe they are the "front line," playing a large role in identifying potential threats to the workplace and/or to workers. Trained in confrontation management, employee assistance professionals can defuse critical situations that might otherwise lead to employee abuse, threats, injuries, and even fatalities (Richardson 1966).

Employee assistance professionals should also be utilized to help employees through the shock and grief associated with serious accidents of all kinds as well as violent incidents. This is helpful even for employees who are not personally injured but who are emotionally upset and hurt by an incident (Richardson 1996). At New York State Electric & Gas, Dr. Joe Sandonato, the health and safety manager, says that employees are encouraged to use the employee assistance program. Even "witnessing a heart attack or severe injury can be very upsetting. We ask supervisors to be alert for employees that need extra support. If someone needs counseling, we want them to know it's there for them" (Hans 1997, 9).

Beyond concerns about violence and traumatic incidents, employee assistance professionals can help employees deal with stress. According to Jon Grice, job stress can lead to inattentive behavior, withdrawal, and substance abuse, all of which can lead to hazard exposure (Grice 1995). As Sarah Wortham puts it, "Stress can hinder decision-making. Because employees are distracted, they're more prone to mistakes." Further, she asserts that job stress costs businesses between $100 and $300 billion annually (Wortham 1996).

Additional Staff Professionals

Other staff professionals in areas such as human resources, procurement, and engineering can be crucial for specific parts of the safety and health program.

Human Resources

Human resource staff professionals are the experts on disciplinary systems and performance evaluation systems. Both of these are very important to the safety and health program. Human resource professionals can help ensure that the discipline system is set up to be fair, covering all employees, and that the disciplinary system really supports the safety and health program. To do that, the system must first and foremost carry a message of the importance of working safely and in a healthful manner and downplay a perception of punishment.

The formal accountability system must also provide for specific evaluation of safety and health performance, preferably for actions taken rather than injuries "avoided." The human resource professionals can help accomplish that goal.

Frequently, labor relations are part of human resources. Labor relations professionals can help construct systematic worker participation in the safety and health program without violating any existing collective bargaining unit agreements or the National Labor Relations Act.

Procurement

Contracting personnel can help ensure that unsafe or unhealthful equipment and materials do not enter the workplace. They can also set up the contracts system to help ensure that contractor company workers who work at the worksite are adequately protected (see discussion of contracting in Chapter 12).

Engineering

Engineers can help design or redesign workstations and or equipment to better prevent or control the potential hazards.

All of these staff professionals should be made to feel part of the safety and health program and appreciated for their positive contributions. As Brant says, "At our best plants, even the sales and marketing staffs took their turns on worker safety and health committees—and definitely were contributors" (1996).

CONTRACTORS AND THEIR EMPLOYEES

Beyond the aspects of managing contractor companies to ensure the safety and health of their workers who earn a paycheck at your worksite, really excellent worksites are working in partnership with their contractor companies. These worksites are combining employees from contractor companies in the committees and activities that their own employees take part in. This is particularly true where contractor companies are "nested," which is to say that they have long-term contracts to provide ongoing services at the worksite, such as maintenance and/or long-term construction projects. The crossover of experience and expertise is frequently very helpful to both the contracting and the contractor companies and among various contractors.

Contractor personnel can, with the appropriate training and resources (which may be provided by their own companies or by the contracting company), make inspections, investigate accidents, analyze jobs, and plan joint awareness programs. They should be closely involved in emergency planning and drilling for the whole worksite.

KEY POINTS

- If line managers are made full participants in the safety and health program, goals are achieved more readily.
- Line managers can be involved in the safety and health program both in their leadership role in day-to-day activities and as a co-equal to employees from all levels in group activities.
- The top manager's support for line managers' involvement in the safety and health program is crucial both for encouragement and the provision of adequate resources.
- Related professional fields staff in areas such as occupational health, environment, security, and employee assistance should be integrated into the safety and health program. Their similar activities should be carefully coordinated with the safety and health professionals.
- Engineering, human resources, procurement, and other staff professionals should understand the importance of their roles in the safety and health program.

- The safety and health program is strengthened by having the involvement of contractor companies and their employees.

When line employees, the top manager, safety and health professionals, line managers, other staff professionals, and contractor companies and their employees are all fully involved in the safety and health program, success in achieving not only the safety and health goal but most other goals of the workplace is virtually assured.

REFERENCES

Brant, Robert J. 1996. Personal conversation.

Grice, Jon. 1995. "The Relationship Between Job Satisfaction and Workers' Compensation Claims." *CPCU Journal* (Fall). Chartered Property Casualty Underwriters Society.

Hans, Mick. 1997. "Avoid the CPR Scramble." *Today's Supervisor* (February): 9.

OSHA. Undated. Unpublished manual, *Managing Worker Safety and Health*, Chapter 10, "Establishing the Right Medical Program for Your Worksite: The Occupation Health Delivery System." Washington, DC: Office of Cooperative Programs.

Richardson, William A. 1996. Manager, Employee Assistance and Equal Opportunity Counseling Program for the Naval Surface Warfare Center at Dahlgren, Virginia, personal conversation.

Wortham, Sarah. 1996. "Hard-hitting Tips to Coach You Through Stress." *Today's Supervisor* 60, no. 7: 14–15. Itasca, IL: National Safety Council.

15

The Totally
Involved Workplace

A worksite that has total involvement from every segment of its population will find the continual quest for excellence within reach every day of the year. This type of involvement allows, as Burns put it in 1964, "people at each level . . . [to] bring to bear their particular experience and expertise to help the organization solve its problems and achieve its goals" (1964).

In the totally involved workplace, the top manager not only has made clear the priority for worker safety and health protection but has followed up by showing his or her personal priority through visible involvement and ensuring the ability of others to keep to that same priority. The line managers and supervisors have clear roles in the safety and health program, including both their own personal demonstration of priority through their visible involvement and by ensuring that those they manage have what they need to be effectively involved. Hourly or salaried non-exempt workers assume the leadership of the implementation of the safety and health program. They are joined by contract workers in the activities of and decisions about the safety and health program. They are supported by staff professionals of many types and skills as well as by the safety and health professionals who guide through influence and expertise.

Not unlike the classic systems of the management loop explored in Part I, total involvement concepts can help to achieve other organizational goals such as high quality and productivity as well as excellence in the protection of worker safety and health.

The totally involved workplace builds upon the closed loop foundation of classic management systems and opens the way for effective use of management systems to assess and prevent or control exposure to potential hazards in the worksite.

REFERENCE

Burns, Robert K. 1964. "Management—A Systems Approach." *ASSE Journal* (December).

Part 4

*Systems
Approaches to
Analyzing and
Preventing or
Controlling
Hazards*

16

Introduction to Systems Approaches to Hazards

The point of the safety and health program is to know all the potential hazards that workers could be exposed to and either prevent or control them. Every other part of the overall safety and health program exists to support this objective. Over the years a number of systems have been developed to achieve this objective. Some are used more frequently than others. These systems may be used one way by some worksites and another by other worksites. Worksites may also call systems by different names, adding to the confusion that can occur.

THE VPP

The 1988 revision of the VPP requirements, based on what OSHA staff had learned from six years of experience, organized requirements into six major elements. Of these, two concerned preventing and controlling hazards: hazard assessment and hazard correction and control. These topics were further divided into sub-elements. Hazard assessment sub-elements included:

- Analysis of changes to the workplace
- Comprehensive health and safety surveys
- Routine self-inspections
- Routine examination and analysis of hazards associated with jobs, processes, or phases
- Employee reports of hazards
- Accident/incident investigations
- Medical program

Hazard correction and control sub-elements in OSHA's VPP included

- Means for eliminating or controlling hazards
- Disciplinary action or reorientation for those who break safe work rules
- Emergency planning
- Ongoing monitoring and maintenance of equipment
- Systematic initiating and tracking of hazard correction (OSHA 1988, 26343–26344)

OSHA Voluntary Guidelines for Safety and Health Program Management

When OSHA drafted its guidelines for safety and health program management in early 1989, six months after those revisions to the VPP, it approached the components discussed in this part of the book as two separate elements of the four major elements of the guidelines and called them "worksite analysis" and "hazard prevention and control" (OSHA 1989, 3909–3910) In this regard, they closely followed the organization of the requirements of the VPP.

In the comment section of the notice publishing the guidelines, OSHA introduced worksite analysis as follows:

> The identification of hazards and potential hazards at a worksite requires an active, ongoing examination and analysis of work processes and working conditions. Because hazards are by nature difficult to recognize, effective examination and analysis will approach the work and working conditions from several perspectives. (OSHA 1989, 3913)

And in the comments on hazard prevention and control, the agency added, "Effective management prevents or controls identified hazards and prepares to minimize harm from job-related injuries and illnesses when they do occur" (OSHA 1989, 3914).

The language used in these comments indicates that OSHA staff members were still thinking of worksite analysis as hazard identification and discrete from hazard control. When the manual to explain implementation of the guidelines was drafted, however, the sub-elements of the major element called "worksite analysis" were divided into two chapters, one on establishing a hazard inventory and the other on "catching the hazards that escape controls." The chapter on hazard prevention and control was placed between these two chapters (OSHA undated).

This approach led to the concept of one nearly seamless system that inventories hazards, plans for prevention or control, and then catches the hazards that elude controls. That more seamless approach is what we will follow in this part.

For the hazard inventory, we will discuss the use of comprehensive surveys, change analysis, job hazard analysis, process hazard analysis, and phase hazard analysis. For hazard prevention or control, the topics will be engineering controls, work practices, personal protective equipment, administrative controls, and the role of accountability in hazard control. We will also cover hazard correction tracking, preventive maintenance, unplanned event preparedness, and the medical program as supplemental tools of hazard control. For dealing with the hazards that elude controls, we will consider inspections, employee reports of hazards, accident/incident investigations, and hazard and incident trend analysis.

Obviously, these categories are not perfectly distinct from each other. For example, sometimes new discoveries of potential hazards are made during self-inspections or trend analysis. Often, employees will bring up a situation that everyone had been unaware of. Comprehensive surveys and ongoing routine hazard analysis will also find hazards with slipped controls. Medical programs, emergency planning, and preventive maintenance play parts both in establishing hazard inventories and in catching hazards that escape controls. But, for the most part, all of these systems serve the functions that we have described, if they are implemented correctly.

References

OSHA. 1988. *Federal Register* 53, no. 133 (July 12): 26339–26348.
OSHA. 1989. *Federal Register* 54, no. 16 (January 26): 3904–3916.
OSHA. Undated. Unpublished manual, *Managing Worker Safety and Health*. Washington, DC: Office of Cooperative Programs.

17

The Hazard Inventory

Establishing an inventory of potential hazards does not necessarily mean that an actual list is drawn up, but it does mean that, to the extent feasible, all the potential hazards of the worksite are sought out. Without a good understanding of what the potential hazards to worker safety and health are, it is difficult to design and implement an effective program of systems to protect workers' safety and health.

Understanding the routine hazards and the hazards well-known in the industry of the worksite is only the beginning. The excellent protector of worker and safety and health strives to develop new understanding of potential hazards in the industry that may not be well understood by others. Excellent protection also involves understanding potential hazards that may be routine in other industries but which are rare in the industry of the worksite. This additional understanding prepares the worksite for what otherwise might be totally surprising occurrences that result in human suffering and wasted dollars.

The OSHA guidelines describe the tools to be used to accomplish this.

So that all hazards and potential hazards are identified:
(A) Conduct comprehensive baseline worksite surveys and periodic update surveys;
(B) Analyze planned and new facilities, processes, materials, and equipment; and,
(C) Perform routine job hazard analyses. (OSHA 1989, 3909)

In establishing the inventory, we look at the whole worksite and everything in it, including all the processes. The tool we use to begin this process is not as important as starting the work. OSHA has chosen to begin with comprehensive surveys in their baseline stage and we will follow that example. It can also be argued logically that the hazard inventory begins with planning for the control of hazards introduced by changed materials and equipment before their arrival at the worksite.

Therefore, this section will examine comprehensive surveys of the physical plant, analysis of all changes to the worksite to discover what potential hazards might be brought to the work as part of the change, and ongoing analysis of jobs and high-hazard or very complicated processes. It will also cover analysis of the phases of work that should be used in some industries where multiple employers, rapid changes, and overlapping operations are involved.

Each of the systems provides the ability to understand hidden potential hazards and to make adjustments and additions to the systems to prevent and control them.

COMPREHENSIVE SURVEYS

In the comment section of the notice that announced the OSHA guidelines, OSHA explained the comprehensive survey as follows:

> A comprehensive survey of the work and working conditions at a site permits a systematic recording of those hazards and potential hazards which can be recognized without intensive analysis. . . . Subsequent comprehensive surveys provide an opportunity to step back from the routine check on control of previously recognized hazards and look for others. (OSHA 1989, 3914)

Comprehensive surveys are frequently confused with routine inspections or compliance audits and there are, certainly, similarities and areas of overlap. But the comprehensive survey is meant to be an exhaustive review of the physical plant and the conditions of work. While it is not something that is done frequently enough to be considered routine, it is done systematically. The methods used are similar to the gathering of data for the emissions inventory that is required for the Environmental Protection Agency's air quality standards (Mansdorf 1995, 67).

Those who wish to achieve excellence in protecting the health and safety of their workers, beyond the need to gather information about compliance with government regulations, will use the comprehensive survey to discover any potential hazards, so that planning for prevention or control can be done.

Comprehensive surveys set up the original baseline of potential hazards and periodically update the inventory of potential hazards requiring planning for prevention or control. Many worksites put the hazard inventory into a computer database (Mansdorf 1995, 67). When hazard exposures occur, the database is also helpful for hazard correction tracking (Brant 1996).

Scope

When baseline comprehensive surveys are done by industrial hygienists, every substance, no matter how small the quantity, is inventoried; its need is ascertained and whether it is appropriately controlled is determined.[1] The environment is tested for every possible contaminant. Most areas are checked for noise levels. Notations are made not only of potential hazards but also where they occur and how many workers could potentially be exposed. For the periodic surveys that update the inventory, checking against the baseline inventory is done to determine changes and the impact of those changes.

In describing the process for inventorying hazards to industrial hygiene, Zack Mansdorf suggests following the process flow from receiving to shipping, but also making sure that research and development and maintenance are also inventoried (Mansdorf 1995). For a com-

---

[1]Of course, if change or pre-use analysis is in place, most, if not all, of these substances would have been approved before their arrival onto the worksite. The survey would only be picking up those that somehow eluded the mechanism for change analysis.

prehensive survey that covers all potential hazards to workers' safety and health, even office and storage areas and unused buildings or old equipment should be checked.

For safety, the process flow is also followed; buildings no longer in use are checked for signs of recent entry and analyzed for possible need for additional protection. Storage racks are checked to see if they are rated for the weight they are bearing. Stability of floors and roofs is checked.

All work areas should be checked for any obvious ergonomic problems. The comprehensive survey should leave no stone unturned nor any corner unexamined, but it does not need to go too far into depth in any one place.

Job and process analyses are not usually a part of the comprehensive survey, since they should be ongoing and routine. The comprehensive surveyors may check records of routine analysis, however, and might recommend that particular analyses be scheduled sooner than planned in the routine analysis system.

Frequency

Comprehensive surveys should be done every eighteen months to three years, depending upon the nature of the industry and the speed of change. Most systematic comprehensive surveys are done every other year. These surveys are both extensive and time consuming. Some large worksites—such as the Pantex Plant in Amarillo, Texas, which both constructs and disarms nuclear weapons—perform ongoing comprehensive surveys rather than attempt to cover the whole worksite in one effort. This approach allows the Pantex Plant needed flexibility with a large geographical site and nearly 4,000 workers.

At Pantex, segments of the plant are surveyed in each effort, rather than the whole plant.

While the danger in the ongoing survey is that there is a temptation to let the survey fall back more into the scope of an inspection or compliance audit, it is certainly possible to perform good surveys in this manner. It is important to select well-qualified teams and to provide some "fresh eyes" even if they come from a "sister" plant. It is also important to keep good records of the survey findings.

Appropriate Surveyors

The unpublished OSHA manual points out that while inspections are often done by line employees at the site, "comprehensive surveys should be performed by people who can bring to your worksite fresh vision and extensive knowledge of safety, health and industrial hygiene" (OSHA undated, 7-1). While many safety and health functions can be carried out by line managers and employees, this is one function that should be led by safety and industrial hygiene personnel, preferably with appropriate education and certifications. These professionals should be supported in the survey by medical personnel—nurses, physicians, or both. Depending upon the type of worksite, security and other related specialists might also be helpful additions.

If a large team can be supported by the worksite, it is good to have one or two line personnel who are very familiar with the plant and work processes being surveyed. It is also important, where possible, to bring in someone with enough familiarity with the industry to be useful, but with "fresh eyes" that might catch something that otherwise is missed because the surveyors have become accustomed to seeing it.

CHANGE ANALYSIS

Any change in the workplace has the potential of introducing hazards to worker safety and health. OSHA listed the changes needing analysis as new or planned facilities, equipment, materials, and processes (OSHA 1989, 3909). Other changes, such as those having to do with shift work or downsizing, can also introduce new hazards. The concept is to begin the analysis for potential hazards while the change is still in the planning phase.

OSHA's unpublished manual goes into more detail.

Anytime you bring something new into your worksite . . . you unintentionally may introduce new hazards. If you are considering a change for your worksite, you should analyze it thoroughly beforehand. This change analysis is cost-effective in terms of human suffering and financial loss it prevents. Moreover, heading off a problem before it develops is less expensive than attempting to fix it after the fact.

An important step in preparing for a worksite change is considering the potential effect on your employees. Individuals respond differently to change, and even a clearly beneficial change can throw a worker temporarily off-balance—literally as well as figuratively—and increase the risks of accidents. You will want to inform all affected employees of the change, provide training as needed, and pay attention to worker response until everyone has adapted. (OSHA undated, 7-6 to 7-7)

OSHA's point about informing and, where necessary, training employees affected by the change is well taken. Excellent protectors of worker safety and health, however, will also involve employees in the planning for

change and the analysis of potential hazards. Line operators can help select new equipment, analyze it for potential hazards, and set up the standard operating procedures for it. For example, at Mobil Chemical Company,
line operators are sent to visit the manufacturer to help
analyze and debug equipment. They provide both the
manufacturer and company engineers with important
information about how the equipment will be used at the
plant (Brant 1996).

Building or Leasing Facilities

When new facilities are to be built, safety and health professionals should be involved in the review of architec-
tural plans and should visit the building site frequently
during construction to make sure that any potential hazards are prevented or properly controlled. The same is
true for renovations to existing structures.

When leasing of existing buildings is contemplated, a
thorough survey of hazards and potential hazards should
be done by safety and health professionals to inventory the
need for hazard correction as well as hazard control. Hazard correction and any needed adjustments for hazard
control should be accomplished before the facility is actually occupied. The survey should also cover environmental hazards as well, such as toxic wastes that could have an
adverse impact over the long term on worker health. Most
sophisticated companies do this systematically.

Installing New Equipment

Safety and health professional sign-off on new capital
expenditures is pretty standard in large and sophisti-

cated companies. How seriously the sign-off is taken by either the engineers planning the new equipment or the safety and health professionals is another question. At one Midwestern fertilizer plant, the safety manager traveled so heavily and was stretched so thin that he sometimes gave others (without his professional expertise) authority to sign off for him on new equipment. He also rarely had time to do a thorough analysis.

Ideally, not only should the safety and health staff have time to review the specifications for new equipment, but both they and at least one key operator who will be using the new equipment should have a chance to see it and try it out, either at the manufacturer or at another plant where it has already been installed. That way they can see how those specifications actually work in a simulated or real work situation. As OSHA points out, "(a)n equipment manufacturer does not know how its product will be used at your worksite. Therefore, you cannot rely totally on the manufacturer to have completely analyzed and prepared controls or safe procedures for the product" (OSHA undated, 7-7)

Introducing New Materials

Usually the material safety data sheet (MSDS) is the place to start with new materials. Most sophisticated companies will substitute less hazardous materials where they can. Not all MSDSs are equally well done. It is helpful to have an industrial hygienist make further checks on ingredients that are new to the site or new in this sort of combination. A qualitative risk assessment should also be done to decide the priority for new sampling.

Starting New Processes

As OSHA points out:

New processes require workers to perform differently. Consequently, new hazards may develop even when your employees are using familiar materials, equipment, and facilities. Carefully develop safe work procedures for new processes. After operators become more familiar with these new procedures, perform routine hazard analysis . . . to discover any hidden hazards. (OSHA undated, 7-8)

Since the development and promulgation of OSHA's process safety standard, most companies falling under that standard are involved in sophisticated process hazard analysis. However, many that are not covered should be doing analyses to make sure that their processes are not producing unnecessary hazards. Process hazard analysis should start before the process is actually used at the site.

People Changes

One aspect of change that is frequently overlooked, in terms of analyzing the possible adverse impact on worker safety and health, is changes in human resource policies and/or downsizing. William Bridges points out that it is not so much the change as the transition that is difficult for humans. "*Change* is situational: the new boss, the new team roles, the new policy. *Transition* is the psychological process people go through to come to terms with the new situation" (Bridges 1991, 3). Even when the change is considered "good," it means an ending and a loss of what was. Letting go of the past may produce a feeling of confusion and that something is wrong. As a result there is an increased level of turnover during major organizational changes (Bridges 1991, 5).

Any time employees are distracted, their ability to concentrate on doing their jobs well is decreased. When that happens, hazards controlled by work practices may slip out of their controls. Injuries may result. It helps to understand this going into any major change and to plan for increased employee assistance with stress, as well as safety and health awareness activities.

Some human resource changes are more directly connected with potential hazards, however. When the work shift system changes, employees may have to change the biological rhythm of their lives. Workers may lose sleep for a while until their bodies adjust. Their alertness may be adversely affected. Some say that automobile accidents go up right after the switch to Daylight Savings Time, which is attributed to the loss of only one hour of sleep. Research indicates that one-and-a-half hours forward change is about the most that a body can assimilate without "jet lag." Reverse rotating eight-hour schedules may well be the worst to adjust to (Westfall 1996, 74).

Where line employees serve on safety teams, changing shifts may require adjusting those teams to make sure that there is coverage for every shift. At a plant in rural Ohio, shifts were changed and one of the new shifts was left with no inspection team members. No one noticed until several inspections had been missed. Safety and health professionals and medical personnel should be involved in analyzing shift changes before they occur so that possible hazards introduced by the planned changes can be understood and prevented or controlled.

The same thing can happen with reengineering or downsizing. It is important to analyze every change to consider the possible impact on the safety and health of workers and plan accordingly.

Multiple Changes

Where multiple changes occur, the interaction between the changes may produce potential hazards that each individual change alone might not. All of this should be taken into consideration when changes are planned.

Job Safety Analysis (JSA)

Job safety analysis (JSA) is also known as job hazard analysis (JHA) and job safety hazard analysis (JSHA). For the sake of simplicity, we will refer to it here as JSA. It consists of a step-by-step, in-depth analysis of the tasks of a job, breaking each task down to its smallest increments and searching for all possible hazards within each increment, including consideration of the MSDS information as well. When all the possible hazards of the task are listed, the means of prevention or control of those hazards are also listed. To be effective, the analysis must border on the ridiculous in terms of its depth. That way, no surprises can occur.

OSHA suggests continuing with the following sequence:

Now determine whether the job could be performed differently to eliminate the hazards. Would it help to combine steps or change the sequence? Are safety equipment and other precautions needed? If a safer way of performing the job is possible, list each new step, being as specific as possible about the new procedure. If no safer way to perform the job is feasible, determine whether any physical changes will eliminate or reduce the danger. These might include redesigning equipment, changing tools, adding machine guards, using personal protective equipment, or improving ventilation. Establishing a personal hygiene routine may be appropriate where toxic dust is a hazard. (OSHA undated, 7-9 to 7-10)

Once the analysis is complete, the job procedures can be written or revised to reflect the way the job will be performed.

In some companies, a practice has grown up of combining JSAs and standard operating procedures (SOPs).[2] In fact, you will hear employees refer to JSAs in a way that means SOP. The danger here is that an appropriately in-depth analysis would be far too cumbersome to ever use successfully as a procedure. Therefore, what happens is that the JSA is smoothed out and covers only the hazards that obviously need prevention or control.

But, neither should the JSAs be allowed to gather dust once they are completed. If they indicate a need to revise the SOPs, they should be used to do so. In an appliance plant in the Midwest, beautiful JSAs with sketches were completed for a number of jobs. They were in a file cabinet. They had not been used to revise the procedures or to retrain workers, so they had no impact and no value.

In the workplace striving for excellence, hourly workers should be involved in the JSA, the revision of procedures, and the training of workers in the new procedures.

Process Hazard Analysis (PHA)

Much the same as with the analysis of jobs, the analysis of processes for potential hazards to workers is called either

---

[2]Part of the confusion may be that manufacturers provide SOPs with new equipment. These SOPs are based on the manufacturers' analyses of the equipment, including safety and health hazard controls. Any changes to those SOPs would result from the initial change analysis rather than JSAs.

process safety analysis or process hazard analysis. Both have the same meaning.

Since the process safety standard—Process Safety Management of Highly Hazardous Chemicals 1910. 119(e)—was promulgated, much has been written about this systematic approach to chemical hazards. We will, therefore, concentrate here on why some industries not now covered by the standard may need to use process hazard analysis. "OSHA believes that any business aiming for a comprehensive safety and health program will benefit from conducting a process hazard analysis" (OSHA undated, 7-10).

Any process in a workplace that may present hazards should be analyzed in step-by-step fashion to collect all the information about potential hazards to workers (and to the environment) so that planning can be done to prevent or control those hazards. This is particularly true where a process may present potential hazards that are not involved in any job tasks that would be analyzed in routine and ongoing JSAs, such as a noisy or hot process in an area where workers are not involved in the process but work nearby or pass through with great frequency.

Who Should Perform PHAs

OSHA advises that the analysis be carried out by a team.

> OSHA believes that a team approach is the best approach for performing a process hazard analysis, because no one person will possess all of the necessary knowledge and experience. Additionally, when more than one person is performing the analysis, different disciplines, opinions and perspectives will be represented, and additional knowledge and expertise will be contributed to the

analysis. At least one member of the team should be an employee who has experience with and knowledge of the process being evaluated. (OSHA undated, 7-12)

Analysis Procedures

OSHA also suggests charting the flow of the process, then inventorying hazardous substances used or produced by the process—including raw materials, intermediate products, final products, byproducts, and wastes—and planning prevention or control of each potential hazard. In addition, the agency recommends that all the equipment used to assemble the raw materials, to process them, and to move out the products, byproducts, and wastes at the end of the process be analyzed for potential hazards to the workers involved in the process, working nearby, or passing through the area (OSHA undated, 7-13 to 7-14).

In all of these areas, it is important to look at combinations of system failures to see what potential hazards might result, using such well-known techniques as "what if?" or "fault-tree" analysis. When fatalities and catastrophes occur, so often we hear something like "Three things went wrong at the same time—how could we have planned to prevent that?" The answer is that everything that could possibly go wrong should be considered as going wrong *at the same time,* unless your analysis can demonstrate otherwise. And anything that is possible and could present danger to workers should be considered a potential hazard to be prevented or controlled.

OSHA suggests using what-if, checklist, "failure mode and effect analysis" (FMEA), or fault-tree analysis. The checklist appears to be a more organized form of what-if analysis, As OSHA says, "For more complex processes, the 'what if' study can best be organized through the use of a 'checklist'." As part of the checklist, they further recommend a very formal team composition and a number of component substudies (OSHA undated, 7-14 to 7-15).

FMEA also seems to focus on what in the process may go wrong. All the components that could fail are listed and analyzed for their potential modes of failure, the effects of failure, and detection factors.

Fault-tree analysis starts at the other end with all the remotely possible undesirable outcomes and then works its way back to find out what has to happen to bring about that outcome (OSHA undated, 7-14 to 7-15).

Once the process analysis is completed, any needed changes to the process or the way that workers interact with the process must result. If changes are needed, there should also be training for the workers involved to understand why the changes are necessary and how the new precautions will help protect them from exposure to hazards. Even there, the work is never complete. Routine analysis requires periodic updating or redoing. The process safety standard requires that the process hazard analysis be updated at least every five years. OSHA suggests that those who are not covered by the standard but have processes that could benefit also update their analyses every five years (OSHA undated, 7-15).

Phase Hazard Analysis

In some industries—such as construction—the production of the "product" proceeds in phases involving different and/or overlapping activities by different employers. Other industries—such as chemical plants or refineries—have certain periods—such as during "turnarounds"—when phases of operations require different employers and different activities. For these situations, routine analysis must be done by phases. That is, each phase of the operation should be analyzed for the potential hazards involved in each activity and for those created by overlapping activities.

For the purpose of discussing this type of routine analysis, OSHA defines a phase as "an operation involving different types of work that present hazards not experienced in previous operations, or an operation where a new subcontractor or work crew is to perform work" (OSHA undated, 7-16). David DeLorenzo, safety and health director for the Sheet Metal and Air Conditioning Contractor's National Association, provided an example. A painting subcontractor may have employees wearing respirators at a worksite who are working very near to employees of another subcontractor involved in another craft or in general labor. These nearby subcontractor employees, although similarly exposed to hazards, will not be similarly protected unless phase planning and coordination have occurred (NSC 1996a).

How dangerous such lack of planning and coordination can be is evident from the fatality that occurred to a member of a trail crew in the Grand Canyon National Park. Crews were assigned to work at different levels of a hairpin-curve filled trail. Workers at one level were dislodging boulders. Another crew was assigned to work directly below them. A 200-pound boulder was dislodged and fell, striking a worker on the lower crew (NSC 1996b).

In describing what should be done, OSHA refers back to other methods of routine hazard analysis:

To find these hazards and to eliminate or control them, you will use many of the same techniques that you use in routine hazard analysis, change analysis, process analysis, and job analysis. One major additional task will be to find those hazards that develop when combinations of activities occur in close proximity. Workers for several contractors with differing expertise may be intermingled. They will need to learn to protect themselves from the hazards associated with the work of nearby colleagues as well as the hazards connected to their own work. (OSHA undated, 7-16)

There is also a need to coordinate some hazard controls between contractor operations. At one large construction site, two carpenters decided to use a scaffold that had been erected for painters. What was not known to the carpenters was that the scaffold was partially disconnected. All of the painters knew that the scaffold could only be used by those authorized to do so, and the authorized painters knew the scaffold was being decommissioned and had no need to use it. However, since the carpenters were not supposed to be using the scaffold, neither their employer nor any of their colleagues had been warned. The lack of communication (and other management controls in both companies) resulted in fatalities.

Many companies also use a work permit system to help coordinate activities and ensure that adequate planning has been accomplished before a job is begun. Good joint analysis, planning, and coordination of phases among employers in these special types of operations will save lives and prevent illnesses and injuries.

Key Points

- Management needs to understand all existing potential hazards to worker safety and health, including hazards that develop from new technology in the industry and hazards resulting from activities or conditions outside the mainstream of product or service operations.

- Comprehensive surveys provide the opportunity to step back from the routine safety and health program activities and look for potential hazards that would otherwise go unnoticed until problems occur.
- Of all the hazard analysis tools, comprehensive surveys have the greatest need for safety and occupational health education and expertise.
- Comprehensive surveys set up the baseline of the hazards inventory, which should be updated periodically.
- Anything to be introduced to the workplace that has the potential to expose workers to hazards should be analyzed to find those potential hazards so that they may be prevented or controlled before the change actually takes place.
- All changes in facilities, equipment, materials, processes, and personnel practices that impact when and where employees will work should be analyzed by safety and health professionals, with the support of occupational health professionals, to ensure that all potential hazard exposures are prevented or adequately controlled.
- Every task of every job should be analyzed for every possible potential hazard on an ongoing cyclical basis with more hazardous tasks being reviewed at least every two years.
- Line operators or personnel providing the service sold should be intimately involved with the analysis of hazards within those jobs.
- Process hazard analysis should be carried out even where not required by standard to ensure that processes do not introduce potential hazards that will not be caught by other routine hazard analysis.

- Phase hazard analysis allows worksite managers with multiple and overlapping operations—including those by different employers—to determine potential hazards and plan to prevent or control them before the new phase of activity begins.

With systems for comprehensive surveys, change analysis, job hazard analysis, process analysis, and, where needed, phase hazard analysis all in place and operating well, the continuously updated hazard inventory should be in place.

REFERENCES

Brant, Robert J. 1996. Personal conversation.

Bridges, William. 1991. *Managing Transitions.* Reading, MA: Addison-Wesley Publishing Company.

Mansdorf, Zack. 1995. Developing a Hazards Inventory. *Occupational Hazards* (September). Cleveland: Penton Publishing.

NSC. 1996a. "Construction Subcommittee Makes Progress in Programs." *OSHA Up-to-Date* 25, no. 11 (November): 4.

NSC. 1996b. "Death in National Park Draws Citations." *OSHA Up-to-Date,* 25, no. 9 (September): 2.

OSHA. 1988. *Federal Register* 53, no. 133 (July 12): 26339–26348.

OSHA. 1989. *Federal Register* 54, no. 16 (January 26): 3904–3916.

OSHA. Undated. Unpublished manual, *Managing Worker Safety and Health,* Chapter 7, "Establishing Complete Hazard Inventories," and Chapter 9, "Catching the Hazards That Escape Controls." Washington, DC: Office of Cooperative Programs.

Westfree, Peggy. 1996. "Too Tired to Work?" *Safety and Health* 154, no. 3: 74–76.

18

Basic Tools of Hazard Prevention and Control

The second step in our systems flow is the planning and implementation of prevention or controls. This involves both technical and management approaches. The management aspects of applying both technical and management skills are covered in this chapter. OSHA recommends:

So that all current and potential hazards, however detected, are corrected or controlled in a timely manner, establish procedures for that purpose, using the following measures: (A) Engineering techniques where feasible and appropriate; (B) Procedures for safe work which are understood and followed by all affected parties, as a result of training, positive reinforcement, correction of unsafe performance, and, if necessary, enforcement through clearly communicated disciplinary system; (C) Provision of personal protective equipment; and, (D) Administrative controls, such as reducing the duration of exposure. (OSHA 1989, 3909–3910)

Unless complete prevention can be achieved—wherein the potential hazard is completely removed from the worksite—most hazard control involves a substantial amount of management. In fact, most hazard control involves a combination of the menu of controls available and the management systems that support them, including enclosures, barriers, personal protective equipment, work practices, and the systems of enforcement, discipline, and positive reinforcement.

ENGINEERING THE CONTROL

Much has been written about the hierarchy of controls, which should be well understood by sophisticated companies. There is still much concern, however, that too little attention is paid to *designing in* hazard prevention and/or control. In early 1996, the National Safety Council proposed to create an Institute for Safety Through Design with the purpose of promoting the benefits and defining "the methods of including decisions affecting safety, health and the environment in all stages of the design process," because "business and industry need more emphasis on safety, beginning in the engineering and design stages of operations" (Manuele 1996, 22).

Usually the easiest means of prevention and/or control of a potential hazard is whatever can be designed into the facility, equipment, materials selected, or processes before installation and/or use. Hank Lick, manager of industrial hygiene at Ford Motor Company, described Ford's approach to noise control as "Buy it quiet, keep it quiet, and fix the rest" (Megan 1996, 50). Changed slightly to read "buy it safe, keep it safe, and fix the rest," this would be a succinct expression of the sophisticated employer's approach to the whole area of hazard prevention and control.

Designing in hazard prevention or control is usually referred to as "engineering controls." OSHA's unpublished manual provides these three principles for engineering controls:

1. If feasible, design the facility, equipment, or process to remove the hazard and/or substitute something that is not hazardous or is less hazardous;

2. If removal is not feasible, enclose the hazard to prevent exposure in normal operations; and,

3. Where complete enclosure is not feasible, establish barriers or local ventilation to reduce exposure to the hazard in normal operations. (OSHA undated, 8-2)

These principles translate into careful planning based on the best possible knowledge of potential hazards. The concept is to put as much of the hazard control into the design as feasible to reduce the amount of control required by such human actions as work practices, administrative controls, or personal protective equipment (PPE).

OSHA gives several examples of their three stages of engineering controls. For elimination of the hazard, it cites:

Redesigning, changing or substituting to remove the source of excessive temperatures, noise or pressure; redesigning a process to use less toxic chemicals; redesigning a work station to relieve physical stress or remove ergonomic hazards; or designing general ventilation with sufficient fresh outdoor air to improve indoor air quality and generally to provide a safe, healthful atmosphere. (OSHA undated, 8-2)

For enclosure of hazards, the agency describes:

Complete enclosure of moving parts of machinery; complete containment of toxic liquids or gasses from the beginning of the process using or producing them to detoxification, safe packing for shipment, or safe disposal . . . .; glove box operations to enclose work with dangerous microorganisms, radioisotopes, or toxic substances; and complete containment of noise, heat, or pressure-producing processes. (OSHA undated, 8-3)

For barriers or local ventilation, it discusses:

Ventilation hoods in laboratory work; machine guarding, including electronic barriers; isolation of a process in an area away from workers, except for maintenance work; baffles used as noise-absorbing barriers; and nuclear radiation or heat shields. (OSHA undated, 8-3)

WORK PRACTICES

Once a potential hazard is allowed into the workplace, whether or not it is enclosed or barriered, human practices will be necessary at some point to control hazard exposures. Even enclosed processes require maintenance to keep them operating smoothly or repair them when something goes wrong. When that happens, the enclosure is broached and work practices must take over.

All types of engineering design controls depend upon sound work practices to keep them in place and functioning properly. An example is a ventilation system. If it is allowed to collect dust and to crack, the engineering design will be overcome by human error and poor management. The work practices support for engineering controls can be crucial. Even the tragedy at Bhopal might have been avoided had the alarm system that was designed to alert operators of danger not been disconnected by human action.

Work practices, for our purposes, also include general workplace rules, housekeeping practices, and standard operating procedures, which have an impact on safety and health. All of these rules are usually better followed when those who are required to follow them have a part in their development.

General Workplace Rules

"Rules convey the expectations of behavior," according to Howard Spencer. Their "goal is to influence error-free behavior" (Spencer 1996, 10). Most workplaces have general workplace rules that, in the safety and health area, usually forbid horseplay or violent behavior at a minimum. In fact, all too frequently rules are phrased negatively, perhaps even as long lists of don'ts. "Humans react better to positive statements" (Spencer 1996, 10).

Some employers also put broad safety rules—such as reporting all injuries and illnesses that occur on the job and requiring the adherence to all safety precautions—in the general rules. These general safety rules are usually found in the employee manual. Most worksites require newly hired employees to sign off on the rules as a record that they have read and understood them.

General Housekeeping Rules

All workers should be following general housekeeping rules concerning keeping their work areas free of tripping or slipping hazards and generally neat and clean. In workplaces where dust may be toxic, these general rules should also include wetting down dust and/or wiping equipment clean. General housekeeping rules usually also include keeping emergency exits and walkways clear.

Standard Operating Procedures (SOP)

All procedures in the workplace should be written, provided to workers, and kept in an accessible place for those who are expected to follow them. They should also include any needed safety and health precautions.

Before standard operating procedures (SOPs) are developed[1] or revised, job safety analyses (JSAs) should be performed to ensure that all potential hazards in the job have been analyzed, and hazard prevention and controls have been planned. It is helpful to have some of the operators who will be performing the jobs assist in the JSA. Once the JSA is complete, the procedures can be developed, once again using some of the operators to make sure that the procedures make sense in terms of the reality of the job (for more on JSAs, see Chapter 17).

Training in the new or revised procedures should educate all operators in the potential hazards and how to

---

[1] When new equipment has SOPs developed by the manufacturer, that usually means that an analysis of potential safety and health hazards has already been accomplished by the manufacturer. That analysis should be corroborated by the purchaser's own change or pre-use analysis. See Chapter 17 for more information on pre-use analysis.

protect themselves and others from exposure. SOPs should be reviewed and revised periodically in conjunction with ongoing routine JSAs.

All work practices require the support of good systems of training, reinforcement, and provisions for correction or discipline. Workers must understand why the practices are necessary as well as how to follow them. They must also understand the importance that management places upon following the practices.

PERSONAL PROTECTIVE EQUIPMENT (PPE)

James Tye, the former director general of the British Safety Council, once remarked on the American tendency to "hang things on people—helmets, gloves, shoes." He recounted visiting a large automobile factory where workers were decked out in protective earmuffs. He asked why, since all the noise came from one corner of the plant, the source of noise was not removed so people would not need to wear so much equipment. Although he said he received no real answer, he speculated that it was because the United States can be so litigious and that company lawyers had recommended making workers responsible for their own protection (Wortham 1996, 41).

Whether or not this is true, Mr. Tye makes a good point about the responsibility placed on workers. Protective clothing and equipment can reduce hazard exposure to a great extent; however, they also depend on the following of work practices for their effectiveness.

Because the provision of PPE is regulated by OSHA standard and each employer is required to evaluate the entire workplace for the need for PPE, not much explanation is needed for sophisticated workplaces. A few points about PPE, however, deserve some emphasis.

Workers need training in the use of PPE that thoroughly explains the need for the PPE and precisely how it helps control their exposure to hazards. They also need to understand how to care for and maintain the PPE.[2]

Acceptance of PPE is easier when workers have a role in determining what types of PPE are needed and have a range of choices, where feasible. Jim Vinson, Director for Safety and Health at Boeing in Seattle, Washington, says, "At one time we didn't ask the employees, we just went out and bought the equipment and put it in the tool rooms. The employees had no options." He said that the result was that much of the equipment did not fit and that it was difficult to get the employees to use it. Once workers were used to help evaluate and select it, he says, "We have a lot better compliance today than we've ever had in the past" (Swanson 1996, 60).

PPE should be provided by the employer in sufficient quantities and sizes to meet all the workers' needs and should be stored near the work area to encourage use. Two examples, both concerning fall protection, illustrate this. At a shipyard in Louisiana, an employee committee highlighted a problem for gantry crane operators who sometimes, but not often, needed to leave the cab and walk out onto the crane arm itself. Since the fall protection equipment was 70 feet down on the ground and

---

[2]It is discouraging to see respirators, in particular, that have been left out in the workplace where they can gather, inside the face piece, the very fumes or dusts that they are designed to keep away from the respiratory tract. Although the author has seen this in recent years, the most vivid memory is of a Texas spray paint booth in 1982, where a paint-caked respirator was lying on the floor. The spray painter was interviewed about his respirator and was found to have understood very little about why he was required to wear it or how it must be used and maintained to protect him. Management was charged with providing the appropriate information and training for him. One year later on a return visit, the same painter was interviewed again. This time he could explain why the respirator was necessary and how to use and maintain it. He also produced a clean, shiny respirator to show off.

some ways away, they would forego the protection and get the job over with as quickly as possible. The employee committee recommended placing fall protection equipment in each crane cab. Thereafter, crane operators were much more likely to take proper precautions when working outside the cab of the crane.

Sherry Casali reports that one employee group where she consulted on safety observed that only 60 percent of workers used appropriate fall protection when it was required. One problem was that the equipment was in a tool room at the front of the plant, a trip requiring as much as 20 minutes from some work areas. When lockers containing the fall protection equipment were placed throughout the facility, compliance with the requirement to use the equipment rose to 85 percent in only one month (Swanson 1996, 63).

Brant adds that it works best to assign responsibility for storage and maintenance to each worker who is required to use PPE, so that everyone using it will take ownership for it (Brant 1996). That, of course, requires that each worker be trained well in the reasons why PPE is needed and how to maintain and store it. Adequate and convenient storage must also be provided.

ADMINISTRATIVE CONTROLS

Administrative controls—such as worker rotation or lengthened work breaks—are sometimes necessary when other controls just do not provide the desired protection. This is particularly true of extreme temperature hazards when combined with seasonal changes. In Chapter 13 an example is given of continuous evaluation resulting in efforts that brought a formerly high level of heat stress cases to zero at a paper mill. One of the remedies was to rotate workers more frequently out of the hot areas in the summertime. But other efforts, such as replacing the bottom of a boiler, were combined with this administrative one.

Administrative controls can also reduce the stress on workers produced by PPE that may become uncomfortable (or less protective) after several hours—such as respirators or goggles in hot weather conditions.

The Role of Accountability Systems in Supporting Controls

As noted above, work practices and use of PPE require prescribed human behavior. This makes them more vulnerable to human error. Human error must be controlled by management techniques. Management of human behavior is three-pronged, relying on adequate training, positive reinforcement of that training, and, when necessary, the enforcement of prescribed behavior.

Adequate Training

In order for workers to follow rules and work practices, including those involving PPE, they must first know what the rules are and then understand why they are necessary. Interactive training is the best way to get this important information to workers and ensure that they understand it. It is also vital, in this type of training, to use some sort of technique to ascertain how much of the information is understood.

The standard method, having someone stand up in front of a group of workers and read the rules and work practices and then have workers sign their names to a statement saying they have received training and have understood it, is probably the least effective method of teaching the practices and rules.

One of the most effective ways for workers to understand rules and work practices is to be involved in their development. However, it is not usually practical to involve all the workers who will need to follow those rules in their development. It does help if all workers know that people just like themselves were involved in rule or procedure development, particularly if those who worked on the rules help with the training about them.

For ascertaining whether the training information is understood, the best method is having the workers demonstrate their knowledge rather than taking a written test. Giving workers the opportunity to teach other workers also helps reinforce what they have learned. Effective adult education is discussed in Chapter 23.

Positive Reinforcement Systems

The general category of positive reinforcement can be divided into three types: incentives, positive feedback, and performance evaluation. Use of one does not necessarily mean the exclusion of either of the other two. In the safety field, incentives have been used for hourly or nonexempt salaried workers more widely than positive feedback or performance evaluation. But the two other methods are beginning to get more use from sophisticated employers.

Incentive Programs

Incentive programs usually involve providing material rewards for achieving a safety-related goal, such as no injuries. Much has been written about safety incentives in recent years. They are based on the psychological concept of connecting a change in behavior with a reward to increase the chance that the behavior change will occur (Smith 1995, S-5). They are also a tangible demonstration that a company is willing to put money into the safety and health program. Many consider incentive programs as a way of making "sober old safety" fun (Smith 1995, S-13).

Most of the articles being written about safety incentives, however, include information about the limitations of incentive programs. Everyone seems to agree that a good program of hazard control and employee training, possibly even employee assimilation of safety as a personal value, must come before any kind of safety incentive program (Hartshorn 1995; Knapp 1996; Minter 1995; Smith 1995). Other concerns are about the durability of incentive programs, their impact on reporting injuries and illnesses, and whether they actually achieve real behavior changes.

According to Stephen Minter, "many incentive programs seem to lack staying power. When safety awards are introduced, injuries go down, but then after some period of time, injuries begin to creep back up. Safety officials are left puzzled why a program that worked so well has become ineffective" (Minter 1995). Krause and McCorquodale report that "company representatives often exclaim, 'We don't understand it. This year we are doing exactly what we did last year, but accident rates are out of control!' " (Krause and McCorquodale 1996)

One reason this occurs may be related to the reason that these programs appear to work for so many worksites. That is that they are novel and fun. Their newness wears out after a while and the fun is reduced as the program grows "old."

Both Daniel Hartshorn and Scott Geller recommend having employee involvement in the development and implementation of the award program (Hartshorn 1995;

Knapp 1996). "If employees feel they are a part of the decision-making process, there will be greater program acceptance and fewer complaints" (Hartshorn 1995). Many companies have employee awareness committees that develop and revise or change incentive programs on an ongoing basis. That may help avoid the lack of novelty that could lose employee interest.

One of the keys to making a safety incentive program work is to induce peer pressure to change behaviors. Hartshorn feels that setting up incentive programs for work groups instead of individuals enhances the team effort and can discourage employees from abusing workers compensation benefits (Hartshorn 1995). Others worry about the negative impact of peer pressure on the reporting of injuries and illnesses. According to Smith, "A major criticism of incentive programs over the years has been that employees are sometimes discouraged from reporting accidents by co-workers unwilling to risk blowing the safety record" (Smith 1995, S-8) That is why so many safety experts recommend rewarding safe behaviors or safety activities rather than the absence of injury (Knapp 1996).

Jim Spigener, of Behavior Science Technology, suggests that incentives be activity-based rather than results-based, so that employees have more control over whether they achieve the rewards. He points out that employees may not necessarily have to work safely not to have an injury during any specific time period and that to reward an employee who has not worked safely sends precisely the wrong message (Kedjidjian 1995, 44).

The answer to the basic question of whether safety incentives programs actually accomplish what they are supposed to do is not really clear. Krause and McCorquodale point out that managers would never even try to improve quality or production with incentives of the same type used in safety and state categorically,

"Neither safety bingo nor the myriad of related incentive schemes has ever 'worked' anywhere to actually improve safety performance." They point out further that incentive programs may actually harm safety performance objectives, cost a lot, get ridiculed by employees, and beget the expectation that regular incentives are an "entitlement" (Krause and McCorquodale 1996, 32).

But Krause and McCorquodale define incentives as "the promise of cash or tangible goods—such as barbeque utensils, wheelbarrows, tool boxes—to be distributed (or withheld) based on individual or group injury frequency rates." They specifically exempt from their condemnation the distribution of awareness devices— mugs, jackets, and hats with the company or team logos—that are not contingent upon numerical goals and recognition lunches and dinners to celebrate good work and accomplishment (Krause and McCorquodale 1996, 34).

On the other hand, incentive "success" stories are not difficult to find. *Occupational Hazards* cited three such examples in its June 1995 issue. The Perry Equipment Company in Texas, the Cherokee Sanford Group in North Carolina, and the Arrowhead Mountain Spring Water Company in California all claimed to have reduced both injuries and compensation costs significantly through incentive programs that were based either all or in major part on rewards for lack of injury. How many injuries may have gone unreported and unclaimed by injured workers is unknown. The safety manager at one of the three companies admitted that there were occasions of unreported injuries but said that such instances were discouraged and were in violation of company policy (Smith 1995, S-16).

Krause and McCorquodale offer a success story of their own concerning PPG's Lake Charles, Louisiana plant. PPG phased out its incentives programs and replaced them with more individual recognition for positive safety behaviors. Surprisingly, employees were not upset by the discontinuation of their rewards for lack of injury. "Although the employees liked receiving incentives, they were not aware what achievement helped garner the prize. In other words, since no perceived linkage existed between achievement and incentive, the reward had little meaning." For the next three years, as management emphasized the importance of reporting injuries, the numbers rose, indicating the suppression of reporting during the years of incentives. After that the injuries began to go down again, and, with no incentive for not reporting them, PPG felt that they at last had made a real difference (Krause and McCorquodale 1996, 36).

PPG's story is echoed by that of Hercules, Inc. at its paper chemicals plant, where a 1991 incentive program was discovered to have only motivated employees to hide injuries. When the safety committee decided to reward employees for specific safety-related activities (such as attending work-related safety meetings, meeting housekeeping standards, and suggesting and helping to implement safety improvements), the actual number of serious injuries dropped by two-thirds (Knapp 1996).

Research indicates that the ratio of serious injuries to minor injuries is anywhere from 1:30 to 1:300 (Snyder, Loafman, and Fleming 1996, 28). If a company with an incentive program based on lack of injuries notices that minor injuries are running less than 30 to each serious injury, there is a good chance that some injuries are not being reported. In any case, it seems clear that the safest approach to incentive programs, if they are desired, is to base them on positive safety actions and to keep away from rewards for working without (reported) injuries.

Positive Feedback

In their discussion of why not to use incentives, Krause and McCorquodale referred to the provision of positive recognition for safety activities. Many companies have turned to this with good results whether it is part of a formal behavior modification program or just good management practice. The concept is fairly simple: Determine what actions or activities have a positive impact on safety and health, make sure employees know what they are and why they work, and set up a system of observing employees and providing positive feedback to let them know they are doing what is desired or more. Low-key rewards may also be a part of positive feedback systems but are not necessary. Most human beings respond quite positively to feedback telling them what they have done well.

Dan Petersen compiled information from ten positive feedback experiences. These were not specifically related to safety and health but were for behavior changes. The reinforcing systems used were mostly just positive feedback, praise, and recognition. One used unspecified rewards along with praise and constructive feedback. Another combined profit-sharing bonuses with praise. A third combined impact on pay with praise and recognition. All of them achieved the behavior change desired. Four also achieved cost savings. Three resulted in increased productivity (Petersen 1988, 238–239).

Petersen also compiled thirty-five results of studies of safe behavior reinforcement. Of these, twenty-five used only feedback, praise, and recognition. Percent improvements were from 8 to 98. Petersen concluded, "It is possible to measure safety performance through observations of employee behavior. This may be a much more reliable technique than the use of accident statistics, in the short term, for determining the effectiveness of a company's safety program effort" (Petersen 1988, 240–241). It is clear that taking the time to notice what employees are doing and letting them know about what they are doing *right* can be a major factor in safe work.[3] (See also the brief discussion of positive reinforcement in Chapter 7.)

Accountability Systems

While systematic and formal accountability is part of the management loop described in Part 2, it can play a role in supporting work practices and general safety rules if employees at all levels are evaluated for their adherence to rules and safe work practices as part of their performance appraisals. The performance appraisals, in turn, must be the basis for decisions on bonuses, salary increases, and promotions. At the supervisory and managerial levels, the appraisal should also concern the example set, positive reinforcement provided, and accountability required for those working under the employee evaluated. Individual performance appraisals, however, are unlikely to be useful for hourly employees in worksites with authorized collective bargaining agents since the union culture is adverse to individual worker appraisals. (For more information on formal and informal accountability systems, see Chapter 7.)

Enforcement of Prescribed Behavior

The reverse side of positive reinforcement is enforcement. The key to enforcement should be sending a message that the safety and health of workers is a high priority and that procedures designed to be protective of that

---

[3]In a questionnaire study by Rosa and Steven Simon, a negative correlation was found for safety reward systems and low worker compensation costs. The questions used concerned whether promotions consider safety, the motivational quality of awards, and the safety rewards system (Simon 1995). It was not clear exactly what the questions were or how the employees surveyed may have interpreted them.

safety and health may not be ignored or bypassed for the sake of any competing priority. The enforcement system should clearly send the message, "We care about you too much to allow you to take risks."

Unfortunately, the vast majority of workplaces use their enforcement system to place blame and assign punishment. As Goldberg says, "traditionally, safety has been managed and regulated on a blame basis. Many operational managers did not understand the real causes of accidents. . . . The standard procedure: Wait for an accident and then place blame. Those accused were usually the people injured in the accident" (Goldberg 1996, 35).

At a Great Lakes plant that manufactures transportation equipment, a discussion between unions and management about the disciplinary systems started right off with accidents. One of the employee representatives pointed out that there were so many rules that an injured employee was sure to have violated one of them whether or not it had anything to do with the injury. A suggestion by a consultant that the company drop the use of discipline in connection with accidents until its more beneficial use—to stop at-risk behavior—could be established was met with "we can't take the manager's right to discipline away," as if accidents were the only reason for the use of discipline and as if discipline is to be used like a lion trainer's whip.

By contrast, the Safety Manager of a VPP Star site explains, "When we are investigating an accident, the concept of discipline for the injured employee is not part of the investigation. We want to know how it can be prevented" (Strain 1995).

We tend to forget the close relationship of the words "discipline" and "disciple" and the positive meaning of discipline as "training that develops self-control, character, or orderliness and efficiency" (Preston and Topf 1994).

By the time an accident has occurred, it is really too late for discipline. Discipline should be an every day reality. And it should mostly be self-discipline. At the Dow Magnesium Extrusion plant in Denver, formal discipline is seldom used because Dow employees watch out for each other, reminding about safe work procedures and making sure they are followed.

Many safety and health leaders are trying to take the punishment aspect away from discipline by substituting time off *with* pay for time off without pay for employees who have more than one infraction of the safe work practices. The emphasis is on giving the employee some time to think about whether he or she could make safety as important personally as it is to the employer (Brant 1996; Lea 1995, 36). Jim Richardson, human resources consultant, suggests that the employee who has been suspended with pay be given a written questionnaire that asks why the problem exists, what the employee will do to fix it, and when the change in behavior will occur. In this way, the suspension will open up a dialogue about changing behavior and serve as a coaching tool rather than punishment (Tapas 1996, 9).

At the worksite with excellent worker safety and health protection, employees know what disciplinary steps can be taken for violations of safety rules and safe and healthful work practices but will tell you that discipline is rarely used because employees help each other remember to follow those rules and practices.

KEY POINTS

- The best time to prevent or control a hazard is during the design stage.
- If hazards cannot be "designed out," look for ways to enclose them or place barriers between them and workers.

- Work practices, including rules and operating procedures, work better when those who are required to follow them have a clear understanding of why they are needed and have a part in their development.
- Workers are more likely to use required personal protective equipment (PPE) if they have a role in the selection of specific PPE, and if the PPE is kept in areas near where it is likely to be used.
- Appropriate human behavior requires the support of adequate training and accountability systems.
- Positive accountability, including ongoing positive feedback, incentives, and performance evaluations with impact on bonuses and promotions, can have a stronger impact on behavior than enforcement.
- Enforcement systems should be clearly understood and used fairly and consistently to emphasize the importance of rules and practices rather than to place blame and punish after damage is done.
- By the time an accident has occurred, it is really too late for discipline.

Establishment of the best feasible hazard controls combined with effective training and accountability systems to manage human behavior should result in an effective hazard prevention and control program that can be supplemented by systems for hazard correction tracking, unplanned event preparedness, preventive maintenance, and medical programs.

REFERENCES

Brant, Robert J. 1996. Company Manager for Safety, Health and Loss Prevention, Mobil Chemical Co., personal conversation.

Goldberg, Allan T. 1996. "Moving Past the Blame Bias: Safety as a Business Asset." *Professional Safety* 41, no. 1: 35–36. Des Plaines, IL: ASSE.

Hartshorn, Daniel B. 1995. "How to Reward Safe Workers." *Safety + Health* 152, no. 12: 84–86. Itasca, IL: National Safety Council.

Kedjidjian, Catherine B. 1995. "What Do Your Employees Think About Your Safety Program?" *Safety + Health* 152, no. 11: 42–46. Itasca, IL: National Safety Council.

Knapp, Sue. 1996. "How to Design Incentive Programs That Work." *Today's Supervisor* 60, no. 7: 8–9. Itasca, IL: National Safety Council.

Krause, Thomas R., and Robert J. McCorquodale. 1996. "Transitioning Away From Safety Incentive Programs." *Professional Safety* 41, no. 3: 32–36. Des Plaines, IL: ASSE.

Lea, Kathy. 1995. "Safety and Health Q&A." *National News Report* (Winter): 36–37. Falls Church, VA: VPPPA.

Manuele, Fred. 1996. "Can We Catch Hazards Before We Create Them? An Interview with Fred Manuele." *Professional Safety* 41, no. 2: 22. Des Plaines, IL: ASSE.

Megan, Graydon. 1996. "Sound Advice for a Quieter Workplace." *Safety + Health* 153, no. 2: 48–52. Itasca, IL: National Safety Council.

Minter, Stephen G. 1995. "A Safe Approach to Incentives." *Occupational Hazards* 57, no. 6: 171–172. Cleveland: Penton Publishing.

OSHA. 1989. *Federal Register* 54, no. 16 (January 26): 3904–3916.

OSHA. Undated. Unpublished Manual, *Managing Worker Safety and Health*, Chapter 8, "Establishing Hazard Prevention and Control Programs." Washington, DC: Office of Cooperative Programs.

Petersen, Dan. 1988. *Safety Management: A Human Approach.* Goshen, NY: Aloray.

Preston, Ron, and Michael Topf. 1994. "Safety Discipline: A Constructive Approach." *Occupational Hazards* 56, no. 3: 51–54. Cleveland: Penton Publishing.

Simon, Rosa A. 1995. "Innovative Applications of Organization Development Technologies for Improving Safety Performance." Presented at the annual conference of the American Society of Safety Engineers, Peabody Orlando Hotel, June 19.

Smith, S.L. 1995. "Safety Incentives: A Program Guide" (S-5 to S-10). "Saving Dollars With Incentives" (S-13 to S-16). *Occupational Hazards* 57, no. 6. Cleveland: Penton Publishing.

Snyder, Gail, Betty Longman, and Elizabeth Fleming. 1996. "Safety Process a 'Plus' at Shell Western." *Occupational Hazards* (September): 2–28.

Spencer, Howard W. 1996. "Who Cares, Or Rules on Rules." *Insights Into Management* 8, no. 1: 10, 16.

Strain, Roger. 1995. Personal conversation with the author, November.

Swanson, Sandra. 1996. "How to Motivate Workers to Wear PPE" (60–62). "Employees Get Involved in PPE Issues" (63). *Safety and Health* 153, no. 3. Itasca, IL: National Safety Council.

Tapas, Tina D. 1996. "Discipline with Respect One Step at a Time." *Today's Supervisor* (November): 8–9.

Wortham, Sarah. 1996. "Forty Years on the Safety Front." *Safety and Health* 154, no. 4: 40–42.

19

Supplemental Tools for Hazard Control

Several systems supplement and support the program of hazard prevention and control: hazard correction tracking, preventive maintenance, unplanned event preparedness, and medical programs. While they are not necessarily direct systems for hazard prevention and control, they have a major impact on keeping hazards controlled.

HAZARD CORRECTION TRACKING

Hazard correction tracking systems are important to follow up on hazards that are usually found through the systems that we will discuss in Chapter 20. Hazards needing correction, however, can also be found using the systems to establish the potential hazard inventory.

A good tracking system provides assurance that every existing hazard found in the worksite will be corrected, by getting it back under its designed controls or by establishing new, more effective controls for it.

Tracking systems are based on the concepts of documenting the hazard found and then documenting all the steps involved until the existing hazard is corrected. As OSHA points out:

Documentation is important because:

- It keeps management and the Safety Department or the person in charge of safety and health aware of the status of long-term correction items;
- It provides a record of what occurred, should the hazard reappear at a later date; and
- It provides timely and accurate information that can be supplied to an employee who reported the hazard. (OSHA undated, 8-8)

To this list should be added that it helps you ensure that the hazard is actually corrected. At a large California construction site, a safety professional responded to an employee report of a dust hazard from a grinding operation. The action taken was to put in a procurement request for a different type of part than was usually purchased to improve the healthfulness of a grinding operation. Once this was completed, the safety professional considered the matter closed. Many months later, nothing had happened and the employees thought that no one cared about their health. One of them mentioned this to an evaluator in response to questions about the speed and adequacy of response to reports of hazards. On investigation, it was discovered that the procurement request was altered by procurement clerks (because "we always get a different type"), and the new type of part was never purchased.

A good tracking system that held "open" the hazard correction until the new part was actually in place would have alerted the safety professional that something had gone wrong long before the problem was actually discovered. As Roger Strain, of Weyerhaeuser, points out, "Tracking well was something we learned from the VPP. It is important to track all corrections to closure in order to hold whoever is responsible accountable for getting it done" (Strain 1995).

Most sophisticated companies have computerized their tracking systems, but sometimes not all hazards found are entered into the system. This occurs because companies have redundant systems of many types to discover existing hazards, some less formal than others. It is important to remember that *some* tracking system must be in place for each system that discovers hazards. The same system does not necessarily have to be used for all of them.

OSHA describes three different types of tracking systems: notations on the report form, tracking by committee minutes, and tracking by separate form. The agency clearly prefers to see the tracking done on the original report form because it is less easy to "lose" the hazard (OSHA undated, 8-8 to 8-9). Whatever the system, it is important to minimize the necessity of any transfers from one system to another, since that is the most likely way to lose track of a hazard correction.

Some companies, such as Mobil Chemical, add one more step to the written closure, sending a safety or health professional to check to make sure that the correction actually occurred (Brant 1996).

PREVENTIVE MAINTENANCE

Safety and health leaders have long recognized the connection between well-maintained facilities and equipment and a safe and healthful work environment. As OSHA says, "... good preventive maintenance plays a major role in ensuring that hazard controls continue to function effectively ... [and] keeps new hazards from arising due to equipment malfunction" (OSHA undated, 8-13). OSHA's official guideline covering maintenance is to "provide for facility and equipment maintenance, so that hazardous breakdown is prevented" (OSHA 1989, 3910).

This approach to maintenance is based on the goal of zero breakdowns. It requires good solid knowledge of equipment performance and the early warning signs of wear that can lead to breakdowns, production disruptions, and, probably, more costly repairs. "Preventive maintenance" is probably the oldest name for this type of planning and hazard control, but it is also called "predictive," "planned," or "productive" maintenance. Whatever it is called, it requires a careful accumulation of maintenance and repair information and history, trend analysis of breakdown history, planning for routine checks and replacement, making checks of various levels of complexity, and replacing parts before trouble arrives.

Graydon Megan describes three levels of complexity in checking equipment and facilities. The first level is what he calls "no tools required." This consists of a simple inspection to see if there are any leaks, visibly worn or damaged parts, or loose fittings. The next level of maintenance check requires entry into machinery to check for such things as "belt tension and condition, tightness of key fasteners, gib tightness, and ram alignment." The most complex level of checking involves using "sophisticated instruments" to measure noise, vibration, overheating, and electrical changes (Megan 1996, 55).

At the former Texaco Chemical Company plant in Port Arthur (now owned by Huntsman), a battery of complex

measurements made for preventive maintenance purposes includes testing the strength of electrical poles to
ensure that they can withstand hurricane wind force and
will not be the cause of fires or explosions if they fall
(Stegall undated). This type of meticulous care in assuring well-maintained equipment and facilities results in
smoother operating, more productive, safer, and more
healthful worksites.

Unplanned Event Preparedness

Even with the best planning and implementation of hazard controls, sometimes unplanned events occur. At that
point, our ability to react to minimize danger and damage is of the utmost importance. Most sophisticated companies put a lot of effort into emergency planning and
preparation. Not so many, however, take time to understand, plan, and test employees for reaction to smaller
unplanned events. Yet an emergency situation may simply be the outgrowth of a series of unplanned occurrences that went (at least officially) unnoticed.

Emergency Planning

The OSHA guideline puts planning and preparation on
equal balance with training and drills, saying, "Plan and
prepare for emergencies, and conduct training and drills
as needed, so that the response of all parties to emergencies will be 'second nature'" (OSHA 1989, 3910). The
analysis and planning must come first, however. Since
much is written and even mandated on this subject, we
will avoid the basics and just touch on the extras that are
being added by the leaders in safety and health.

The average place of employment will have some sort of emergency planning, even if it is only for fires. This planning should include the aftermath of an emergency or "post crisis." When everyone has returned to work, an intervention session led by a counselor should be scheduled within 24 to 72 hours to allow people to talk about their feelings. Dr. Ken Wolf points out, "When people talk through their feelings, they take control of the situation" (Hans 1996, 9).

The sophisticated workplace plans for all emergencies that could conceivably happen. Before an emergency plan is developed or updated, careful analysis should be done to ensure that no type of conceivable emergency has been left out. OSHA suggests considering all possible events in the categories of natural disasters, disasters caused by forces outside of your workplace, and disasters caused by failure of hazard controls at your workplace (OSHA undated, 8-15).

Natural Disasters

Wind, water, brush fires, and earthquakes are the leaders in natural disasters and have a tendency to provide big surprises every fifty years or so. It pays to find out as much as you can about the history of natural disasters in your area. Floods in the central part of the country in 1994 and 1995 reached dimensions thought to be impossible with modern flood control measures. In the middle of this century, Hurricane Betsy managed to head right up the Mississippi River, bringing new disasters to new areas.

It also pays to learn about the side effects or aftermaths of these disasters. At the Texaco plant on the Gulf of Mexico mentioned previously, startup after the plant had been under flood waters from hurricanes involved controlling such new hazards as snakes and biological hazards in the waters and mud left behind (Stegall undated).

Disasters Caused by Human or Human-Caused Forces Outside the Workplace

What is out there in the neighborhood? Are there chemical plants that could conceivably release enough toxic air contaminants to produce emergency situations at this workplace? Are there refineries? Given wind patterns and the types of toxic contaminants, a potentially dangerous neighbor could be miles away. If so, emergency planning should include organizing the companies in the area to plan, together and with area emergency response organizations, for emergencies that may involve more than one of the companies.[1]

Is the worksite in the path of airport landings and take-offs? If so, planning may be needed for the possibility of airplane crashes into the workplace. Are there any main rail lines nearby that carry long-distance freight or rail yards where freight cars sit for periods of time either empty or holding unknown and possibly volatile materials?

Is there any reason why the worksite might be a target for a terrorist act? Surely the employees of the Social Security Administration in Oklahoma City did not think it likely that someone would or could blow up their building. Nor did the hotel and white-collar companies in New York's World Trade Building expect that someone would try to blow up theirs. Some private American companies have been targeted for political reasons at their overseas plants. Terrorist attacks are not as remote a possibility as it might at first seem.

One means of protection from terrorist attack is in the restriction of uncleared vehicle traffic to distances that

---

[1]Many chemical plants all over the country have organized Local Emergency Planning Councils (LEPCs) for this very purpose. One may already be established in your area.

preclude vehicle bomb attacks on buildings such as that at Oklahoma City. Workplaces with restricted entry, requiring company identification or passing through a metal detector or both, have a better chance of preventing either terrorist attack or violence aimed at specific workers.

Violence at the workplace is the second most frequent cause of occupational fatalities and the most frequent for women workers (42 percent of fatalities in women and 19 percent in men.) There is a tendency to believe that violence only happens to convenience store clerks, but nine percent of fatalities from workplace violence occurred in manufacturing plants. Mass homicides have even occurred in financial institutions where distraught borrowers carried out terrible revenge (Kedjidjian 1996, 42). Many employers say that there is nothing that can be done to prevent or minimize the effects of this type of hazard. Other employers are busy doing both.

In planning for prevention or minimization of attacks aimed at specific workers, the help of security, human resource, and employee assistance experts should be enlisted. Some companies screen potential employees carefully for past violent or verbally aggressive behavior. Employee assistance counselors can work with employees who seem to be under a lot of personal stress to help keep problems from building up to a dangerous point.

General workplace rules must include a complete prohibition on violence of any sort in the workplace. Convair has a "zero tolerance" policy, whereby every reported threat, exchange of harsh words, or scuffle is tracked and addressed. Employees are encouraged to report these incidents just as they would any other hazard, accident, or near-miss incident (LaBarr 1994).

Perhaps the "zero tolerance" policy would have saved lives and injury in the Dearborn, Michigan post office where a violent employee killed a co-worker, injured two others, and then took his own life. He had been passed over for a promotion. The woman who had received the promotion had written a letter to the Postmaster reporting that the violent employee had threatened her life. The Postmaster reportedly did talk to the two individuals but did nothing else, not even consulting with the union. Six weeks later, after a verbal altercation over the playing of a radio, the violent employee shot the radio player, wounded the woman who was promoted and the supervisor that promoted her, and then killed himself (Smith 1993).

Mike Peltier, of the National Safety Council, recommends that supervisors, particularly those who have responsibility for disciplining or firing workers, have training in conflict management and learn how to spot the early warning signs of a potentially violent worker (Kedjidjian 1996, 44). Company employee assistance counselors could provide training, both formal and informal, and a number of management consulting companies provide formal training (Richardson 1996).

Threats should be taken seriously. Sometimes the families of seriously disturbed and disgruntled former employees can be enlisted to help you. Mobil Chemical Company was successful in asking some of these families to keep track of the activities and mindset of the former employees with known grudges against the company (or former supervisors or co-workers) and alerting company security when and if there were danger signs. Such an arrangement can provide some advance warning.

According to Joe Kinney of the National Safe Workplace Institute, the endangered employee, when there is a specific target, can be helped by some simple things such as relocation of the workstation or alteration of that employee's work schedule. Providing photos of the stalker or harasser to security and reception personnel can also help spot trouble before it is too late (Kedjidjian 1996, 45–46).

Failure of Hazard Controls in Your Workplace

Sometimes hazard control failures occur because planning was not extensive enough. It pays to have an inventory of materials used anywhere on your premises. If you have a pool on the premises or in your office building, chlorine is being used and stored. If your workplace has large areas of lawn or garden, you may have periods of time when fertilizers and pesticides are being used in large quantities. Given the right quantities and circumstances, these everyday items can produce emergency situations.

Emergency Practice

The equal partner of emergency planning and preparation is practice. Once the emergency plan is developed and implemented, employees need the opportunity to practice what they are expected to do, no matter if a particular employee's only "job" is to go to a safe place to be counted. Emergencies place extraordinary stress on all who are caught up in them. Frequent practice for emergencies helps employees get through them, doing what they are supposed to do to minimize danger of harm to themselves or others. Since different types of emergencies may require different behavior, all types should be practiced, and evacuation should be practiced at least every year. (For more information on training and practice for emergencies, see Chapter 24.)

Other Unplanned Events

A myriad of unplanned events go on in every workplace, if not every day, then frequently. These usually are responded to by the workers on the line in one way or another that keeps the unplanned event from becoming an emergency. What the sophisticated workplace needs is to understand those unplanned events and to analyze their potential for producing injuries and illnesses or even possible emergency situations.

Most of these workplaces require and expect near-miss reporting and investigation, but some are, like Occidental Chemical, asking employees to report *anything* unplanned that occurs (Driscoll 1994). The key is to make sure that employees understand that they will not experience any adverse reaction if they report unplanned events for which they may be partially responsible or at least perceive themselves to be so.

The information employees can provide about the things that go wrong in small doses may allow planning to prevent serious injury or catastrophic event. The safety manager of a highly sophisticated and very successful safety and health program at a large chemical plant said, after investigating a serious injury, "It took about 200 little things going wrong all at the same time, something we had never seen in 60 years of that particular operation, to injure this employee." The more that can be discovered about the "little things that go wrong," the better able you are to protect your employees.

Some innovative and sophisticated employers are now providing "operations drills" to practice response to less-than-emergency, unplanned events and to test worker and supervisor skills and knowledge in practice. Possible scenarios include a malfunctioning overhead crane; elevated chlorine level; loss of power to the power bus feeding essential utilities, fire alarms, and waste treatment facilities; bulging drum containing waste; toxic contaminant leak; prohibited chemical in laboratory, indicator gauge out of specification limits (Stalnaker 1996). (For more information, see Chapter 24.)

MEDICAL PROGRAM

The medical program can actually support both the establishment of the hazard inventory and the hazard prevention and control program. The VPP requirements current in mid-1996 place the medical program with hazard assessment rather than hazard correction and control (OSHA 1988, 26344). The guidelines, however, place it with hazard prevention and control: "Establish a medical program which includes availability of first aid on site and of physician and emergency medical care nearby, so that harm will be minimized if and when injury or illness does occur" (OSHA 1989, 3910). The emphasis of this guideline appears to be the minimization of harm when it occurs.

When OSHA prepared its draft manual, a whole chapter was devoted to the site medical program, which it called "the occupational health delivery system" or "ODS." "This term [ODS] will help you remember that a comprehensive program is more than a after-the-fact response to work-related injuries and illnesses. It also includes activities that uncover the safety and health hazards in your business and that help you plan for prevention or control" (OSHA undated, 10-1).

OSHA lists three types of activities for the medical program: prevention of hazards, early recognition and treatment of work-related illness and injury, and limiting the severity of work-related illness and injury. The VPP requirements that the Department of Energy (DOE) adapted from OSHA in the early to mid-1990s included all three activities and specifically mentioned nurse or physician involvement in job hazard analyses and comprehensive surveys (DOE 1994, 14).

Prevention

One of the classic ways to prevent occupational illness or injury is to ensure the overall healthiness and conditioning of the body. More and more companies are turning to wellness programs to encourage physical fitness, smoking cessation, low-fat diets, and stress reduction. Some companies with repetitive motion jobs are also offering stretch and exercise breaks.

In addition to the classic concepts of wellness, for prevention of injury or illness, workplaces are finding it particularly helpful to involve occupational health nurses or occupational physicians in job hazard analysis and comprehensive surveys from the ergonomic point of view (see Chapter 18). When occupational health personnel who treat employees know what their work and work areas look like and what sort of potential hazards they face, occupational illness can be recognized in early stages. Training in the known potential hazards of the industry and the early symptoms of occupational illness is important for occupational health providers involved in a worksite.

Early Diagnosis

If nurses and physicians understand the work and the potential hazards involved in it, they can do a better job of spotting early symptoms of occupational illness before too much harm has been done.

It is also helpful to have occupational nurses or physicians do trend analyses on employee visits to the first aid station, nurse's office, contract clinic, or hospital. Sometimes symptoms that resemble those of common infectious diseases may turn out to be symptoms of occupational illness. If a trend analysis picks up similar symptoms from a particular area or kind of work, then the industrial hygienist may want to take a closer look at that area or job to see if there are health hazards that have not yet been identified for the hazard inventory.

Limitation of Harm

Another classic use of medical personnel is for the limitation or minimization of harm. It pays to have well-thought-out access to emergency medical help as part of all emergency planning, but occupational physicians and nurses can and should be used for much more. They should help plan for the selection of light duty jobs for injured or temporarily impaired workers and should monitor the medical care provided to those workers before their return to work. Sometimes just the knowledge that someone from the company is checking on their well-being and showing an interest in getting them back to productive work can make a big difference in how fast such workers do return to work.

The medical program and occupational health professionals can offer much more than they are currently expected to do to help protect workers.

KEY POINTS

- Hazard correction tracking should never be allowed to fall short of tracking to complete correction.
- Hazard correction tracking systems should be designed where possible to eliminate shifting from one document or system to another so that uncontrolled hazards do not get "lost."

- Zero breakdowns is the goal of preventive maintenance.
- All equipment and facilities should be thoroughly analyzed to determine frequency of maintenance and replacement of parts.
- All possible, rather than probable, emergencies should be analyzed, covering natural disasters and those caused by forces outside worksite control as well as failures of worksite controls.
- Violent behavior by employees or targeting employees can be planned for and prevented to a certain degree.
- Emergency situations are frequently the accumulation of smaller unplanned events that have escaped hazard analysis.
- Encouraging employees to report *all* unplanned events will help provide information for potential hazard analysis.
- Practicing reactions to serious but not emergency unplanned events as well as emergencies can locate weaknesses and provide a better prepared workplace.
- Joint planning and practice with community emergency response organizations and other area worksites can help both prevent and better prepare for large-scale emergencies affecting the worksite.
- Occupational physicians and/or nurses should have access and be accessible to the worksite for hazard analysis, early recognition and treatment of occupational illness, and limiting the severity of harm from occupational injury or illness.
- Occupational health professionals can assist with job hazard analysis, comprehensive surveys, and trend analysis.

REFERENCES

Brant, Robert J. 1996. Company Manager for Safety, Health and Loss Prevention, Mobil Chemical Co., personal conversation.

Department of Energy. 1994. *Voluntary Protection Program, Part 1. Program Elements*. Washington, DC: Office of Safety and Quality Assurance, Office of Occupational Safety.

Driscoll, William. 1994. Corporate Vice President for Safety, Occidental Chemical Corporation, personal conversation, May.

Hans, Mick. 1996. "After the Smoke Clears, Who's Minding the Employees?" *Today's Supervisor* (October): 8.

Kedjidjian, Catherine B. 1996. "Work Can Be Murder for Women." *Safety and Health* 153, no. 3: 42–45. Itasca, IL: National Safety Council.

LaBarr, Gregg. 1994. "Workplace Violence: Employee Safety Under Fire." *Occupational Hazards* 56, no. 11: 23–28. Cleveland: Penton Publishing.

Megan, Graydon P. 1996. "How to Set up a Plant-Maintenance Program." *Safety and Health* 153, no. 4: 52–56. Itasca, IL: National Safety Council.

OSHA. 1988. *Federal Register* 53, no. 133 (July 12): 26339–26348.

OSHA. 1989. *Federal Register* 54, no. 16 (January 26): 3904–3916.

OSHA. Undated. Unpublished Manual, *Managing Worker Safety and Health*, Chapter 8, "Establishing Hazard Prevention and Control Programs," pp. 8-1 to 8-25, and Chapter 10, "Establishing the Right Medical Program for Your Worksite: The Occupational Health Delivery System," pp. 10-1 to 10-26. Washington, DC: Office of Cooperative Programs.

Richardson, William A. 1996. Managing Director, Macro International, and Manager, Equal Opportunity and Employee Assistance Counseling Program, Naval Surface Warfare Center, Dahlgren Virginia, personal conversation.

Smith, S. L. 1993. "Violence in the Workplace: A Cry for Help." *Occupational Hazards* 55, no. 10: 29–33. Cleveland: Penton Publishing.

Stalnaker, C. Keith. 1996. "Using Operations Drills to Improve Workplace Safety." *Professional Safety* 41, no. 2: 29–32. Des Plaines, IL: ASSE.

Stegall, Robert. Undated. Interview in a videotape presentation, "Managing Worker Safety and Health." VPPPA, Falls Church, VA.

Strain, Roger. 1995. Safety and Health Manager at the Valliant, OK, plant, in an interview with the author, November.

20

When Hazards Get Away from Their Controls

The freshest concept in the unpublished OSHA manual is the one of differentiating between the activities to assess the potential hazards and those that find hazards that are meant to be controlled. The only potential hazard that can be guaranteed not to ever expose workers to harm is the hazard that is prevented by total removal from the worksite. And as long as it remains virtually impossible to "foolproof" hazard controls—since as Duane Barns of Dow is fond of saying, "The fools will get you every time" (Barns 1992)—they can be expected to fail occasionally.

If the attempt to protect workers from occupational hazards is viewed as a war, the work that goes into compiling the hazard inventory and establishing hazard controls would be the strategic and fortification work. The activities involved in catching hazards that have slipped their controls are where the real battles are fought.

One example of a technical hazard control that has allowed its target hazard to "escape" might be a ventilation system that has not been well maintained, as mentioned previously. At a fertilizer plant, the ventilation system had been broached in numerous places for spot readings, leaving it full of small holes. It had also been allowed to accumulate dust over a period of weeks during heavy production. As a result, it had lost its full capacity to draw air contaminants away from the workers and the hazard was no longer well controlled.

An example of work practice controls failing was found at a refinery where a sleepy but hurried worker on the second part of a rare double shift left his vehicle motor running while he investigated a possible malfunction on the line. He had been trained and knew the rules about sources of ignition, but he should not have been working in the sleepy condition he was in. In this case, the worker was badly burned when the engine set off escaping fumes.

These situations are usually discovered through a combination of routine self-inspections and industrial hygiene monitoring, employee reports of hazards, accident/incident investigations, and trend analyses of accidents and hazards found. Since most of these sub-elements are the best understood of all of those listed in the OSHA guidelines, our discussion will only touch on aspects that are not as well understood or that demonstrate a sophisticated approach to a traditional tool.

ROUTINE GENERAL INSPECTIONS

Safety inspections are, next to accident investigations, the most frequently used safety and health program tool. But OSHA considers routine inspections to include routine health hazard checks as well and so has included routine industrial hygiene monitoring and sampling in this category. The guidelines call for "regular site safety and health inspections so that new or previously missed hazards and failures in hazard controls are identified" (OSHA 1989, 3909) The comment section expands upon this:

> Once a comprehensive examination of the workplace has been conducted and hazard controls have been established, routine site safety and health inspections are necessary to ensure that changes in conditions and activities do not create new hazards and that hazard controls remain in place and are effective. Routine industrial hygiene monitoring and sampling are essential components of such inspections in many workplaces. (OSHA 1989, 3914)

The unpublished OSHA manual also differentiates between inspections *generally*—which it says refers to "looking closely at something to see if it meets requirements"—and this specific kind of inspection, which is a "general inspection of every part of the worksite to locate any hazards that need correction" (OSHA undated, 9-2). So in defining the routine general inspection, OSHA also specifies its scope—the whole worksite. At the same time, the emphasis should be on routine matters rather than making sure that every nook and cranny be examined as in comprehensive surveys. The key is to find hazards that have slipped the controls planned for them, whether that involves machinery and equipment or work practices.

Frequency

The other key concept is that it be *routine*, not just when the mood strikes or when something has gone wrong.

OSHA offers some ideas on frequency as well, recommending that medium and large fixed worksites be completely inspected every quarter, with inspections occurring every month. Smaller fixed worksites should be completely inspected every month. Construction sites should be inspected "weekly because of the rapidly changing nature of the site and its hazards" (OSHA undated, 9-2). Office areas can be inspected quarterly.

For routine monitoring and sampling, the frequency should be set by a qualified industrial hygienist on the basis of data from the comprehensive surveys, change analysis, or routine job or process analysis.

By using line employees to make inspections each week or month, the worksite can be checked for routine hazards more frequently than if safety and health professionals were required.

Who Should Inspect

Because these inspections are for routine matters, they require inspectors who can recognize routine hazards. Once trained in the kinds of things that can go wrong and how safety controls are supposed to work, anyone familiar with the worksite can perform inspections. OSHA suggests providing training that is the equivalent of its #501 course, "A Guide to Voluntary Compliance in Safety and Health" (OSHA undated, 9-4). Most sophisticated worksites will design their own training. Even routine industrial hygiene monitoring and sampling can be done by line employees with adequate training. Safety and health professionals should be involved in the design and provision of training but should then be resources to these inspectors and leave the actual inspections to production and maintenance workers (or office staff in their areas.)

Many sites prefer using workers that do not work in an area to inspect it, feeling that they will look at the area with "fresh eyes." Others feel most comfortable with managers, supervisors, or workers from the area, feeling that they will be the most familiar. A combination may work best.

Written Guidance and Inspection Reports

These inspectors will need written guidance about the procedures of their inspections that remind them where to go and what to look for, as well as helping them keep from overlooking anything. Most employee inspectors use checklists specifically developed for their worksites. Many of these allow the inspectors to record the hazards found, the assigned responsibility for correction, and, when the correction is completed, a notation that the correction has occurred, right on the checklist.

It is important that there be a record of all of these inspection results. As OSHA says, "In all but the smallest and least dangerous of workplaces, written inspection reports are necessary to record hazards discovered, responsibility assigned for correction and tracking of correction to completion" (OSHA undated, 9-5).

EMPLOYEE REPORTS OF HAZARDS

The OSHA guidelines call for providing "a reliable system for employees, without fear of reprisal, to notify management personnel about conditions that appear hazardous and to receive timely and appropriate response; and encourage employees to use the system." This is "so that employee insight and experience in safety and health protection may be utilized, and employee concerns addressed" (OSHA 1989, 3909).

Setting up systems for employees to report hazards increases the number of "eyes" looking for hazards. The success of employee reporting depends upon the offering of appropriate systems, encouragement to use them, timely and appropriate responses and actions, hazard correction tracking, and ensuring that employees who report hazards do not suffer from any type of reprisal or harassment.

Types of Systems Used

Numerous systems have proved successful for worksites. Most sophisticated worksites use multiple systems to ensure that everyone will be able to get attention. An employee idea to improve the control of a potential hazard, for example, may need a different system of reporting and response than a hazard that has slipped out of its controls.

Reporting to the Supervisor

The most classic system provides that the employee report the hazard to his or her immediate supervisor. This works well where employees have good relationships with their supervisors and can rely on them to take their reports of hazards seriously. It also requires that the supervisor be able to effect the hazard correction either through his or her own authority or through contacts with others.

It is difficult to track reports received this way to ensure that complete correction is accomplished and to trend hazards. Another possible problem may arise as teamwork takes hold of more and more worksites. In those worksites, there will be fewer employees who actually have a supervisor. At this point, however, there are still millions of worksites where reporting to the supervisor is the major system or the only system.

Filling out a Complaint or Report of Hazard Form

Some worksites have complaint or report of hazard boxes at intervals around the worksite where forms can be obtained, filled out, and dropped in a slot for pickup and delivery to the safety and health department. This system usually allows for anonymity, which may be desirable. It is also easy to provide for hazard correction tracking when a written system is used. Its success will depend upon whether workers know about it and are encouraged to use it, how frequently the forms are picked up and acted upon, and, of course, what kind of response is received.

Suggestion Program

Many suggestion programs have a safety and health component. This is frequently where workers can use their creativity to suggest solutions to long-standing safety and health problems or call attention to potential hazards that are not yet in the hazard inventory. Like the report form, it also is easy to provide for hazard correction tracking, since the suggestion is in writing.

On the other hand, the suggestions may not always be treated with a sense of urgency and may utilize someone other than a safety and health professional to make decisions about them. Further, a frequent complaint about suggestion systems is that even some suggestions that win awards never get implemented. Another complaint is that the emphasis is on saving money rather than preventing injuries and illnesses. As with any desirable activity for line employees, suggestion systems must be taken seriously by management to be effective with workers.

Maintenance Requests

Many workplaces allow line employees to fill out requests for maintenance repairs. These systems usually have some sort of marking to indicate that health or safety is involved. Some of the workplaces require that the employee's supervisor sign off as well. The success of the system depends upon how the maintenance supervisor makes priority decisions and what kind of backlog maintenance is experiencing. If both the employee and the supervisor have to sign, the relationship between them will have a bearing on whether the employee will bother and whether the request actually gets to maintenance. If employees are properly trained about what type of problems should be reported on maintenance forms and why, they should be able to use the forms effectively without going through their supervisors.

A drawback to using maintenance forms without any other system is that they are only useful for items that maintenance can fix. These forms are not helpful in terms of calling attention to unsafe or unhealthful practices and do not provide for employee ideas of how hazard controls could be improved.

Reporting to a Safety Committee Representative or Union Representative

Many places that have employee or joint safety and health committees encourage employees to report hazards to the committee member in their area. Employees usually feel comfortable talking things over with a peer. This is even more true in a union environment where workers are accustomed to carrying their concerns to a representative. It is hard to track both the concerns and the correction of hazards in these oral systems, but it can be done if committee members and/or representatives make notes on the hazards reported and put them into a tracking system.

Hot Lines

Telephone numbers to safety and health hot lines are more and more frequently found. These are usually manned by safety and health professionals who decide upon the response. At Allied Signal's Kansas City Division, however, in a program called, "3999 Comments, Please!", the calls go to the president of the division, who responds personally to each one. In this case, the phone system hot line is for more than health and safety and is open for all employee concerns.

Telephone systems have the advantage of providing a feeling of immediacy, since the reports can be made so quickly and easily. Real immediacy, of course, depends upon the timeliness and appropriateness of the response. Also a hotline or other telephone system, much as oral reports to representatives, requires a little extra effort to make sure that the concerns get documented, tracked, and trended.

Giving the Employee the Authority to Deal with Hazards

In many sophisticated workplaces, the employee is empowered and encouraged to make as many corrections himself or herself as possible. In these workplaces, the employee not only has the right but the responsibility to stop work that involves hazard exposure. It is more of a culture than a reporting system and can result in employees using any of the systems above to accomplish corrections that they are unable to effect themselves.

Encouraging Employees to Report Hazards

No matter how many and what kind of systems are provided to employees to report hazards, they are unlikely to do so unless they are convinced that management really wants them to. In places where employees have not traditionally reported hazards, some incentives might be needed to get employees to start making the reports. The incentives need not be expensive and can be fun. For example, the supervisory unit with the most reported valid hazards in a quarter could win a pizza lunch or catered barbeque. Of course, some system other than reports to supervisors would have to be used.

It is also important to avoid having the hazard reporting system look as though it might be encouraging employees to report one another. If hazardous practices are something that you feel will be important to report, it is best to make sure that adverse disciplinary action is not connected to these hazard reports. OSHA also suggests that you avoid placing policy statements about the hazard reporting system and the disciplinary system too close together on the bulletin board or employee handbook (OSHA undated, 9-8).

Encouragement should also to be given to supervisors and lower-level line managers. They will respond well to being recognized for having employees who report hazards. For the most part, however, the greatest encouragement for hazard reporting is prompt and appropriate response.

Timely and Appropriate Response

The only way to have a successful set of systems for employees to report hazards is if they can see that their concerns are taken seriously. When reports of hazards sit on someone's desk or in a suggestion box for days or weeks or months the system can quickly die. Employees need to see something positive happening promptly. Safety and health professionals should be involved in deciding how fast a hazard will be corrected. If they decide that the correction can wait, the employee should be notified and have that fact explained to him or her.

William Kincaid recounts a story about a complaint of an unusual odor in an automobile assembly plant. The IH who went to check on it found no contaminants in the air but noted that near the end of the assembly line, where the odor had been reported, the brand of gasoline going into the cars had recently been changed and probably had changed the odor released when filling the cars. Since everything was fine, the IH said nothing to the workers on the line and left. Workers became concerned that something was being hidden from them. By the end of the day, 100 of them had gone to the clinic with an array of symptoms that were determined to be imagined (Kincaid 1996, 42).

Appropriate and timely response includes taking care to respond even when the employee is mistaken and no real hazard exists. Employees who report non-valid hazards need to understand why no action is taken. Even when the hazard is reported anonymously, some response should be provided. This is usually accomplished by posting the response in the area where the hazard was reported.

Hazard Report Documentation

Wherever possible, reports of hazards should be collected and documented for two reasons. The first and most important is so that the hazards identified can be tracked until they are completely corrected (see Chapter 19 for a more detailed discussion of hazard correction tracking.)

The other reason is to provide information for hazard trending. If you can track the reports of hazards received over a period of time, it is possible that a trend or pattern may show up that could lead to improved hazard inventory or methods of prevention or control (trend analysis is discussed below).

Protection from Reprisals

It is really just an extension of encouragement to ensure that employees do not suffer even the most subtle harassment. At one large construction site, a worker who reported hazards found himself being assigned the dirtiest jobs and the loneliest ones far too often to be simply a matter of chance. When this is the case, workers soon learn to forgo reporting even though the site manager says he or she wants it to be done. The policy must be clear that reprisals will not be tolerated and any cases found must be dealt with swiftly.

On the other hand, if supervisors are recognized by upper levels of management when their employees report valid hazards, they are much less likely to feel the need to punish workers who do report hazards (see Appendix 4).

The key is for everyone to understand that hazard controls are not perfect and do let hazards slip out on occasion. The best workplaces, however, find them quickly and get them back under control or design better controls. And to do this successfully, every worker must notice and then correct or report hazards.

ACCIDENT/INCIDENT INVESTIGATIONS

Accidents can be very tragic and, at best, make us very uncomfortable. However, they are also opportunities to learn. As Dan Petersen says, "Every accident opens a window through which we can observe the system . . ."

(Petersen 1988, 15). The OSHA guidelines put it this way, "Provide for investigation of accidents and 'near miss' incidents, so that their causes and means for their prevention are identified" (OSHA 1989, 3909).

Just about every worksite that has had accidents has some sort of accident investigation procedure. It may be just having the injured employee's supervisor fill out a form, such as the OSHA first report of injury form or its equivalent. Incidents or near misses are not as frequently investigated. And even the accidents that are investigated do not always provide good information about their causes and means for prevention.

Since much has been written about accident investigation, this section will briefly cover some of the basic information such as the difference between accidents, incidents, and near misses, who should be involved in investigation, and what results to look for from a successful accident investigation.

Definitions

OSHA provides definitions of accident, incident, and near miss that differentiate between the three terms. *Accidents* are unplanned and undesired events that result in personal injury or property damage. *Incidents* are unplanned and undesired events that adversely affect the completion of a task. *Near misses* are incidents where no injury or property damage has occurred but where a slight difference in position or timing would have meant that damage or injury could have occurred. OSHA goes on to say that an illness that results from a single exposure is a "personal injury" but that illnesses resulting from long-time exposure do not fall into this category (OSHA undated, 9-12).

These definitions are by no means standard. Many worksites use near miss to cover property damage accidents where no injury occurred. At one large manufacturing site in Kansas City, employees were asked to report near misses and most of the reports received were of hazards, rather than occurrences where injury or damage was narrowly avoided.

Investigating Incidents/Near Misses

Taking the time to carefully investigate incidents without personal injury and near misses where no damage has been done can reduce the numbers of accidents with personal injury. Like accidents with personal injury, these incidents and near misses provide a window on the failings of the systems to keep workers protected from hazards. Investigations should be done in the same way as for personal injuries.

Who Should Investigate

Although most workplaces ask the supervisor of the injured employee to investigate the accident, at more sophisticated workplaces this assignment is usually augmented or replaced by an investigation team with extensive accident investigation training. These teams are much more effective when they include operations employees. Employees, because they live with potential and existing hazards every day and know the imperfections of technical and managerial systems to prevent hazard exposure, are very valuable in helping to get past the obvious causes to the underlying managerial system failures that are the real causes of accidents and incidents.

As was discussed in the example about the accident investigation committee in Chapter 8, employees must have good direction, training, and resources to be able to provide effective investigations.

Accident Investigation Results

The result desired from an accident/incident investigation is to learn enough to feel confident that you have done all that is feasible to prevent harm in the future. That is difficult to accomplish if there is a rush to judgment on the cause (or more likely, causes) of the accident/incident. Dan Petersen has compared accident investigation to the attempt to diagnose an illness, pointing out that the accident and any unsafe acts or conditions involved in it are only symptoms, not the cause. "We must look behind that act and conditions to determine why." When causes are diagnosed and treated, a permanent (or at least, better) control can be effected. "The function of a safety professional . . . is similar to that of a physician: diagnose symptoms to determine causes, and then treat those causes or suggest appropriate treatment to management" (Petersen 1988, 15-16).

Roger Strain, Safety and Health Manager at Weyerhaeuser's Valiant, Oklahoma plant, provides guidance and assistance to other Weyerhaeuser plants and sometimes to plants in other companies. About accident investigation he says, "It is important not to stop too soon with the causes of accidents if you want to make sure, as we do, that you have planned for the best future prevention." He tells a story of looking at an accident report that found the cause of an injury to be sawdust on the floor, and the prevention to be sweeping up the sawdust. When he decided to investigate further, he found that an engineering control for sawdust on the floor, a vacuum system, was not functioning. The vacuum bag was full and the hose was split. Further, there was no system in place to keep the vacuum system running. Therefore, sawdust would just accumulate on the floor again and possibly cause another injury (Strain 1995).

Everyone talks about "root causes," but it is not always clear that the term is profoundly understood. A southwestern weapons plant describes the difference between "direct cause" and "root cause" as the difference between saying the cause of the accident was that the employee was not trained in the safety precautions of the job and saying that the cause was that the employee was not trained because of a less than adequate apprenticeship program. While it is true that the second version is more in depth than the first, the digging is not very deep and also raises questions as to whether the investigator looked at everything instead of just the injured employee. As James Thomen points out, "Seeking root cause can lead to finger pointing, however subtle. Excellence in safety cannot be achieved within such a culture" (Thomen 1996, 31).

At a chemical plant in upstate New York, an employee was blinded for several days when he attempted to dislodge an obstruction in a nitrogen line without shutting it off first. The employee admitted that he was supposed to shut off the line. Further, he had signed a statement that he had been trained in the necessity to shut off all lines before opening them. The accident investigation team, however, did not stop with the obvious. They asked some more questions and discovered that not only this worker but all of the workers under one foreman's supervision had made it their practice not to take time to shut off small lines while working on them, only the larger lines. Their careful work led them to the problem supervisor and those who held him accountable rather than a problem employee.

Even when the injured employee is a "repeater," there is usually more to look at than just that employee. Robert Pater believes that not enough is done in looking at the human, task, and organization factors that may be involved in repeated accidents and incidents rather than just believing that an employee is "accident prone." Pater's human factors consist of injury history, body conditioning, whether medications are being used, body mechanics, learning style, pace of work, self-image, aging, and emotional issues.

Pater's task factors are job design, workstation layout, lighting, climate, pacing, and frequent or prolonged exposure to hazards. His organizational factors include management ability to learn from incidents and near misses, medical management, effective training, appropriate and accessible personal protective equipment, adequate staffing so that employees are not working "thin and hard," appropriate job procedures, and employee assistance programs. All of these aspects should be analyzed to see if there are opportunities to help keep accidents from happening to the same worker again (Pater 1996, 22).

TREND ANALYSIS

The OSHA guidelines call for the analysis of the patterns of accidents as well as the causes of each individual accident. "Analyze injury and illness trends over time, so that patterns with common causes can be identified and prevented" (OSHA 1989, 3914). The unpublished manual adds to this concept saying that accident logs are not the only useful source of pattern information. "Any records of hazards can be analyzed for patterns. Examples are inspection records and employee hazard reporting records" (OSHA undated, 9-15).

In fact, even first aid records and records of visits to the nurse's office for seemingly unrelated illnesses can sometimes provide clues as to problems caused by as yet undetected hazard exposure.

Injury/Illness Trends

The key to all pattern analysis is to have enough data so that patterns, if any, can emerge. If accidents with personal injury only happen a few times each year, then several years of data should be accumulated and analyzed rather than attempting to do so with monthly, quarterly, or even annual information. Another important factor is to analyze the data in ways that are meaningful to the safety and health professional staff. Many workplaces are utilizing computer programs to provide data compilation, but safety and health professionals may not find much of interest in these data and never use them to decide further courses of action.

The key to analysis may not be what part of the body was injured but what equipment or type of task was involved. It can also be what shift or what geographical area of the plant. Before setting up or revising a computerized program, the safety and health professional should look at accident reports for a sizable period of time and note what factors are intriguing. Then those factors can be built into the program to speed up the selection process before analysis.

It is important to note that data compilation and display are not analysis. The safety and health professional should be using the display to make decisions about what should be analyzed. If nothing further is done with data than display it for everyone to see, it is likely that no analysis is being done.

In addition to accidents, similar injuries or illnesses over a period of time are always of interest. Tracing each back to look for further similarities such as time, place, equipment, and body part can help diagnose inadequate hazard controls or previously unidentified hazards. As OSHA says, "Any clue that suggests a previously unnoticed connection between several injuries or illnesses is worth further investigation" (OSHA undated, 9-15).

Hazard Trends

One good thing about trending hazards is that usually there will be a faster accumulation of hazard exposure reports than actual injuries or reported illnesses. Therefore, the trend analysis of hazards can be done more frequently. Hazard records collected from inspection reports and employee reports of hazards can provide the ability to spot trends *before* someone suffers harm. Repeat hazards indicate inadequate controls and should lead to analysis of the controls in place to see what feasible stronger controls there could be. The causes of hazards can be investigated using the Hazard Analysis Flow Chart found in Appendix 3.

KEY POINTS

- Hazards are only completely controlled when they are prevented by being totally removed from the workplace.
- A key to excellence in hazard control is using systems to locate and correct the hazards that escape controls and to look for ways to strengthen controls.

- Routine general inspections cover the whole worksite to locate hazards that need correction but do not need to cover the site with the depth of a comprehensive survey.
- The whole worksite should be covered by routine, general inspections every quarter in general industry and more frequently in construction.
- Line employees can do effective inspections with appropriate training.
- Records should be kept of inspection results so that hazards can be tracked to completion and data accumulated for hazard trend analysis.
- Using multiple systems may be the best method for ensuring that all existing hazards are reported and that employees' ideas about improvements get serious consideration.
- Whenever possible, employee reports of hazards and suggestions for improved controls should be written so that they can be tracked and trended.
- Management must ensure that no employee suffers even informal harassment for reporting hazards.
- Managers and supervisors should be recognized for having employees who report valid hazards.
- Management encouragement of employee reports of hazards may involve incentives but prompt and appropriate action in response to reports of hazards is the best encouragement.
- Even when employees are mistaken about the nature of a suspected hazard, they should be told why no correction is needed.
- Accidents and incidents or near misses are opportunities to learn more about protection of workers from hazard exposure.
- Appropriately trained and equipped employees make excellent accident/incident investigators.

- It is important not to stop too soon in the investigation of accident causes and particularly to avoid laying all the "blame" on the injured employee.
- When enough data has been accumulated, the pattern of both injuries/illnesses and hazards noted can be helpful in determining where better controls need to be developed.
- Computer data compilation and display is not trend analysis but can be used to get analysis started.

When the hazard inventory is completed, a program of controls is in place and supported, systems to catch the hazards that escape controls and provide information about areas of needed improvement in controls, the systematic approach to hazard analysis and prevention or control is in place.

REFERENCES

Barns, Duane. 1992. Unwritten presentation at a Department of Energy workshop on the VPP.

Kincaid, William H. 1996. "10 Habits of Effective Safety Managers." *Occupational Hazards* (November): 41–43.

OSHA. 1989. *Federal Register* 54, no. 16 (January 26): 3904–3916.

OSHA. Undated. Unpublished manual, *Managing Worker Safety and Health,* Chapter 9, "Catching the Hazards That Escape Controls," pp. 9-1 to 9-26. Washington, DC: Office of Cooperative Programs.

Pater, Robert. 1996. "Breaking the Chain of Accident Repetition." *Professional Safety* 41, no. 2: 20–23. Des Plaines, IL: ASSE.

Petersen, Dan. 1988. *Safety Management: A Human Approach,* second edition. Goshen, NY: Aloray.

Strain, Roger. 1995. In an interview with the author, November.

Thomen, James R. 1996. "Root Cause: Holy Grail or Fatal Trap?" *Professional Safety* 41, no. 9 (September): 31–32.

21

Systematically Approached Hazards

Hazard analysis, prevention, and control means a great deal more than being in compliance with standards. Not only do they require technical understanding of hazards and methods of control, but they also require both systematic methods to identify all the potential hazards and a systematic approach to methodically plan and implement prevention of hazard exposure.

Keeping hazards controlled also means systematic tracking of all the hazard exposures until they are safely recontrolled, a system of preventive maintenance that keeps engineered controls in place and working and prevents other equipment from becoming hazardous, and planning and practice of emergency situations and unplanned events that could turn into emergency situations. It is supported by occupational health professionals who keep the workforce healthy, diagnosing problems before they are serious or widespread and limiting the severity of any harm that might befall employees.

Finally, since hazards that are controlled may sometimes escape those controls, providing a safe workplace requires that hazards are systematically located and re-controlled before harm is done.

Once all of these systems are in place, building on the management loop and involvement of everyone in the workplace, excellence is only a matter of keeping up the systems and ensuring that everyone knows what they need to know to carry out their responsibilities and help to protect themselves and others.

Part 5

Learning to Own Safety and Health

22

Introduction to Learning Ownership

Occupational safety and health training was once described as the "backbone of the body" of managing worker safety and health because it affects every part of the other elements of managing worker safety and health (Sherrill 1994). It certainly is true that if those companies that have achieved excellence in protecting their workers have learned one thing, it is that all the players must clearly understand what must be done *and why* before they can be expected to fully support any effort. That support and effort, along with being able to see positive results, is what brings about a sense of ownership, which always accompanies true excellence. That is, everyone involved in creating the excellence feels a sense of responsibility and pride in the accomplishment.

The mere providing of safety training cannot be relied upon to accomplish the understanding required for ownership, but providing excellent training not only can but does much to instill the sense of ownership.

THE ROLE OF TRAINING IN THE VPP REQUIREMENTS

Early in the VPP history, OSHA switched from a requirement for "an employee training program in safe work practices" (OSHA 1982, 29027) to a requirement that employees and supervisors "understand" potential hazards and their own various roles and duties in protecting themselves and others (OSHA 1985, 43813). This change showed that OSHA was beginning to think of training in terms of its desired results rather than an exercise in providing information to workers by talking to them or giving them something to read. This change was further emphasized by providing the OSHA staff who reviewed VPP applicants' programs at their sites with questionnaires that included questions for employees about what they understood rather than just their opinions.

THE ROLE OF TRAINING IN THE OSHA VOLUNTARY GUIDELINES

In the comment section of the notice announcing the Safety and Health Management Program Guidelines, OSHA begins the discussion of training, the final element, by saying:

> Education and training are essential means for communicating practical understanding of the requirements of effective safety and health protection to all personnel. Without such understanding,

managers, supervisors, and other employees will not perform their responsibilities for safety and health protection effectively. (OSHA 1989, 3915)

There are many regulatory requirements for safety and health training, but in this fifth, brief part of this book, we will take the management systems perspective of training. As such, we will only be looking at the components and methods that help employees at all levels "learn" ownership. Finally, we will look at how the components we have discussed in the four parts fit together to produce excellence.

REFERENCES

OSHA. 1982. *Federal Register* 47, no. 128 (July 2): 29025–29032.
OSHA. 1995. *Federal Register* 50, no. 209 (October 29): 43804–43817.
OSHA. 1989. *Federal Register* 54, no. 16 (January 26): 3904–3916.
Sherrill, Leigh. 1994. Member of the OSHA VPP staff and instructor for the OSHA course on evaluating safety and health programs, in an unwritten presentation at the VPPPA Conference in Phoenix in September.

23

Methods to Ensure Learning

A lot of what is called "training" may not result in the learning intended. According to John Cheeseman, an education specialist for the Ontario Natural Resources Safety Association, anywhere from 20 to 80 percent of what people are taught in a classroom is lost in the transfer to the workplace and thus is never useful to the job (Minter 1996, 33). One of the problems may be that the training is not thought through. According to McGehee and Thayer, training should be put in perspective as a means to an end and not as an end in itself (Petersen 1988, 53). The question must be asked, What do we want this training to achieve?, followed by What is the best way to achieve this learning?

Ensuring that appropriate learning occurs requires a determination of what the objectives of training are, understanding how people learn, providing stimulating learning opportunities, and evaluating the achievement of learning.

Determining Training Objectives

As Mager points out, "I cannot emphasize too strongly the point that an instructor will function in a fog of his own making until he knows what he wants his students to be able to do at the end of the instruction" (Petersen 1988, 60).

Determine objectives for the training benefits with the same care exercised in determining training needs. If you have been careful to ensure that training is needed before you start to plan training, articulating the objectives for the training will follow more easily.

In Figure 23-1, Lippy and Livingston provide three important characteristics of a learning objective and some examples of each, making the point that objectives must be observable, measurable, and state the condition under which performance will be demonstrated (Lippy and Livingston 1996, 6).

Beware, however, of the training objective that sounds good until you really think about it. For example, "By the end of the presentation, the students will be able to name all the different types of respirators available from the tool room." It is unlikely that the ability to name the respirators is really what you hope to accomplish. Do you want the students to know which respirator to use for which job or do you want them to know what respirators are available from the tool room and which have to be specially requested from somewhere else?

In the unpublished OSHA manual, there is a list of five basic learning principles (OSHA undated, 11-2). The first principle is that the "trainee must understand the purpose of the instruction." Determining the objectives of the training goes hand-in-hand with preparing and pre-

1. **It is observable,** it can be demonstrated. Here are some examples:

- To identify
- To define
- To compare

- To describe
- To explain
- To find

2. **It is measurable** and expressed in units of achievement. Some examples:

- With 90 percent accuracy
- Within 10 minutes
- Following all EPA regulations

3. **It states the conditions under which performance is to be demonstrated.**
Example:
Find the Material Safety Data sheet for all of the chemicals on your lead job site within 10 minutes.

Figure 23-1. Characteristics of a learning objective. *Source:* Bruce Lippy and Dennis Livingston. University of Maryland's Environmental Health Education Center and Community Resources, Inc., 1996.

senting the perceived purpose of the training. To understand why training will be useful, students will have to understand what the training is supposed to enable them to know or do. Putting the objectives side by side with the purpose to be presented to the students may help clarify your thinking for both.

Of course, not all training is classic classroom style. Emergency and operational drills are also training. These also need clear objectives. The major objectives for these practices or exercises will probably include testing whether the workers in the drill or practice know what they need to in order to respond quickly and appropriately, giving the workers a chance to practice what they have learned, and also discovering whether the plans for the emergency have appropriately covered everything needed. But whatever the learning experience that you set out to create, determining your objectives in advance is an absolute must.

How People Learn

We have a tendency to think of safety and health training as taking place in a classroom or auditorium where one or more "experts" lecture about the chosen subject. Dan Petersen refers to this method as the "oldest, cheapest, and least effective technique available to a trainer." He further cites McGehee and Thayer in a statement that the lecture method, "one-way communication" to "passive listeners," is "of minimal value in promoting attitudinal or behavioral change" (Petersen 1988, 61).

Figure 23-2 illustrates one trainer's summary of learning research. Note that the more the trainee is involved in the training process, the more information is retained. Regardless of whether the percentages shown in the figure are precise, common sense tells us that the more we are involved in something, the more we will remember it.

Besides the necessity of student understanding of the purpose of the training, OSHA's training and learning principles, mentioned above, include:

- Organizing the order of presentation to harmonize with the order students will be expected to follow in using the information
- Provision of immediate practice and application of the newly acquired skills
- Provision of feedback on the results of their practice
- Provision for individual differences in learning

MOST PEOPLE LEARN:

10% OF WHAT THEY READ

20% OF WHAT THEY HEAR

30% OF WHAT THEY SEE

50% OF WHAT THEY SEE AND HEAR

70% OF WHAT THEY TALK OVER WITH OTHERS

80% OF WHAT THEY USE AND DO IN REAL LIFE

90% OF WHAT THEY TEACH SOMEONE ELSE

Figure 23-2. How people learn. *Source:* William A. Richardson, Macro Inc., 1996.

Concerning the latter, OSHA says:

We are individuals, and we learn in different ways. A successful training program incorporates a variety of learning opportunities, such as written instruction, audiovisual instruction, lectures, and hands-on coaching. Also, we learn at different speeds. The pace of training should recognize these differences. One effective way to learn is by teaching others. (OSHA undated, 11-3).

As early as 1983, Mobil Chemical's plants in Covington, Georgia were using hourly workers to provide most of the safety and health training to other employees. At

Allied Signal's Kansas City Division, the local union has taken the responsibility to provide some of the safety training, also using hourly workers as instructors. Of course, in both cases, professional trainers provided train-the-trainer training to the worker-instructors. Employees should also help determine when training is needed and even what their colleagues need training in. Trying out new equipment or procedures with a group of employees before changes are made at the workplace will help you determine not only changes that might need to be made before introduction to the workplace but will also help you design the training for the larger group of employees who will be working with the changed equipment or procedures. (For more on change analysis, see Chapter 17.)

Lippy and Livingston also provide a list of principles for adult learning, shown in Figure 23-3, which they base on writings of T. W. Goad and M. S. Knowles. As you read through these principles, you may very well find yourself referring to your own experience and agreeing that they fit you very well. Adults need to be self-directed and involved in the learning process, relating everything they learn to their own experiences.

Unfortunately, the frequently used technique of either telling employees something or having them read it and then sign to acknowledge that they have been trained, ignores most of both the OSHA and the Lippy–Livingston principles for training adults. In the next section we will talk about ways to make learning more interesting.

PROVIDING STIMULATING LEARNING EXPERIENCES

Increasing the chance that the training you provide will stimulate the learning process depends on the methods

1. **Adults learn by doing, they want to be involved.**

   Adults are motivated to learn as they develop needs and interests that learning will satisfy. This is why doing a needs assessment is so important.

2. **Problems and examples must be realistic and relevant.**

   Adult learning is centered around life or work. This means that the best framework for organizing adult learning are life and work situations, not academic or theoretical subjects.

3. **Adults relate their learning to what they already know.**

   This is critical. Where children's minds can be approached as sponges or blank chalkboards, adult minds should be seen as warehouses brimming with lots of useful stuff and a fair amount of clutter, too. Experience is the richest resource for adult learning.

4. **An informal environment is best.**

5. **Variety stimulates and tends to open up all five of the learner's senses.**

6. **Grading systems tend to produce negative results.** The testing approach should be explained beforehand and documented, whatever is chosen.

7. **A trainer for adults tends to be more of a facilitator than a teacher.** Adults have a deep need to be self-directed, so the trainer needs to engage in a process of asking questions and helping the class to develop the answers, rather than transmitting the knowledge to them.

Figure 23-3. Principles of adult learning. *Source:* Bruce Lippy and Dennis Livingston. University of Maryland's Environmental Health Education Center and Community Resources, Inc., 1996.

that are used to convey information and techniques for trainers to use.

Learning Methods

One of the aspects of providing a stimulating experience for learning is the method used to convey information. Petersen calls these "learning methods" and he divides them into four types: lecture, conference, case, and role playing (Petersen 1988, 61). To these could be added "student teaching" and "practice" as techniques. All of these methods may be used separately or in conjunction.

Lecture

Lecturing students or trainees is the most frequently used method. It is a very fast and economical way of putting information before the students. In its most classic sense, where the "expert" lecturer stands at a podium before a large group of people and takes few or no questions, it is the least interpersonal and probably the least effective method of encouraging the retention of the information presented. But in smaller, more informal settings, where questions can be answered and observations shared, it is somewhat more effective.

Sometimes there is little choice but to present information in the speediest and most economical way, and there are ways to make the experience more effective. The dynamism of the lecturer is crucial for the lecture method. Prestige also plays an important role. When we have respect for the lecturer and curiosity about the subject, we tend to retain more of what is said. It is also true that a very dynamic speaker with charisma and dramatic and/or humorous flair will hold our attention and help us remember more of the information presented.

When a lot of information must be provided through the lecture method, it helps to provide a variety of speakers and some presentations through a different medium, such as film or videotape. Film or videotape should be used to increase the learning experience by visually and aurally taking the trainees out of the classroom and into interesting areas where they can experience more about what they are being taught.

Demonstrations as part of a lecture are also helpful. Seeing something done, as opposed to just hearing the doing described, aids learning.

And even in the "worst" example of the lecture, the large impersonal setting, we have all heard a speech or lecture that rings in our minds for a long time. And people will pay to watch entertainers stand before them and "present." So while there may be problems with the lecture method, there is also no doubt that the goal of imparting needed information can be achieved through this method. When training is planned, however, care should be taken to ensure that this method in its most restrictive mode is not overused.

Conference
The conference method emphasizes group discussions, empowering a group to work through a problem, brainstorm, or compile lists from the group members' individual experiences. In the conference method, the trainer is more a facilitator than a lecturer. The trainer leads the discussions, referees, records, encourages, and generally gets the group to do the work.

For this method to work by itself, the students need to have a lot of information on the subject before they come into training. It may be life experience, work experience, or knowledge from other training or education, but they must have something to share with each other to make the training useful. Sometimes this type of training method is used in conjunction with the lecture so that a certain amount of training is imparted, and then the group is led through discussions relating this new information to other experience or learning that they already have.

Case

In this method the trainees are given cases or problems to study and then resolve or critique. This is usually done in small groups, although it can be performed by a large group as a whole when time is of the essence. Here again, the trainer is a facilitator, guiding the group and encouraging everyone to participate. In this method, trainees may be using information obtained by experience, other training, lectures, conference group work, reading, or audiovisual presentation.

This method takes skillful preparation in terms of the cases or problems to be used. Sometimes a problem that is not well constructed can obstruct the hoped-for learning experience. For example, at one training session, a small group was asked to critique the content of several passages of a report in the hopes that they would learn some of the pitfalls of report writing. Instead, because of a lack of clarity on a subject the case developer thought not important, the group went off on a tangent about the supposed report writers, assuming a totally different identity for those writers than intended and reacting to what they felt were inappropriate recommendations. The group learned nothing that was intended by the exercise.

Role Playing

Role playing requires the trainees to act out parts in situations that should provide a simulated experience to help learning. Role playing perhaps serves best when used in lieu of real-life demonstration or practice for newly learned techniques involving interpersonal relations. When trainees really put themselves enthusiastically into the assumed role, approaching problems as they would if they were the assumed identity, Janus and King find that private shifts in attitude can result (Petersen 1988, 62).

Among adults, however, there is much aversion to putting themselves into the limelight in this manner without knowing exactly what will happen. Some may even consider it childish to watch. If the role playing is tightly constrained and scripted, it loses spontaneity and most of its ability to teach, so the trainees must have the ability to bring their own experience into the role playing.

A danger, although probably rare, is that someone may agree to play a role and then sabotage the role-playing effort. In one instance, a female trainer got acceptance from a trainee to play the role of a worker while she played the role of an interviewer demonstrating how to put a worker interviewee at ease and find out what the worker knew about protection from safety and health hazards. The trainee she selected (on the advice of those who knew him) proceeded to evade the questions and suggest that they go get a drink, playing his audience for laughs. The trainer played it out but concluded it quickly. She explained good-humoredly to the group that neither she nor anyone else doing this type of interview, as far as she knew, had ever come across such a response in a real situation. She pointed out to the group that if they came across someone who responded in such a manner, the best thing would be to politely close the interview as soon as possible and move on to the next person.

Another problem is that role playing is very time consuming. In a training session, usually only a handful of the trainees would be able to take part, at most. Watching role playing may provide some information to the other students, particularly if they are watching at least one experienced person dealing with the simulated problem, but not the same intensity of experience as the few who go through the exercise personally. There are a few times when it works to have two or three people playing roles just among themselves without an audience or a facilitator involved, but since it could get off track pretty quickly, it is best to have a facilitator nearby.

Student Teaching

Sometimes when there is a lot of material to be presented and the trainees can work in small groups outside of the training sessions, it can be effective to assign some of the information presentation to them. They would need to be residential, meaning that they all are staying in the same place overnight while they are in training, or they would all be in the same general place between training sessions that take place over a period of time.

Small groups can be given assignments to review the material separately or together and then decide how to present it to the rest of the training class in a specified period of time. They are usually allowed to determine the method they want to use to present the information (depending upon the available resources) and who will go before the group. In one such situation, where five groups were given this type of assignment, one group put on a skit to illustrate the most important parts of the information, another found an exercise for the rest of the group to participate in, and the other three had each of their members present lecturettes.

These groups usually do not have a precise sense of how much time to allow for presentations; thus, keeping them to strict time periods may mean cutting off some of what they have planned and thereby losing part of the information for the whole group. Occasionally, a group will not understand what they are charged with presenting and present something totally different. Topics that groups do work on to present, however, they usually really learn and remember well.

Practice

Although practice, like student teaching, is not listed as one of Petersen's training methods—and a case can certainly be made that it is not a method of imparting information but rather a method of retaining information—it is an important training tool. Practice is very beneficial when the learned information is about how to do something, such as operating equipment, responding to unplanned events, filling out a form, or taking a sample, but less so when the information imparted deals with interpersonal relations. That is where role playing, discussed above, comes into play.

Practice may involve simulations such as the computer simulators used for flight training or similar situations. It may also involve the actual equipment that workers will use, but in circumstances where others are able to ensure that no harm is done.

Practice is particularly important when it comes to learning what to do in stressful, hazardous situations such as emergencies or other unplanned events. The stress of an unusual situation, especially one where there may be life-threatening aspects, impacts the ability to remember what to do or to make good decisions. It requires, therefore, that the actions needed to ensure minimal damage and harm be second nature to those who must take them. The only way to ensure that is to practice over and over so that the actions require little decision making.

Practice requires feedback on the results of the practice. Otherwise, the trainees could be practicing a wrong version of what they were taught or be retaining the wrong information.

Combination

The most effective training will probably use some combination of the methods described above, particularly for all-day or multiple-day sessions. Training could start with a lecturette either by an in-person speaker or by videotape. That could be followed with the conference method, working through a problem or compiling experience information from the group. The group discussion could lead into case studies. The group could practice what they have learned either through actual or simulated use of equipment or forms, or through role playing. For learning in segments, each segment could consist of two or more of the methods.

Some Helpful Training Techniques

No matter what the method used for imparting information, certain techniques can be used to help the learning process. These include humor or drama, rewards for trainee contributions or participation, visual and aural interest, handouts, and comfortable and practical room setups.

Drama

When cleverly done, drama can add considerable retention to the learning process. Drama can be achieved in a number of ways. The drama may occur from actually acting out a situation in the classroom, or it can be a dramatic story that carries home the point to be made. It can also be pictures or sounds that carry dramatic impact.

An acted-out situation need not be overly dramatic in and of itself. Take, for example, the speaker who had lectured to the law school class about the difficulties that eye witnesses have in actually remembering what they see. In the midst of the lecture, a stranger enters the room, walks to the podium, hands the professor something (which is immediately placed on a shelf in the podium out of sight), whispers in his ear, and then walks out. The whole episode has taken perhaps a minute. The class has no reason to believe that this has anything to do with them or the lecture. The professor now asks them, "What happened just now? What did the man bring to me? Describe it. What did he look like—how tall, what weight, what color hair and eyes, what kind of clothing?" As the class stumbles through the answers, finding out that different people saw different things or simply can't remember even though they were all eye witnesses, each individual student gets a dramatic boost to his or her ability to remember the difficulty witnesses have in making accurate descriptions and, probably, identifications.

At Mobil Chemical Company's La Grange, Georgia plant, hazard communication courses start off with a tall can sitting on a table in the front of the room. The course facilitator acts as if it were not there as the introduction to the session begins. Then the can begins to shake and move. A smallish training or safety and health professional comes out of the can covered in children's play goop or shredded paper and slithers over tables and the class participants. After the class recovers from the humor and excitement, the facilitator drives home the point that exposure can happen unexpectedly and awfully fast. By the time someone has been exposed to a toxic substance, it is too late to find out about it. All workers need to know about potential toxic substance hazards and what to do to protect themselves before exposure occurs. The drama has helped make the point.

A popular speaker for groups of refinery/petrochemical workers is a man who recounts how his mistakes led to a terrible accident at a refinery. His understated but dramatic recounting of the burns and their treatment, the visual drama of his reconstructed face, the story of the emotionally painful changes in his life because of the accident has greater impact on those workers as they go through their routine operations than any amount of statistics, rules, discipline, or exhortations. Drama carries the point.

Humor

Like drama, humor helps memory. Speakers classically believe that they need to start off a presentation with a joke, and not necessarily one that has anything to do with their subjects. As long as the speaker tells jokes well and chooses one that does not offend, start-off jokes probably help more than they hinder, since they can break the ice for the speaker and the audience. Using humor to help make points and enable better retention of those points, however, is a little different than simple joke telling.

Patt Schwab tells of a group of truckers trying to pass a commercial driver's license exam. At the time, only 60 percent of the truckers taking the exam nationally were passing it. Most of the questions concerned names for parts of the truck or problems that a truck might have. Schwab found that humorous alternate definitions to contrast with the correct ones helped them remember the correct ones. The class enjoyed such fun definitions as "brake lag" meaning coming back late from a coffee break or "slack adjuster" being another name for a supervisor. In this way, she was able to help them remember the right definitions to the extent that 98 percent of those students then passed the exam (Schwab 1996).

She also points out that such well-known nicknames as "dead-man switch" are really helpful to convey information and help those who receive information retain it.

She recommends that, when using humor to help get a safety message over, the humor be "sandwiched" between serious points—making the point seriously, adding something humorous that is on the subject, and then returning to the serious point.

Schwab warns that humor should not mock serious matters or the proper way to do things. Improper ways are fair game as long as they are theoretical, not directed at someone personally. Personal stories and quips work best. She believes that humor is aided by exaggeration. "Anything worth telling is worth exaggerating! Never let truth get in the way of a good story!" (Schwab 1996)

Rewarding Contributors

In addition to providing humor with the information needed to pass the trucker's test, Schwab also gave "prizes" to class members who spoke up, showed leadership, or caught her "notorious" misspellings on the flip chart (Schwab 1996). Although people enjoy being actively involved in training, they may be a little reluctant to get started, and an interactive course with no one willing to interact is deadly. Humorous rewards for those who do contribute may help get the interaction going.

A corporate safety and health manager for a wood products company presented toothpicks to the participants of a safety training class when those participants added something to the discussion. He, too, must have believed in the importance of exaggeration, since he described the toothpicks (which he had just picked up in the hotel coffee shop) as having been handcrafted from the finest oaks in Maine. Before long, class participants were reminding him when he forgot to give them a toothpick for speaking up. They did not really believe that the toothpicks were particularly special; they just liked being recognized for their contributions.

Rewards might be small pieces of candy or simply having a flip chart page on the wall where names of those who contributed and how often would be marked as the contributions were made.

Visual and Aural Interest

It is helpful to have something interesting to see or hear to help stimulate interest and to augment the ways to learn the information. If a slide or overhead projector shows a summary of what the lecturer is saying, then, as Figure 23-2 indicates, the training participants have an additional means of learning—reading as well as hearing. It helps if the slide or overhead transparency is visually interesting with color and/or border designs. Any lettering on the slides or overheads must be large enough to be seen at the distances from which trainees will be viewing. For example, if the trainees are 25 feet away, the lettering should be at least one inch high and about one-eighth inch thick. At between 50 and 100 feet the letters should be at least two inches tall and one-quarter inch thick (Lippy and Livingston 1996, 28).

As mentioned earlier, films and videotapes can provide sounds and sights from beyond the classroom that help keep the training participants stimulated.

Handouts

Handouts to provide additional information and practical examples may also help the trainees remember the information they have been given. According to Adele McCormack, Conference and Education Coordinator for the VPPPA, the one thing that workshop attendees always seem to want more of is handouts (McCormack 1996). While sometimes providing a whole manual of reference material may be called for, usually nothing so bulky to carry and store is necessary. Practical examples are the best handouts.

Comfortable and Practical Room Setups

The setup of the training room should be keyed to the type of training methods to be used. It is hard to work in small groups if the class is arranged in rows or around one large table. Round tables lend themselves to group efforts. Space to get up and move around between the tables facilitates small group presentations.

Evaluating the Learning Achieved

Some sort of evaluation of training is needed to find out if the training has been successful. A lot of training evaluation is based on feedback, either informally during the sessions or by an evaluation form filled out at the end of training. Much can be learned from these, particularly about the methods and techniques used and the skills of the trainers in presenting. Probably of more importance is the evaluation of the results of training, determining how much impact the training had on actual knowledge, behavior, or overall results.

Evaluation of training will be greatly aided by having good, clear training objectives. If the objectives have been developed well, it should be fairly easy to evaluate how well those objectives were achieved.

Feedback

A lot can be learned from informal feedback during the presentation of materials. The body language of the participants can tell you whether they are alert and involved or if their minds are drifting elsewhere. Their involvement in questions, observations, and group activities also tells you whether they are alert and learning. If they continue to talk about the subjects discussed during their breaks and over meals, that's another good sign.

Sometimes trainees will tell you how much they are enjoying and learning. But more often than not, you will need to encourage them to provide feedback by requesting that they fill out an evaluation questionnaire at the end of the training. Such questionnaires should ask for evaluation of relevance and appropriateness, pacing and clarity, and enjoyment, and also provide room for comments or open-ended questions (Lippy and Livingston 1996, 33). Montante calls this type of feedback "reaction evaluation" and feels that it is a gauge of emotional reaction to the training (Montante 1996, 34).

Many trainers follow up with an additional evaluation three months after the training is completed. This follow-up evaluation asks if the training has been useful, what the practical applications were, and for suggestions on how the training could be made more useful (Richardson 1996).

Evaluating Training Impact

Montante points out that there are three aspects of the evaluation of impact: knowledge, behavior, and results (Montante 1996, 34). The evaluation of each of these will be different.

Knowledge

Much of the attempt to judge the results of training is concentrated on knowledge, which usually is evaluated by written tests, either before and after or just afterwards. People do not like tests very much but may find the experience of missing the right answer traumatic enough to remember that one or those several parts much better than all the rest. This method is probably the easiest to use.

Behavior

Behavior can sometimes be tested if the skill involves proficiency that lends itself to written or oral testing. Behavior can also be reported by self-observation from the trainees. The most usual means of evaluating behavior is to observe it, either generally noting that the group of employees appear to be performing correctly or specifically asking each trainee to demonstrate the learned behavior.

Results

What Montante calls results are broader and more general than how much one trainee has absorbed. His results look more at the overall goals intended by safety and health training to begin with, such as changes in losses, claims, injury and illness rates, waste, productivity, quality, and cost performance. In fact, these are so broad that one type of training may not have much impact by itself. Even if the training was so important that it is expected to have an impact on these more general results, it is difficult to separate the impact of training from the impact of other factors. Still, sometimes much can be inferred from obvious changes to these more general measures.

KEY POINTS

- If training is not effective, much of it will be forgotten before it can be used.
- Determining training objectives before the training is developed helps articulate the purpose of the training and makes evaluation of the training easier.

- Training objectives should be observable, measurable, and state the conditions under which performance would be demonstrated.
- The more ways the trainee is involved in learning, the more likely he or she is to retain the information taught.
- Adults have a strong need to be involved and to relate what they are learning to their own experiences.
- The best approach to training methods is to combine them for variety and for the different values of each method.
- Information retention is helped by humor or drama.
- Trainees respond well to encouragement and recognition for speaking up and taking part in training activities.
- Evaluation of training is necessary to determine whether the training has been successful in its purpose.
- Evaluation can be achieved through formal and informal feedback from the trainees, testing of knowledge, observation of behaviors, and/or analysis of impact on desired safety and health results.

REFERENCES

Lippy, Bruce, and Dennis Livingston. 1996. Train-the-Trainer Program, Plasterers' and Cement Masons' Lead-Based Paint Abatement Course, University of Maryland's Environmental Health Education Center and Community Resources, Inc., developed for the Plasterer's and Cement Masons' International Association (OP & CMIA) under EPA grant Cx823839-01-0.

McCormack, Adele C. 1996. Personal telephone conversation with the author, July.

Minter, Stephen G. 1996. "Safety Training That Sticks." *Occupational Hazards* 58, no. 7: 33–36.

Montante, William M. 1996. "Effective Training: The Missing Links." *Professional Safety* 41, no. 1: 32–34. Des Plaines, IL: ASSE.

OSHA. Undated. Unpublished manual, *Managing Worker Safety and Health*, Chapter 11, "Safety and Health Training," pp. 11-1 to 11-12. Washington, DC: Office of Cooperative Programs.

Petersen, Dan. 1988. *Safety Management: A Human Approach.* Goshen, NY: Aloray.

Richardson, William A. 1996. Managing Director, Macro International, Inc., personal conversation with the author, August.

Schwab, Patt. 1996. "Good Humor = Good Safety Training." *Retail, Trades and Services Section Newsletter:* 1–2. Itasca IL: National Safety Council.

24

Learning for Ownership

Employees at all levels of a company need knowledge about protecting themselves and others from occupational hazards and the skills to work safely and healthfully. Knowledge and skills will result from appropriate orientation and ongoing training, drills, safety meetings, and training supplements such as awareness programs and safety and health communication. Appropriate training includes the basic knowledge and skills both to understand responsibilities and the everyday hazards of the job and to handle unplanned events, including emergencies.

SAFETY AND HEALTH TRAINING IN ORIENTATION TO THE JOB

There are certain basic things that must be taught to everyone at the worksite. First, every single employee must know what his or her responsibilities under the safety and health program are (see Chapter 6 for examples of assigned responsibility). Second, all line employees must know what potential hazards they face and how to protect themselves and others. All managers must know, at least generally, what kinds of potential hazards their employees could be exposed to and the protections set up to keep them from actual exposure.

Line employees, including supervisors and those managers who are in the main service or production areas frequently, require the most safety and health training. This training starts with orientation for employees new to the worksite and for employees who are starting new jobs. It should consist of two parts, one general and one specific to the job to be learned. Orientation should be followed by practice of the tasks required by the job, including the safety and health precautions.

General Orientation

When employees at any level begin to work, they should have safety and health subjects integrated into their orientation to the new worksite. These subjects should include:

- Their safety and health rights and responsibilities along with any other worksite rights and responsibilities, including company policy towards violence of any sort or threats of violence while on company property.

- The company and worksite safety and health policy, including the priority placed by management on working safely and healthfully.
- The overall goal of the safety and health program, so that the new employee can understand what the worksite is trying to achieve.
- Any safety and health objectives that are pertinent to the work that the employee will do.
- The different types of emergencies that could occur and what to do in each type.

All new employees, no matter where they will be working, should be given tours of the worksite, during which general information about potential hazards and the mechanisms or systems to prevent exposure are covered along with information about the product flow and how quality and productivity are maintained. This provides each employee with enough knowledge to move safely about the plant in areas other than where that employee is specifically employed.

Specific Orientation

More specific orientation to the actual tasks and skills to be learned should include the safety and health precautions as part of the work procedures. For office workers, this should include ergonomic information. Time should be taken to fully demonstrate any personal protective equipment that might be used on the job and a chance given to practice putting it on (and cleaning and storing it, if that is part of the employee's duties). Employers seeking excellence will insist that every employee have thorough knowledge of all the potential hazards of a job, including safety hazards of equipment and procedures— not just high-hazard chemicals.

It helps if co-workers either conduct or play a part in this specific orientation. Seeing them perform work safely will make a strong impression about the relationship of safe procedures to succeeding at the job. Hearing them explain why those safe work procedures are followed will also make a stronger impression than if a manager or safety and health professional explained it.

Although workers who are just changing jobs will not need the general orientation, they should have orientation to the specific tasks of a new job, including the same kind of safety and health information as provided to a new employee.

Both general and specific orientation should be presented in such a way that the new employees are encouraged to ask questions and get involved in the discussion about this important information.

Practice

Employees new to the worksite or new to a job need the opportunity to practice what they have been taught with a supervisor or experienced co-worker nearby to remind them of anything they may have forgotten and to make sure that no bad habits get started. The practice period will vary depending upon the complexity of the job being learned and by the new employee's ability to absorb and use the information about the job. It should continue, with perhaps less frequent observation as time goes by, until the supervisor or co-worker is reasonably sure that all the routine occurrences have been encountered and successfully mastered.

Ongoing Safety and Health Courses

Besides the initial safety and health training of orientation, worksites should provide various types of ongoing safety and health training. The content will depend upon the types of worksite activities and potential hazards. Much training is required by standard. Most worksites, no matter what industry, benefit from ongoing ergonomic, industrial vehicle, generic defensive driver, and lockout/tagout training.

As an example of one company's safety and health training programs, Figure 24-1 shows a listing of the safety and health courses available for non-managerial employees at Allied Signal's Kansas City Division, which manufactures electrical, electronic, electromechanical, mechanical, rubber, and plastic components.

• 40-hour Hazwoper	• Back Injury Prevention
• General 24-hour Hazwoper	• Ambulance—Outside
	• Utility Vehicle
• Hazardous Material Information	• Ladder Safety
• Overhead Crane & Rigging	• Machine Guarding
• In-plant Vehicle Refresher	• Rigging for Heavy/Special Loads
• General Orientation— Right to Know	• Electrical Safety, Maintenance General
• High Risk Chemical Users	• Electrical Safety, Maintenance Overview

Figure 24-1. Allied signal Kansas city division safety and health training for non-exempt associates. *Source:* Allied Signal Kansas City Division Master Training List, DOE VPP Application.

In addition to many of the same courses shown in Figure 24-1, ICF Kaiser Hanford (which manages engineering, construction, maintenance, and waste transportation and handling as a subcontractor) offers courses in hazardous waste operations; aerial lift operation; asbestos; behavior-based safety; blood-borne pathogens; confined space; defensive driving; excavation, trenching and shoring; fall protection; first aid/CPR; fire extinguisher, lockout/tagout; noise control and hearing conservation; hoisting and rigging; and scaffold safety for non-exempt workers (Palmer, 1996).

Manager and supervisory industrial safety training at Westinghouse's Waste Isolation Pilot Plant in New Mexico includes thirty-one modules (see Figure 24-2 for a list of some of those modules). Most of these subjects would be relevant for managers in any kind of manufacturing. Many, such as Regulatory Requirements, Safety and Accountability, Manager and Supervisor Responsibilities, Fire Protection, What You Can Do to Prevent Accidents, How to Analyze Tasks for Hazards, Housekeeping, Safety Meetings, and Safety Goals, would be good for managers in all types of endeavors.

Kaiser offers its managers a course—Manager's Safety Training Phase II—which is provided by Westinghouse Hanford. It is designed to teach upper and middle level managers their roles in safety and health, including setting meaningful goals, employee involvement, and the importance of daily commitment (Palmer 1996).

DRILLS

Drills are particularly important to prepare for unplanned events, especially emergencies. They provide the opportunity to practice the special behaviors and tasks required by unplanned events in a low-stress envi-

Training Modules:

- Regulatory Requirements
- Safety and Accountability
- Manager and Supervisor Responsibilities
- Landlord* Responsibilities
- Fire Protection
- Subcontracts and Safety
- What You Can Do to Prevent Accidents
- Incident Reporting Requirements

- How to Analyze Tasks for Hazards
- Electrical Safety
- Hazardous Materials
- Housekeeping
- Work in High Places or Confined Spaces
- Safety Meetings
- Monitoring the Safety Program
- Safety Goals

Figure 24-2. Westinghouse Waste Isolation Pilot Plant industrial safety management and supervisor training program. *Source:* Waste Isolation Division, Industrial Safety, MAS-123, pp. 4–5.

ronment. They also provide the opportunity for management to observe how well their plans and training have prepared the workforce for potentially hazardous unplanned events and to make adjustments before anyone is actually exposed to hazards.

Emergency Drills

Most workplaces have regular fire evacuation drills, but many have other potential emergencies and should plan for those and provide drills as well (see Chapter 19 for

---

*Landlord is the term used for the manager assigned responsibility for a building's maintenance and housekeeping.

information on planning for emergencies). Emergency drills should include evacuation drills at least once each year to ensure that the whole workforce can be evacuated in an orderly and timely fashion.

Many continuously operating worksites prefer to have drills in place, testing their alarm systems without ever actually evacuating. A West Coast chemical plant felt that enough unplanned chemical reactions occurred to make drills unnecessary for their most likely emergency. Interviews of the workers at the plant revealed that (1) at least one worker thought that he should get into his car and go home if a fire broke out in the plant while he was outside unloading a rail car;[1] (2) the emergency alarm could not be heard in the warehouse; (3) a temporary worker planned to don self-contained breathing apparatus and help contain any possible chemical spills when, although he said he had been trained for such action by another employer, he had received no training from this employer to be involved in these operations. It was clear from these responses that neither the plant nor its employees were actually ready for any type of serious emergency.

Thinking out every part of a possible emergency is a necessity. For example, in plants where explosions are possible, employees need to understand that other explosions can follow the first and may be even more lethal. At one petrochemical plant in the southwest, office employees ran to their windows after a blast was heard, only to

---

[1]This would have bypassed going to an evacuation point where he could have been counted to save emergency personnel the risk of trying to find him in a burning building. Personnel counts are extremely important when entering the building can be life-threatening for emergency personnel. Drills should always include some personnel who are instructed beforehand to go off to areas where they will not be seen—as if they had been injured—so that the accuracy of the count can be tested.

be caught by flying glass when a larger explosion occurred. If they had properly practiced this type of emergency (and frequently office workers are left out of plans for emergencies "out in the plant"), they would have taken cover until an all-clear alarm sounded.

Most sophisticated worksites plan annual emergency scenarios and enlist local emergency organizations—fire, police, hospitals—to help them act out responses. All the entities critique the drill afterwards to see where they could have been better prepared and/or coordinated.

Unplanned Event Drills

Other types of unplanned events can cause emergency situations but not of catastrophic proportions. A new type of drill is coming into use to practice response to these less-than-catastrophic unplanned events. Unlike emergency drills, these drills, which Stalnaker calls "operations drills," can be conducted by the line managers whose employees are involved in the drills. The drills are meant to provide practice dealing with non-routine but not extraordinary events and keeping them from becoming emergency situations. The drills also provide the opportunity to check on the adequacy of procedures and training (Stalnaker 1996).

Drill Scenarios

The idea is to set up a mock unplanned event and to allow the employees involved to react to it as they would the real thing. Some possible drill scenarios are shown in Figure 24-3. As you can see, these are the kinds of things that are foreseen and planned for and yet do not happen frequently enough for employees and their supervisors to have experience handling them.

UTILITY OPERATIONS

During a routine round of the water treatment plant, an operator analyzes a sample and detects an elevated-chlorine level. The drill will determine whether the operator and her supervisor will take appropriate actions to assess and correct the condition.

POWER OPERATIONS

An operator assigned to the control room of a major switchyard hears an alarm that indicates the loss of power to an electrical power bus that feeds essential utility systems, fire alarm systems, and waste treatment facilities. The backup generator does not start. The drill will determine whether the operator will properly assess the cause and take appropriate action, in a timely manner, to return power via an alternate bus.

WASTE OPERATIONS

A waste handler is conducting a routine inspection in a waste warehouse when he finds a drum that appears to be bulging and could be overpressured. The drill will determine whether the operator and his supervisor will notify proper authorities, secure the area, and relieve the pressure. In this drill, employees will handle and open a drum simulated to be overpressured.

CHEMICAL OPERATIONS

A chemical operator enters a building and detects what he thinks is a leak around a valve stem on a chlorine system. The drill will determine whether the operator will properly notify management, understands PPE requirements and how to don the equipment, will tighten the packing nut, and follow established procedures for working with chlorine.

Figure 24-3. Drill scenarios. *Source:* C. Keith Stalnaker. "Using Operations Drills to Improve Workplace Safety." *Professional Safety* 41, no. 2 (1996). Des Plaines, IL: ASSE. Reproduced with permission from The American Society of Safety Engineers.

CHEMISTRY LABORATORY OPERATIONS
A chemist discovers a container of highly hazardous chemicals
not allowed in the laboratory. The drill will determine whether
the chemist will report the incident and properly prepare the
chemical for disposal.

INSTRUMENTATION
An instrument technician reports to the control room supervisor
that the as-found condition of an indicator gauge used to monitor
a critical safety system was out of specification limits. The drill
will determine whether the supervisor takes steps to properly assess impacts of the conditions.

OTHER POSSIBLE SCENARIOS

- Rescue of an injured employee in a confined space.

- Discovery of respirator with the wrong filter cartridge
  installed, after use has started.

- A crane supporting a suspended load of hazardous materials
  becomes inoperable.

- Lockout/tagout: preparing permits, applying protection,
  verifying protection, etc.

Figure 24-3. (*continued*)

Drill Guide

Stalnaker emphasizes the importance of ensuring that
the drill does not embarrass or intimidate those involved. Preparation of a drill guide, an example of which
is shown in Figure 24-4, provides the structure for careful planning of the drill as well as an evaluation instrument after the drill is completed (Stalnaker, 1996).

1) **Name of Drill:** Runaway Overhead Crane in Building 9876

2) **Approvals:**
   Prepared by: _____
                         Author/Dept./Date

   Reviewed by: _____
                         Safety/Dept./Date

   Approvals: _____
                         Facility Manager/Date

                     _____
                         Operations Manager/Date

                     _____
                         Drill Coordinator/Date

3) **References**
   Procedures:#ABCDE—Operation of Overhead Cranes
   #GHIJK—Crane Safety

4) **Objectives**
   To assess operator response to an out-of-control overhead crane. To determine whether proper methods will be used to shut down the crane in an abnormal situation.

5) **Drill Scenario**
   —Operator is operating the radio-controlled crane when the crane can no longer be controlled. This is simulated by giving the operator a radio-control box without a battery ("dummy box") while Monitor #1, a licensed crane user, uses a functioning radio-control unit to operate the crane.
   —With Monitor #1 beside the operator, the operator is told to use the dummy box to pick up a load and move it in an eastward direction. As the operator uses the box, the monitor mirrors the operator's actions, using the control unit to begin moving the load. The monitor tells the operator to

Figure 24-4. Sample drill guide. Drill Guide #12345 *Source:* C. Keith Stalnaker. "Using Operations Drills to Improve Workplace Safety." *Professional Safety* 41, no. 2 (1996). Des Plaines, IL: ASSE. Reproduced with permission from The American Society of Safety Engineers.

stop the crane, yet continues to move the crane to simulate an out-of-control condition.

6) Expected Actions

a) Operator should attempt to stop the crane using the power switch on the dummy box. (Monitor keeps the crane in motion following this action.)

b) Operator should next push (simulate) "emergency crane stop" buttons located on the south, north, and west walls. (Monitor keeps crane in motion following this action.)

c) Operator should now locate and open (simulate) the crane's electrical breaker in the equipment room. (Monitor stops the crane.) At this point, the operator should indicate a need for lockout/tagout of the open breaker. (Monitor acknowledges this need and instructs the operator to continue under the assumption that lockout/tagout has been accomplished.

d) Operator should locate supplies and erect (initiate) a barrier around the suspended load in order to prevent access by other workers.

e) Operator should now contact his/her supervisor, who, in turn, should notify the operations manager. (Monitor terminates the drill and returns the load to its original position.)

f) Operator should review procedures for any additional action.

7) Drill Monitor Assignments and Qualifications

a) Drill coordinator and operations manager: Rove the area of the drill and monitor response.

b) Monitor #1: Must be licensed to use a crane. Stays with the operator at all times. Operates the crane to adhere to the drill scenario. Prevents operator from actually performing the actions that are to be simulated.

c) Operator: Should be licensed and currently authorized to use the crane.

8) Initial Conditions

a) Drill coordinator should obtain concurrence/approval from facility supervisor and operations manager to conduct the drill at the scheduled time.

Figure 24-4. (*continued*)

b) Facility supervisor shall ensure that the drill area is free of excessive traffic and that the crane is available at the scheduled time.

c) Drill coordinator shall announce commencement and conclusion of the drill over the facility's public address system.

9) Materials and Simulation Devices
a) Operable crane radio-control unit;
b) Inoperable (battery removed) crane radio control unit (dummy box).

10) Additional Precautions or Limitations
None.

11) Time Standards
None.

12) Expected Drill Execution Time
Five minutes.

13) Point of Drill Termination
Area around the load has been secured, supervisor contacted, and operations manager notified of the incident.

14) Restoration
Operations supervisor performs a crane function test to ensure that the crane is ready to return to normal service.

Figure 24-4. (*continued*)

Drill Monitors

Each drill should have at least one drill monitor and large-scale operations may need several. The monitor(s) must not be involved in the expected actions of the drill. If a supervisor acts as a monitor, he or she must not be the supervisor at the same time. The actions and responses of the supervisor and some managers are part of what is being practiced in the drill.

The role of the drill monitor is to take whatever actions are needed for the simulation and acknowledge the decision for action taken by the drill participants when those actions should not actually be taken. An example is when, as shown in Figure 24-4, the operator goes to the electrical box and says that he is shutting off the crane at the circuit breaker and also that he is effecting lockout/tagout. The drill monitor's acknowledgment allows the drill to continue without actually taking these actions (Stalnaker 1996).

Drill Debriefing

Just as after an emergency drill, the unplanned event or operations drill should be followed by a debriefing for all the participants in which the drill coordinator goes over what should have happened and what actually did take place. The debriefing is a good place to talk about any ways to improve procedures or training (Stalnaker 1996).

Drill Records

The sample drill record shown in Figure 24-5 provides the official summary of the drill and can serve as a report to others in the plant who have not taken part in the drill. The record should show both the lessons learned and the actions taken for improvement, if any were needed.

Stalnaker reports that one plant conducted 1,100 drills with an operator/supervisor expenditure of 557 hours, or 0.5 man-hours per drill. Since these drills are short, they are inexpensive but can be very effective. As Stalnaker summarizes, "Operations drills are an excellent way to ensure that employees will take actions to prevent abnormal situations from escalating into emergencies" (Stalnaker 1996, p. 32).

Drill Guide #: 12345   Revision: 0   Drill Date: 00/00/00

1) **Title of Drill Guide:** Runaway Overhead Crane in Building 9876

2) **Participant/Employee Role:**
John Smith, Badge #0000, Building 9876 Operations Supervisor
Bill Jones, Badge #1111, Operator in Building 9876 (operated crane)
Sue Black, Badge #2222, Operations Manager
Ken Douglas, Badge #3333, Monitor #1
Mark Barnes, Badge #4444, Drill Coordinator

3) **Were Objectives Met?**
No. The operator took all expected actions in a timely manner, except (D) "Erecting a barrier around the suspended load to protect passersby." The operator did not identify the need to establish a barrier. Notifications by the operator and supervisor were performed in accordance with procedures. The deficiency noted above was discussed with the operations supervisor during the debriefing session. The supervisor conducted a review of all Building 9876 operators on 00/00/00 to review the results and go over the proper steps of dealing with a runaway crane.

4) **Lessons Learned**
Training records needed to verify operator licensing were not available at the start of the drill and delayed it some 10 minutes. In the future, remind the operations supervisor to have records available when the drill is scheduled.

_____

Drill Coordinator/Badge #/Date
cc: Operations Manager

Figure 24-5. Sample drill record. *Source:* C. Keith Stalnaker. "Using Operations Drills to Improve Workplace Safety." *Professional Safety* 41, no. 2 (1996). Des Plaines, IL: ASSE. Reproduced with permission from The American Society of Safety Engineers.

SAFETY MEETINGS

Most fixed-site workplaces have safety meetings each month. Construction and other industries with rapidly changing conditions are more likely to have "tool box" meetings at the start of the first shift of the week. These meetings are excellent places to refresh basic safety and health training—particularly with an eye to the kinds of potential hazards likely to be encountered before the next meeting—to explore new ideas or problems, and to get employees actively and meaningfully involved in safety and health.

Refresher Training

The most frequent use for safety meetings is to provide refresher training on safety and health matters. Refresher training is a good idea because as time goes by, shortcuts and ways of doing things that may not be as protective as they should be of the employees' safety and health can develop. The problem with refresher training is that, improperly handled, it can get to be a meaningless bore and general turnoff. If the meeting is only presenting information that is developed somewhere else and the employees are asked to look at it or listen to it and then sign off that they have been trained, the training is likely to fail in its intent. Safety meetings, just as any other form of training, need to be considered in terms of how adults learn (see Chapter 23).

Safety meetings should also be used to get two-way communication going. Part of the refresher training should discuss the safety and health policy, the goal, and the objectives that involve the employees at the safety meeting. Since the policy is simply the statement of the workplace attitude toward protection of workers, it is good, from time to time, to get a reality check discussion going about whether the written policy really does do what it is supposed to and, if not, how it or the workplace should be changed to bring the two closer together.

To a certain extent, the same is true of the goal of the safety and health program and the objectives that are set to achieve it. It is particularly worthwhile to take time, every so often, to look at the objectives or parts of the objectives that are the responsibility of the workgroup at the safety meeting and check progress toward their achievement and impact on the goal of the worksite. This should be done in a discussion format rather than having someone "present" the information to them. Workers are likely to have their own ideas about the objectives and the progress being made toward them (for more on policy, goal, and objectives, see Part 2.)

New Ideas/Problems

Safety meetings are the best places to introduce new general safety and health requirements and procedures and to allow practice and discussion of these new ideas. It is also one of the best places to find out about potential hazards or other problems that workers may have noted or thought about. Unlike individual reports of hazards/ problems, discussion in the safety meeting allows an exchange of ideas among workers and possible group solutions.

Employee Involvement

Probably the best method of keeping safety meetings interesting for employees is to allow them to take some or all control over what will be presented and how. With the use of the safety, health, and training professionals as a resource, hourly or non-exempt employees can better decide what topics to cover and how material should be presented. Taking the responsibility makes the sessions more interesting. Since the workers preparing the training know what they would like to know about, they are in a good position to know what will make the information more interesting to their fellow employees (for more on employee involvement, see Chapter 11.).

TRAINING SUPPLEMENTS

While not exactly training, awareness programs and any sort of two-way communication about safety and health add to worker knowledge or remind workers of things they have already learned.

Awareness Programs

Awareness programs are closely akin to incentive programs and in fact overlap with them somewhat. The jacket or cup that is given as an incentive probably has a safety slogan or safety reminder of some sort on it that helps awareness on a very simple level. Simple recognition programs similar to those described in Chapter 18 also serve as awareness programs.

In the early 1980s, Gray Tool, a plant producing oil-field equipment, found that its employees needed to be more aware of the hazards they were exposed to and the steps to take to help protect themselves. Managers began quizzing employees on a random basis and providing positive feedback for good answers. Several months later, employees were not only better able to answer the questions but were also doing a much better job of following safe work procedures. A similar but more elaborate program at Motorola in Austin, Texas had managers telephoning employees to ask safety and health questions. Correct answers were rewarded with pizzas. At least, they were until too many right answers made the program expensive (Horn 1993).

Safety and health newsletters or articles covering safety and health activities in more general workplace newsletters can also help awareness, particularly if hourly and/or non-exempt employees are mentioned or quoted in the articles. Posters, electronic signs, and other mechanisms for placing safety slogans in eye-catching places may be of some help in increasing safety awareness as well.

Two-Way Communication

Involving employees in two-way communication about safety and health helps keep what they have learned foremost in their minds. The meetings described in Chapter 12 are possibilities for two-way safety and health communication, as are the safety meetings described above. The important concept is that the communication be two-way. If all communication about safety and health is simply sent out or presented to hourly and non-exempt workers, very little is going to stay with them. If they have a chance to provide feedback, they will retain much more.

KEY POINTS

- Employees must have appropriate safety and health knowledge and skills to take ownership or personal responsibility for safety and health at the worksite.

- Every employee at every level must know what his or her responsibilities are under the safety and health program.
- All line employees must know what potential hazards are faced in the tasks of the job and how to help protect themselves and others.
- Managers must know, at least generally, what potential hazards their employees face and what protections have been put in place to prevent exposure.
- Safety and health must be integrated into both general and specific worksite orientation.
- A practice period for employees new to a job is helpful to ensure that all routine occurrences are successfully mastered in a safe environment.
- Drills provide the opportunity to prepare for unplanned and emergency situations in a comparatively low-stress environment.
- Emergency drills should be run for each type of emergency for which planning has been done and should involve everyone who could conceivably be involved in the real emergency.
- Annual emergency scenarios involving local emergency organizations prepare the community for possible emergencies involving the worksite.
- Operations drills provide a quick and inexpensive means of practicing response to unplanned events that could lead to emergencies.
- Drills offer the opportunity to critique planning, procedures, and training as well as practice.
- Routine safety meetings or tool box talks provide the opportunity to give refresher training, explain and practice new procedures, and involve workers in group problem identification and resolution.

- Awareness programs and safety and health communication that is two-way, allowing workers to offer ideas about problems and resolutions, supplement training by reminding and keeping them actively involved in what they have learned.

Assuring that the right safety and health information is presented through initial, ongoing orientation, courses, and meetings as well as through awareness programs and safety and health communication builds on the effective preparation for ensuring that learning is done. Employees at every level are given the knowledge and skills needed to allow them to take ownership of safety and health at the worksite.

REFERENCES

Horn, Connie. 1993. Hourly worker and VPP Coordinator, Motorola Oak Hill Plant, Austin, Texas, personal conversation with the author, May.

Palmer, Daniel S. 1996. Industrial Safety and Health, ICF Kaiser Hanford, personal conversation with the author, August.

Stalnaker, C. Keith. 1996. "Using Operations Drills to Improve Safety." *Professional Safety* 41, no. 2: 29–32. Des Plaines, IL: ASSE.

25

Learned Ownership

In the workplace with excellent safety and health protection, every employee has an important role to play. Constructing the complete and closed management loop provides the structure for systems to analyze and control hazards. Excellence, however, is difficult to achieve and certainly cannot be maintained for long without total involvement. Total involvement requires knowledge and skills that are acquired through the various types of training. To accomplish this, training must effectively ensure learning and provide appropriate knowledge and skills.

As each part of this system for excellence is built, it both supports and draws support from the other elements of the system. As the system is built, more and more ownership is established for each employee at the worksite—an ownership that accepts personal responsibility for safety and health and is fueled by the knowledge and skills provided through safety and health training.

Author's Afterword: The Future of Excellence

This book is meant to be a snapshot of excellence in worker safety and health protection near the end of the twentieth century. Excellence today is vastly different from excellence fifty years ago and even greatly changed from ten or fifteen years ago. It can be assumed that excellence will continue to change.

Sometimes it is difficult to differentiate between management fads and lasting change. That the global economy has overtaken national economies is a lasting change. That the citizens of nations attempt to reverse that change does not make it a fad. That companies cut back their staffs of professionals to reduce costs and please stockholders for the short term may, however, be a fad. Already, the Society of Human Resource Management says that corporate "downsizing" is declining due to lack of profitability gains (Grimsley et al. 1996).

I expect, however, that we will see outsourcing of safety and health expertise for some time to come as companies cut their own safety and health experts and hire contract firms to provide expert resources to the line managers and employees who will have responsibility for safety and health. Still, I do not believe that this will be a lasting change. While outside experts can provide many important services, the role for safety and health professionals (described in Chapter 13) includes some key elements that will not work as well, or at all, if the attempt is made to provide them through contract companies. These include helping to form the vision of where the safety and health program should be headed, providing continuous evaluation, and acting as the conscience of the worksite for safety and health.

The future of worker safety and health protection excellence will continue, however, to rest with company employees who are in the mainstream of production of goods or services. As the nature of work changes, new safety and health challenges will appear—whether ergonomic, toxic substance, stress, or new hazards that we do not yet imagine. We know enough about technology to understand that it is not as hazard-free as once we might have imagined. It just does not have as many of the old hazards that killed and maimed our workforce. Today's hazards—for example, repetitive motion brought about by high-speed information technology—are going to impact industries such as finance that have never given much thought to worker safety and health.

The very nature of excellence as we understand it, is the ability to continue to learn and grow. The excellent workplace will understand new hazards faster than others. It will begin to develop prevention and controls for those hazards before others have even begun to recognize them.

Safety and health protection excellence is really part of overall management excellence. For the best companies, the line between worker protection and environmental protection will become more and more blurred. Companies on the leading edge of environmental protection are already applying the same concepts covered in this book to the environment, and that includes worker involvement. The additional aspect of involvement for environmental excellence is necessarily that of the community.

The excellent company will have the goals of worker and environmental protection just slightly in front of goals for product or service quality and efficient production. Peter Keen, an international management consultant at the CEO level, has said that future quality will be measured by the quality of relationships, specifically relationships with customers, stockholders, and employees (Keen 1995, 40). The measurement of the quality of the relationship with company employees will be based on injury and illness rates, because it is not only a measure of how much the company cares for the employee, but also a measure of the responsibility that employees take in doing the job well.

Whatever the future of occupational safety and health excellence, one thing is absolutely clear, it will not be the status quo, let alone yesterday's preoccupation with compliance. Companies that expect to achieve excellence will always be ahead of government regulation. The systems described here are the best ways now known to stay open to improvement opportunities and to evolve as excellence evolves.

REFERENCES

Grimsley, Kirsten D., Steven Ginsberg, Margaret W. Pressler, and Heather Salerno. 1996. "WashBiz." *Washington Post*, no. 258 (August 19).

Keen, Peter G. W. 1995. "Future Quality." *Ways*, no. 6 (June–July): 37–40. Toronto: Issues for Canada's Future, Inc.

Appendixes

Appendix **1**

The Voluntary Protection Programs (VPP) Process

THE APPLICATION

OSHA provides application guidelines that describe the information needed for the application and how to organize it. Applications are usually sent to one of the ten OSHA regional offices,[1] where they are reviewed to ascertain whether the applicant site appears to be able to meet the requirements for at least one of the VPP.[2]

In some parts of the country, backlogs of six months to two years developed from the time of application until

---

[1] This may change to Area Offices as OSHA is "reinvented" and as the need for VPP help increases. By the summer of 1996, Region VI was already shifting most VPP activity to the Area Offices.

[2] At any point in the approval process or after approval any applicant or participating site may withdraw from the VPP without prejudice (OSHA 1988, 26346).

the time an OSHA team could come onsite to verify the application and determine adequacy of the program as implemented. OSHA has attempted to alleviate these backlogs by getting help from other government agencies such as the Department of Energy and the National Aeronautics and Space Agency.[3] In the mid-1990s, OSHA was even training and utilizing safety and health professionals from participating VPP sites as unpaid Special Government Employees.

THE ONSITE VISIT

OSHA, DOE, and the states that offer VPP arrange the date for onsite visits to applicant sites well in advance at a time convenient both for the agencies applied to and the applicants. The team leader contacts the site and explains what the team will need to have in terms of documentation and assistance.

OSHA and state VPP onsite teams usually consist of a team leader, a back-up team leader, a safety professional, and an industrial hygienist. Team size can vary with the size and complexity of the hazards at an applicant site. DOE teams tend to be much larger, with from twelve to twenty-four members, but DOE sites are also much larger (Kanth 1996).

If active compliance officers are used as team members, they are not considered to be compliance officers for the VPP review. OSHA personnel used for VPP reviews were usually from Regional Office staffs, with some assistance from staff at the National Office. In re-

---

[3]As states operating their own OSHA programs started up VPP programs, they would also frequently send state team-members-in-training to assist with federal OSHA VPP reviews.

cent years, however, compliance officers from OSHA Area Offices (where nearly all compliance is carried out) are being used more and more. DOE team personnel include national and field DOE staff, contractors and consultants, hourly workers from other sites, and usually at least one OSHA VPP staffer.

VPP onsite visits generally run from Monday afternoon to Friday morning of one week, although they can be shorter or longer depending upon the size and complexity of the worksite. The visits usually start with a meeting where the applicant site can present orientation information and the team leader can explain what is needed. The teams sample the requested documentation and interview randomly selected and other employees and tour the site. Any hazard seen by the team is explained to the applicant hosts and corrections are expected to be accomplished as soon as possible. The teams are supposed to help the applicant hosts understand which of their systems broke down, allowing the hazard to arise. Any hazard left uncorrected when the team leaves must be corrected within 90 days.[4] The team leader will expect written notification (and possibly pictures) when the hazard is corrected. In some cases, the team leader and possibly one other team member have returned to the site to see the corrections for himself or herself.

The applicant may also be given up to 90 days to make adjustments to the safety and health program systems that will allow approval. Program adjustments that require

---

[4]Although, as of early 1996, all hazards noted by VPP onsite teams had been corrected voluntarily, OSHA does reserve the right to refer an uncorrected hazard, if it seriously endangers the safety and health of employees, to enforcement if management refuses to correct it. Such a referral requires the decision of the Assistant Secretary of Labor for Occupational Safety and Health (OSHA 1988, 26347). The DOE VPP does not provide an inspection exemption.

more than a 90-day period are usually the subject of a Merit Program goal.

APPROVAL DECISIONS

While at the site, the team usually makes the determination as to its recommendation to the Assistant Secretary for approval or denial. Quite often the team will leave a draft report of the visit at the site before they leave. The decision itself must clear the Regional Administrator and is the responsibility of the Assistant Secretary. No approval is final until signed by that official (OSHA 1988, 26347; DOE 1994, 21).

AFTER APPROVAL

Each approved VPP site must send in its annual incidence rates, average employment, and annual program evaluation report each year by February 15 (OSHA 1988, 26342).

All approved sites are reevaluated following the schedules discussed in Chapter 1. If a Merit site is found to be making too little progress towards Star approval or has lost ground beyond the ability to adjust that condition in 90 days, the site will be asked to withdraw. If it completes the term of its approval without achieving its Merit goals or if it has lost ground in areas originally approvable, its approval to Merit will be allowed to lapse.

If a Star site is found to have significantly slipped away from Star level quality so that 90 days is not sufficient time to make adjustments, OSHA may choose to place that Star site on a conditional approval for a one-year period. If, after that time, full Star quality has not been achieved, the site is asked to withdraw.

REFERENCES

DOE. 1994. *Voluntary Protection Program, Part 1: Program Elements.* Washington, DC: Office of Safety and Quality Assurance, Office of Occupational Safety.

Kanth, Sanjeeva. 1996. DOE VPP staff member, personal conversation, August.

OSHA. 1988. *Federal Register* 53, no. 133 (July 12): 26339–26348.

Appendix 2

Further Description of a Safety and Health Program Assessment[1]

INTRODUCTION

There are three basic methods for assessing safety and health program effectiveness. This description will explain each of them. It also will provide more detailed information on how to use these tools to evaluate each element and subsidiary component of a safety and health program.

---

[1]This appendix has been taken from OSHA's undated, unpublished manual, *Managing Worker Safety and Health*.

The three basic methods for assessing safety and health program effectiveness are:

- Checking documentation of activity;
- Interviewing employees at all levels for knowledge, awareness, and perceptions; and
- Reviewing site conditions and, where hazards are found, finding the weaknesses in management systems that allowed the hazards to occur or to be "uncontrolled."

Some elements of the safety and health program are best assessed using one of these methods. Others lend themselves to assessment by two or all three methods.

Documentation

Checking documentation is a standard audit technique. It is particularly useful for understanding whether the tracking of hazards to correction is effective. It can also be used to determine the quality of certain activities, such as self-inspections or routine hazard analysis.

Inspection records can tell the evaluator whether serious hazards are being found, or whether the same hazards are being found repeatedly. If serious hazards are not being found and accidents keep occurring, there may be a need to train inspectors to look for different hazards. If the same hazards are being found repeatedly, the problem may be more complicated. Perhaps the hazards are not being corrected. If so, this would suggest a tracking problem or a problem in accountability for hazard correction.

If certain hazards recur repeatedly after being corrected, someone is not taking responsibility for keeping those hazards under control. Either the responsibility is not clear, or those who are responsible are not being held accountable.

Employee Interviews

Talking to randomly selected employees at all levels will provide a good indication of the quality of employee training and of employee perceptions of the program. If safety and health training is effective, employees will be able to tell you about the hazards they work with and how they protect themselves and others by keeping those hazards controlled. Every employee should also be able to say precisely what he or she is expected to do as part of the program. And all employees should know where to go in an emergency.

Employee perceptions can provide other useful information. An employee's opinion of how easy it is to report a hazard and get a response will tell you a lot about how well your hazard reporting system is working. If employees indicate that your system for enforcing safety and health rules and safe work practices is inconsistent or confusing, you will know that the system needs improvement.

Interviews should not be limited to hourly employees. Much can be learned from talking with first-line supervisors. It is also helpful to query line managers about their understanding of their safety and health responsibilities.

Site Conditions and Root Causes of Hazards

Examining the conditions of the workplace can reveal existing hazards, but it can also provide information about the breakdown of those management systems meant to prevent or control these hazards.

Looking at conditions and practices is a well-established technique for assessing the effectiveness of safety and health programs. For example, let's say that in areas where PPE is required, you see large and understandable signs communicating this requirement and all employees—with no exceptions—wearing equipment properly. You have obtained valuable visual evidence that the PPE program is working.

Another way to obtain information about safety and health program management is through root analysis of observed hazards. This approach to hazards is much like the most sophisticated accident investigation techniques, in which many contributing factors are located and corrected or controlled.

For example, let's say that during a review of conditions, you find a machine being operated without a guard on a pinch point. You should not limit your response to ensuring that a guard is installed. Asking a few questions can reveal a lot about the safety program's management systems. Why was the guard missing? If the operator says he did not know a guard was supposed to be on the machine, follow up with questions about the existence of safe work procedures and/or training.

If he says that the guard slows him down, and that the supervisor knows he takes it off, ask questions about the enforcement of rules, accountability, and the clarity of the worksite objective of putting safety and health first.

Let's say, however, that your insurance inspector or an OSHA inspector is the first person to notice the need for the guard. Or you first notice it when someone is hurt. A different lead-off question is appropriate. Has a comprehensive survey of the worksite been done by someone with enough expertise to recognize all potential and existing hazards?

Analyzing the root causes of hazards, while very helpful during a formal assessment, is a technique that also lends itself to everyday use. Attempt to analyze causes whenever hazards are spotted.

When evaluating each part of your worksite's safety and health program, use one or more of the above methods, as appropriate.

The remainder of this appendix will identify the components found in each element of a quality safety and health program and will describe useful ways to assess these components.

1. *Assessing the Key Components of Management Leadership and Employee Involvement*
   - WORKSITE POLICY ON SAFE AND HEALTHFUL WORKING CONDITIONS
     — *Documentation.* If there is a written policy, does it clearly declare the priority of worker safety and health over other organizational values, such as production?
     — *Interviews.*
       When asked, can employees at all levels express the worksite policy on worker safety and health?
       If the policy is written, can hourly employees tell you where they have seen it?
       Can employees at all levels explain the priority of worker safety and health over other organizational values, as the policy intends?
     — *Site Conditions and Root Causes of Hazards.* Have injuries occurred because employees at any level did not understand the importance of safety precautions in relation to other organizational values, such as production?

- GOAL AND OBJECTIVES FOR WORKER
  SAFETY AND HEALTH
  — *Documentation.*
  If there is a written goal for your safety and
  health program, is it updated annually?
  If there are written objectives, such as an an-
  nual plan to reach that goal, are they clearly
  stated?
  If managers and supervisors have written ob-
  jectives, do these documents include objec-
  tives for the safety and health program?
  — *Interviews.*
  Do managers and supervisors have a clear idea
  of their objectives for worker safety and health?
  Do hourly employees understand the current
  objectives of the safety and health program?
  Site Conditions and Root Causes of Hazards.
  (Only helpful in a general sense.)
- VISIBLE TOP MANAGEMENT LEADERSHIP
  — *Documentation.* Are there one or more written
  programs which involve top-level management in safety and health activities? For example, top management can receive and sign
  off on inspection reports either after each inspection or in a quarterly summary. These reports can then be posted for employees to see.
  Top management can provide "open door"
  times each week or each month for employees to come in to discuss safety and health
  concerns. Top management can reward the
  best safety suggestions each month or at
  other specified intervals.
  — *Interviews.*
  Can hourly employees describe how management officials are involved in safety and
  health activities?

Do hourly employees perceive that managers and supervisors follow safety and health rules and work practices, such as wearing appropriate personal protective equipment?

— *Site Conditions and Root Causes of Hazards.* When employees are found not wearing required personal protective equipment or not following safe work practices, have any of them said that managers or supervisors also did not follow these rules?

- EMPLOYEE INVOLVEMENT
  — *Documentation.*

  Are there one or more written programs that provide for employee involvement in decisions affecting their safety and health?

  Is there documentation of these activities; for example, employee inspection reports, minutes of joint employee-management or employee committee meetings?

  Is there written documentation of any management response to employee safety and health program activities?

  Does the documentation indicate a genuine substance to employee activities?

  Are there written guarantees of employee protection from harassment resulting from safety and health program involvement?

  — *Interviews.*

  Are employees aware of ways they can be involved in decisions affecting their safety and health?

  Do employees appear to take pride in the achievements of the worksite safety and health program?

  Are employees comfortable answering questions about safety and health programs and conditions at the site?

Do employees feel they have the support of management for their safety and health activities?

— *Site Conditions and Root Causes of Hazards.* (Not applicable.)

- ASSIGNMENT OF RESPONSIBILITY
  — *Documentation.* Are responsibilities written out so that they can be clearly understood?
  — *Interviews.* Do employees understand their own responsibilities and those of others?
  — *Site Conditions and Root Causes of Hazards.*
  Was the hazard caused in part because no one was assigned the responsibility to control or prevent it?
  Was the hazard allowed to exist in part because someone in management did not have the clear responsibility to hold a lower-level manager or supervisor accountable for carrying out assigned responsibilities?

- ADEQUATE AUTHORITY AND RESOURCES
  — *Documentation.* (Only generally applicable.)
  — *Interviews.*
  Do safety staff members or any other personnel with responsibilities for ensuring safe operation of production equipment have the authority to shut down that equipment or to order maintenance or parts?
  Do employees talk about not being able to get safety or health improvements because of cost?
  Do employees mention the need for more safety or health personnel or expert consultants?
  — *Site Conditions and Root Causes of Hazards.*
  Do recognized hazards go uncorrected because of lack of authority or resources?

Do hazards go unrecognized because greater expertise is needed to diagnose them?

- ACCOUNTABILITY OF MANAGERS, SUPERVISORS, AND HOURLY EMPLOYEES
  — *Documentation.*

    Do performance evaluations for all line managers and supervisors include specific criteria relating to safety and health protection?

    Is there documented evidence of employees at all levels being held accountable for safety and health responsibilities, including safe work practices? Is accountability accomplished through either performance evaluations affecting pay and/or promotions or disciplinary actions?

  — *Interviews.*

    When you ask employees what happens to people who violate safety and health rules or safe work practices, do they indicate that rule breakers are clearly and consistently held accountable?

    Do hourly employees indicate that supervisors and managers genuinely care about meeting safety and health responsibilities?

    When asked what happens when rules are broken, do hourly employees complain that supervisors and managers do not follow rules and never are disciplined for infractions?

  — *Site Conditions and Root Causes of Hazards.*

    Are hazards occurring because employees, supervisors, and/or managers are not being held accountable for their safety and health responsibilities?

    Are identified hazards not being corrected because those persons assigned the responsibility are not being held accountable?

- EVALUATION OF PROGRAM OPERATIONS
  — *Documentation.* Is there a written evaluation of each major part of the program, as identified in the OSHA Safety and Health Program Management Guidelines (54 FR 3908, January 26, 1989)? Does this written evaluation list what is being done, assess the effectiveness of each program element against the goal and objectives, and recommend changes as needed to make the program more effective or to try alternatives?
  — *Interviews.* Can employees, supervisors, and/or managers tell you how the program is evaluated and revised each year?
  — *Site Conditions and Root Causes of Hazards.* (Only generally applicable.)

2. *Assessing the Key Components of Worksite Analysis*
  - COMPREHENSIVE SURVEYS, CHANGE ANALYSIS, ROUTINE HAZARD ANALYSIS
    — *Documentation.*
    Are there documents that provide comprehensive analysis of all potential safety and health hazards of the worksite?
    Are there documents that provide both the analysis of potential safety and health hazards for each new facility, equipment, material, or process and the means for such hazards' elimination or control?
    Does documentation exist of the step-by-step analysis of the hazards in each part of each job, so that you can clearly discern the evolution of decisions on safe work procedures?
    If complicated processes exist, with a potential for catastrophic impact from an accident but low probability of such accident (as in nu-

clear power or chemical production), are there documents analyzing the potential hazards in each part of the processes and the means to prevent or control them?

If there are processes with a potential for catastrophic impact from an accident but low probability of an accident, have analyses such as "fault tree" or "what if?" been documented to ensure enough back-up systems for worker protection in the event of multiple control failure?

— *Interviews.*

Do employees complain that new facilities, equipment, materials, or processes are hazardous?

Do any employees say they have been involved in job safety analysis or process review and are satisfied with the results?

Does the safety and health staff indicate ignorance of existing or potential hazards at the worksite?

Does the occupational nurse/doctor or other health care provider understand the potential occupational diseases and health effects in this worksite?

— *Site Conditions and Root Causes of Hazards.*

Have hazards appeared where no one in management realized there was potential for their development?

Where workers have faithfully followed job procedures, have accidents or near misses occurred because of hidden hazards?

Have hazards been discovered in the design of new facilities, equipment, materials, and processes after use has begun?

Have accidents or near misses occurred when two or more failures in the hazard control system occurred at the same time, surprising everyone?

- REGULAR SITE SAFETY AND HEALTH INSPECTIONS
  — *Documentation.*
  If inspection reports are written, do they show that inspections are done on a regular basis?
  Do the hazards found indicate good ability to recognize those hazards typical of this industry?
  Are hazards found during inspections tracked to complete correction?
  What is the relationship between hazards uncovered during inspections and those implicated in injuries or illness?
  — *Interviews.* Do employees indicate that they see inspections being conducted, and that these inspections appear thorough?
  — *Site Conditions and Root Causes of Hazards.* Are the hazards discovered during accident investigations ones that should have been recognized and corrected by the regular inspection process?
- EMPLOYEE REPORTS OF HAZARDS
  — *Documentation.*
  Is the system for written reports being used frequently?
  Are valid hazards that have been reported by employees tracked to complete correction?
  Are the responses timely and adequate?
  — *Interviews.*
  Do employees know whom to contact and what to do if they see something they believe to be hazardous to themselves or coworkers?

Do employees think that responses to their reports of hazards are timely and adequate?

Do employees say that sometimes when they report a hazard, they hear nothing further about it?

Do any employees say that they or other workers are being harassed, officially or otherwise, for reporting hazards?

— *Site Conditions and Root Causes of Hazards.*

When hazards are found, do employees ever say they have complained repeatedly but to no avail?

Are hazards ever found where employees could reasonably be expected to have previously recognized and reported them?

- ACCIDENT AND NEAR MISS
  INVESTIGATIONS
  — *Documentation.*

  Do accident investigation reports show a thorough analysis of causes, rather than a tendency automatically to blame the injured employee?

  Are near misses (property damage or close calls) investigated using the same techniques as accident investigations?

  Are hazards that are identified as contributing to accidents or near misses tracked to correction?

  — *Interviews.*

  Do employees understand and accept the results of accident and near miss investigations?

  Do employees mention a tendency on management's part to blame the injured employee?

Do employees believe that all hazards contributing to accidents are corrected or controlled?

— *Site Conditions and Root Causes of Hazards.* Are
accidents sometimes caused at least partly by
factors that might also have contributed to
previous near misses that were not investigated or accidents that were too superficially
investigated?

- INJURY AND ILLNESS PATTERN ANALYSIS
  — *Documentation.*

In addition to the required OSHA log, are
careful records kept of first aid injuries
and/or illnesses that might not immediately
appear to be work-related?

Is there any periodic, written analysis of the
patterns of near misses, injuries, and/or illnesses over time, seeking previously unrecognized connections between them that indicate
unrecognized hazards needing correction or
control?

Looking at the OSHA 200 log and, where applicable, first aid logs, are there patterns of illness or injury that should have been analyzed
for previously undetected hazards?

If there is an occupational nurse/doctor on
the worksite, or if employees suffering from
ordinary illness are encouraged to see a
nearby health care provider, are the lists of
those visits analyzed for clusters of illness
that might be work-related?

— *Interviews.* Do employees mention illnesses or
injuries that seem work-related to them but
that have not been analyzed for previously
undetected hazards?

— *Site Conditions and Root Causes of Hazards.* (Not generally applicable.)

3. *Assessing the Key Components of Hazard Prevention and Control*
   - APPROPRIATE USE OF ENGINEERING CONTROLS, WORK PRACTICES, PERSONAL PROTECTIVE EQUIPMENT, AND ADMINISTRATIVE CONTROLS
     — *Documentation.*

     If there are documented comprehensive surveys, are they accompanied by a plan for systematic prevention or control of hazards found?

     If there is a written plan, does it show that the best method of hazard protection was chosen?

     Are there written safe work procedures?

     If respirators are used, is there a written respirator program?

     — *Interviews.*

     Do employees say they have been trained in and have ready access to reliable, safe work procedures?

     Do employees say they have difficulty accomplishing their work because of unwieldy controls meant to protect them?

     Do employees ever mention personal protective equipment, work procedures, or engineering controls as interfering with their ability to work safely?

     Do employees who use PPE understand why they use it and how to maintain it?

     Do employees who use PPE indicate that the rules for PPE use are consistently and fairly enforced?

Do employees indicate that safe work procedures are fairly and consistently enforced?

— *Site Conditions and Root Causes of Hazards.*

Do you ever find that controls meant to protect workers are actually putting them at risk or not providing enough protection?

Are employees engaging in unsafe practices or creating unsafe conditions because rules and work practices are not fairly and consistently enforced?

Are employees in areas designated for PPE wearing it properly, with no exceptions?

Are hazards that could feasibly be controlled through improved design being inadequately controlled by other means?

- FACILITY AND EQUIPMENT PREVENTIVE MAINTENANCE

  — *Documentation.*

  Is there a preventive maintenance schedule that provides for timely maintenance of the facilities and equipment?

  Is there a written or computerized record of performed maintenance that shows the schedule has been followed?

  Do maintenance request records show a pattern of certain facilities or equipment needing repair or breaking down before maintenance was scheduled or actually performed?

  Do any accident/incident investigations list facility or equipment breakdown as a major cause?

  — *Interviews.*

  Do employees mention difficulty with improperly functioning equipment or facilities in poor repair?

Do maintenance employees believe that the preventive maintenance system is working well?

Do employees believe that hazard controls needing maintenance are properly cared for?

— *Site Conditions and Root Causes of Hazards.*

Is poor maintenance a frequent source of hazards?

Are hazard controls in good working order? Does equipment appear to be in good working order?

- EMERGENCY PLANNING AND PREPARATION
  - *Documentation.* Are there clearly written procedures for every likely emergency, with clear evacuation routes, assembly points, and emergency telephone numbers?
  - *Interviews.* When asked about any kind of likely emergency, can employees tell you exactly what they are supposed to do?
  - *Site Conditions and Root Causes of Hazards.*

    Have hazards occurred during actual or simulated emergencies due to confusion about what to do?

    In larger worksites, are emergency evacuation routes clearly marked?

    Are emergency telephone numbers and fire alarms easy to find?

- ESTABLISHING A MEDICAL PROGRAM
  - *Documentation.* Are good, clear records kept of medical testing and assistance?
  - *Interviews.*

    Do employees say that test results were explained to them?

    Do employees feel that more first aid or CPR-trained personnel should be available?

Are employees satisfied with the medical arrangements provided at the site or elsewhere?

Does the occupational health care provider understand the potential hazards of the worksite, so that occupational illness symptoms can be recognized?

— *Site Conditions and Root Causes of Hazards.*

Have further injuries or worsening of injuries occurred because proper medical assistance (including trained first aid and CPR providers) was not readily available?

Have occupational illnesses possibly gone undetected because no one with occupational health specialty training reviewed employee symptoms as part of the medical program?

4. **Assessing the Key Components of Safety and Health Training**
   - ENSURING THAT ALL EMPLOYEES UNDERSTAND HAZARDS
     — *Documentation.*

     Does the written training program include complete training for every employee in emergency procedures and in all potential hazards to which employees may be exposed?

     Do training records show that every employee received the planned training?

     Do the written evaluations of training indicate that the training was successful, and that the employees learned what was intended?

     — *Interviews.*

     Can employees tell you what hazards they are exposed to, why those hazards are a threat, and how they can help protect themselves and others?

If PPE is used, can employees explain why they use it and how to use and maintain it properly?

Can employees tell you precisely what they are supposed to do and where they are supposed to go in every kind of emergency likely to occur at your worksite?

Do employees feel that health and safety training is adequate?

— *Site Conditions and Root Causes of Hazards.*

Have employees been hurt or made ill by hazards of which they were completely unaware, whose dangers they did not understand, or from which they did not know how to protect themselves?

Have employees or rescue workers ever been endangered by employees not knowing what to do or where to go in a given emergency situation?

Are there hazards in the workplace that exist, at least in part, because one or more employees have not received adequate hazard control training?

Are there any instances of employees not wearing required PPE properly because they have not received proper training?

- ENSURING THAT SUPERVISORS UNDERSTAND THEIR RESPONSIBILITIES

  — *Documentation.* Do training records indicate that all supervisors have been trained in their responsibilities to analyze work under their supervision for unrecognized hazards, to maintain physical protections, and to reinforce employee training through performance feed-back and, where necessary, enforcement of safe work procedures and safety and health rules?

— *Interviews.*

Are supervisors aware of their responsibilities?

Do employees say that supervisors are carrying out these duties?

— *Site Conditions and Root Causes.* Has a supervisor's lack of understanding of safety and health responsibilities played a part in creating hazardous activities or conditions?

- ENSURING THAT MANAGERS UNDERSTAND THEIR SAFETY AND HEALTH RESPONSIBILITIES

  — *Documentation.* Do training plans for managers include training in safety and health responsibilities? Do records indicate that all line managers have received this training?

  — *Interviews.* Do employees indicate the managers know and carry out their safety and health responsibilities?

  — *Site Conditions and Root Causes of Hazards.* Has an incomplete or inaccurate understanding by management of its safety and health responsibilities played a part in the creation of hazardous activities or conditions?

Appendix 3

Hazard
Analysis Flow
Charts

HAZARD ANALYSIS FLOW CHARTS

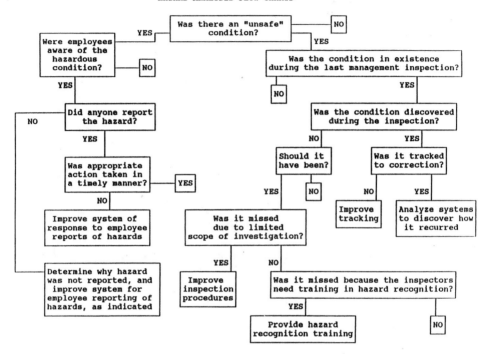

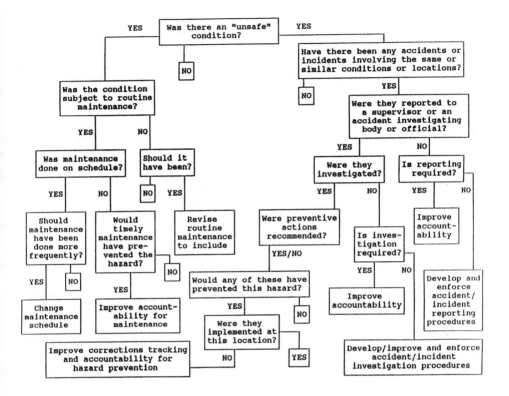

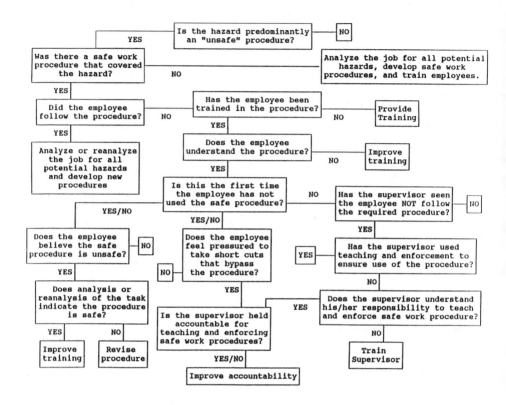

Appendix **4**

Walking the
Fine Line[1]

If you are the owner or top manager of a business, you have delegated certain responsibilities to other worksite managers and supervisors. You want to avoid undercutting their authority, since that would interfere with their ability to carry out those responsibilities. At the same time, you want to demonstrate your own commitment to reducing safety and health hazards and protecting your workforce. How do you walk this fine line?

- Put a complete safety and health program in place.
- Hold your managers and supervisors strictly accountable.

[1]Excerpts from OSHA's undated, unpublished manual, *Managing Worker Safety and Health*.

- Encourage employees to use the routine systems afforded to them by the safety and health program.
- Forge a partnership with your managers and supervisors that encourages employees to speak out and use the systems.

COMPLETE SAFETY AND HEALTH PROGRAM

Each of the methods you use to improve workplace safety and health protection will work even better if complemented by the other techniques of good management.... [A] functioning program is the sum of all those parts. Therefore, it would be a mistake to allow managers to pick and choose, using some program parts and not the rest.

... In providing a complete safety and health program, you give your entire workforce—managers, supervisors, and rank and file employees—the tools they need to work with you in keeping the worksite safe and healthful. A complete program addresses the needs and responsibilities of all employees.

ACCOUNTABILITY

Managers and supervisors held accountable for their safety and health responsibilities are more likely to press for solutions to safety and health problems than to present barriers to problem resolution. They are more likely to suggest new ideas for hazard prevention and control than to oppose new ideas. By holding your managers and supervisors accountable, you encourage their positive involvement in the safety and health program. Your own involvement is then less likely to undercut or threaten their authority....

ENCOURAGING THE USE OF PROGRAM SYSTEMS

You have a full program in place, and you are holding your managers and supervisors accountable for carrying out their responsibilities. The next step is to encourage the rest of your workforce to use the systems built into the program and to do their part.

Encourage employees to take full advantage of opportunities—to become involved in problem identification, problem solving, and hazard reporting. Then, when they do become involved, make sure they get appropriate and timely management feedback, including recognition and reward.

When your program's systems are working well, most safety and health problems will be resolved before your employees feel the need to approach you directly. Big problems may arise, however, that the normal systems cannot handle. Your supervisors probably will understand that these problems are not a reflection on them, and that you are the proper person to address these concerns.

What should you do when an employee brings a problem or suggestion to your attention? Listen carefully! Then tactfully ask what attempts have been made already to solve the problem or submit the suggestion. In other words, what systems—safety and health program mechanisms—have already been used?

Perhaps the employee will respond that he or she has spoken with the supervisor but has gotten no action. This may indicate a problem within your program. Although unlikely, the problem may be a supervisor who genuinely does not care about having a safe or healthful workplace. Rather than approach this situation as a personal matter involving this particular supervisor, focus on how the system is not working. Maybe the supervisor did not understand the issue raised by the employee or could not explain to the employee why no action was necessary. Make clear to the supervisor's manager that you want the problem within the system to be resolved. If the supervisor's attitude is at least part of the problem, give the supervisor and his/her manager a chance to work it out. It is not a good idea to confront the supervisor based on one incident.

Obviously, if your accountability system is going to work, any individual who continues to present barriers to effective safety and health management will have to be held accountable. It is important, however, to try to separate any accountability activity from your immediate response to employee-raised questions, concerns, or suggestions.

Remember, too, that your safety and health systems not only encourage employee involvement in identifying hazards and resolving problems, but also protect those employees from retaliatory and discriminatory actions, including unofficial harassment.

FORGING A PARTNERSHIP

Make sure your supervisors know you understand that not every safety or health problem can be solved at the supervisory level. Call upon your managers and supervisors to help make the employee input systems work. Think of your work units—crews, departments—as teams striving to identify and solve problems through whatever system mechanisms are needed. Your managers and supervisors are the team leaders, working together with you and the other players toward a common goal.

You may wish to reward or otherwise recognize the teams that are most successful at reporting hazards or suggesting new hazard control ideas. Recognition can be based on the number of reports and suggestions or on the quality of employee input. Let your managers and supervisors know that when an employee brings a safety or health matter to your attention, you consider that a good reflection of the supervisor's leadership.

Index

Accessibility of top management, 145–48
Accident/incident investigations, 264–69
  definitions of, 265–66
  results, 267–69
  who should investigate, 266–67
Accident investigation committees, 105, 266–67
Accidents, definitions of, 265
Accountability systems, 79–87, 224–33
  formal, 84–87
    disciplinary systems, 85–86
    informal accountability negating, 82
    performance evaluation, 84–85
    positive reinforcement, 86–87, 225–31
  foundations for, 80–81
  informal, 81–84
    countering negative, 83
    as form of no accountability, 82–83
    negating formal accountability, 82
    positive, 83–84
  key points, 87

managers and supervisors and, 140, 179, 368
positive reinforcement and, 225–31
prescribed behavior enforcement and, 231–33
Active intervention by top manager, 142–44
Activities, evaluation of, 104–5
Administrative controls, 223–24
Adult education. *See* Training
Allied Signal (Kansas City Division), 261, 288, 311
American Society of Safety Engineers (ASSE), 21
Amerson, Ron, 20
Analysis
  change, 201–6
  failure mode and effect, 209, 210
  hazard flow charts, 101, 271, 363–66
  of hazards. *See* Hazard inventory
  human resource change, 204–5
  of jobs, 206–7
  phase hazard, 210–12
  of processes, 207–10
Andrews, Jim, 64

Application, VPP, 337–38
Approval, VPP, 12–13, 90–91, 340
Arrowhead Mountain Spring Water
    Company (California), 228
Assessing program effectiveness,
    343–62
Assignment of responsibilities, 63–77
    accountability for, 80
    basic ongoing, 65–72
    communication of, 76
    ensuring appropriate authority and
        resources, 73–75
    key points, 76–77
    short-term, 72–73
Atmosphere for employee involve-
    ment, 126–29
Attitude towards safety, written policy
    and, 35–37, 39–40
Auditing. *See also* Documentation;
    Evaluation
    evaluation versus, 93–94
Authority
    employee safety culture and, 128
    for meeting responsibilities, 73–74, 75
    of top management, 139–40
Awareness programs, 325–26

Barriers to hazards, 218
Barror, Randy, 159–60, 168
Baseline, establishing, 52
Baseline comprehensive surveys, 198
Bell Atlantic, 37
Benchmark technique, 163–65
Bid process, 151–52
Birthday meals, 148
Brant, Robert, 174, 223
Bridges, William, 204
Burns, Robert K., 52
Bypass (or split level) meetings,
    147–48

Casali, Sherry, 223
Case studies, as training method, 292
Change analysis, 201–6
    building or leasing facilities, 202
    installing new equipment, 202–3
    introducing new materials, 203
    multiple changes, 206
    people changes, 204–5
    starting new processes, 204
Cheeseman, John, 283
Chemical/petroleum industries, 17, 150
Cherokee Sanford Group (North Car-
    olina), 228
Close contact of line workers, 120

Committees. *See also* Safety and health
    committees
    accident investigation, 105, 266–67
Communication
    of assignment of safety and health
        responsibilities, 76
    of objectives of program, 60–61
    of overall goal, 47–48
    of written safety policy, 38–40
Complaints, 259
Compliance inspections by OSHA, 19
Comprehensive surveys, 197–200
    appropriate surveyors for, 200
    frequency of, 199–200
    scope of, 198–99
Conferences
    as training method, 291–92
    VPPPA, 19, 20, 164–65
Conflict management, 245
Consultant firms used for evalua-
    tions, 98
Contracting companies, 150–53,
    184–85
Control of hazards. *See* Hazard pre-
    vention and control
Counseling services, 182–83
Courses. *See also* Training
    ongoing safety and health, 311–12
    professional development, 162–63

Data trending, 169–70
Deckelman, Leroy, 167, 171
De Costa, Ken, 21
DeLorenzo, David, 211
Demonstration program, 13–14
Demonstration site, 13–14
Descriptive goals, 46–47
Disciplinary systems, 85–86, 231–33
Dismissal by contracting compa-
    nies, 153
Documentation, 344–45
    hazard correction tracking and,
        237–39
    hazard reports from employees,
        263–64
    review of, site self-evaluation and,
        100–101
DOE VPP, 14–15
Dow Chemical Company, 37, 152
Dow Magnesium Extrusion plant
    (Denver), 233
Downsizing, 204, 331
Drama, as training technique, 296–97
Drills, 312–22
    emergency, 313–15

for unplanned events, 247–48,
  315–22
  debriefing, 321
  guide, 317–20
  monitors, 320–21
  records, 321–22
  scenarios, 315–17

Education. *See* Training
Emergencies
  drills for, 313–15
  planning for, 241–46
  practice for, 246, 285–86
Emissions inventory, 197
Employee assistance professionals,
  182–83
Employees. *See also* Line employee involvement
  accident/incident investigations,
    264–69
  assignment of ongoing responsibili-
    ties to, 70–71
  change analysis and, 204–5
  communicating safety policy to,
    38–40
  contracted, 150–53, 184–85
  disciplinary systems, 85–86
  hourly and non-exempt, 13, 19, 55,
    82–83, 85, 98, 99, 113, 125, 127,
    133, 154, 155, 159, 166, 173
  interviews, 101, 345
  job orientation, 308–10
  morale of, 19, 145, 155
  participation, 52, 177
  performance evaluation, 84–85
  positive reinforcement, 86–87,
    225–31
  professional coaching of, 167–70
  reports of hazards by, 257–64
    documentation, 263–64
    encouraging to report, 261–62
    protection from reprisals, 264
    response to, 262–63
    systems used, 258–61
  sense of ownership of company, 71,
    122, 131–34
  surveys of, site evaluation and, 102
  violent behavior by, 182, 244–45
Enclosure of hazards, 218
Energy, Department of (DOE), 14–15,
  20–21, 248
Enforcement, 5, 231–33
  formal accountability and, 85–86
Engineering, 71, 184
Engineering design controls, 216–18, 219

Environmental Leadership Program, 21
Environmental staff professionals, 181
Ergonomic hazards, 124, 159, 181, 199,
  249, 309
Escaped hazards, examples of, 31
Evacuation drills, 313, 314
"Evaluating Your Safety and Health
  Program" (unpublished OSHA
  manual), 93, 97–99, 100, 103–4,
  142, 147, 180, 201, 253, 255, 284–85
Evaluation(s)
  of employees, 84–85
  by professional experts, 169–70
  of program, 89–108
    audits versus, 93–94
    benefits of, 91–92
    choosing evaluators, 97–99
    information-gathering tools for,
      99–103
    judgments, 103–5
    key points, 107–8
    ongoing evaluations, 102–3
    ongoing objectives, 95–97
    scope of, 97
    shortcomings of, 92
    short-term objectives, 94–95
    uses of, 105–7
    VPP annual program require-
      ment for, 90–91
    written, 105
  team, 97–99, 102
  of training, 301–3
Example-setting by top management,
  148–49
Excellence, as concept of VPP, 9–10
Experience modifier rate (EMR), 151
Expertise of evaluation team, 98
Experts, safety and health. *See* Profes-
  sional experts
Expressions of power by line employ-
  ees, 121–22
Extraordinary events. *See* Unplanned
  events

Failure mode and effect analysis
  (FMEA), 209, 210
Fall protection equipment, 222–23
Fault-tree analysis, 209, 210
Federal Register, 8, 166
Feedback, training and, 301–2
First-line supervisors, 175
  assignment of ongoing responsibili-
    ties to, 69–70
Flow charts, hazard analysis, 101, 271,
  363–66

Ford New Holland plant (Grand Island, Nebraska), 30, 123
Formal accountability systems, 84–87, 179, 183
  disciplinary systems, 85–86
  informal accountability negating, 82
  performance evaluation, 84–85
  positive reinforcement, 86–87, 225–31
Formal active intervention by top manager, 144
Foundation for employee involvement, 126
Future quality of safety excellence, 332–33

Geller, Scott, 226–27
General housekeeping rules, 220
General orientation to job, 308–9
General workplace rules, 219–20, 244
Goals. *See also* Overall goal of program
  descriptive versus numerical, 44–47
Goldberg, Allan, 232
Government regulations, 166
Grand Canyon National Park, 211
Gray Tool, 325–26
Grice, Jon, 117, 183
Guidelines, OSHA. *See* Voluntary guidelines, OSHA

Handbooks, employee, 38
Handouts, as training technique, 300–301
Hansen, Larry, 29–30
Hartshorn, Daniel, 226–27
Hazard(s)
  getting away from controls, 253–73
    accident/incident investigations, 264–69
    employee reports of hazards, 257–64
    key points, 271–72
    routine general inspections, 254–57
    trend analysis, 269–71
  root causes of, 70, 268, 345–46
Hazard analysis
  flow charts, 101, 271, 363–66
  job (JHA), 206–7, 220, 221
  phase, 210–12
  process (PHA), 207–10
Hazard control failures, 246
Hazard controls. *See* Hazard prevention and control

Hazard correction tracking systems, 237–39
Hazard inventory, 192, 194, 195–214
  change analysis, 201–6
  comprehensive surveys, 197–200
  job safety analysis, 206–7
  key points, 212–14
  phase hazard analysis, 210–12
  process hazard analysis, 207–10
Hazard prevention and control, 30–31, 192–93, 194, 215–52
  administrative controls, 223–24
  engineering the control, 216–18
  hazard correction tracking, 237–39
  key points, 233–34, 250–51
  medical program, 248–50
  personal protective equipment, 221–23
  preventive maintenance, 239–41
  role of accountability systems in, 224–33
  unplanned event preparedness, 241–48
  work practices, 218–21
Hazard trend analysis, 271
Health policy. *See* Written policy
Health professionals. *See* Professional experts
Health training. *See* Training
Hercules, Inc., 229
Hot lines, 261
Hourly and non-exempt employees, 13, 19, 55, 82–83, 85, 98, 99, 113, 125, 127, 133, 154, 155, 159, 166, 173
Housekeeping rules, 220
Human disasters, 243–45
Human resource change analysis, 204–5
Human resource professionals, 72, 183–84
Humor as training technique, 298–99
Huselid, Mark, 123

ICF Kaiser Hanford, 120, 312
Idaho Springs Monsanto plant, 98
Illnesses. *See* Injuries and illnesses
Incentive programs, 225–29
Incident investigations. *See* Accident/incident investigations
Incidents, definitions of, 265
Industrial hygiene (IH) monitoring, 27, 124, 131, 159
Industry participants, VPP, 17, 18
Informal accountability systems, 81–84, 179
  countering negative, 83

as form of no accountability, 82–83
  negating formal accountability, 82
  positive, 83–84
Informal active intervention, 142–43
Information-gathering tools, for evaluations, 99–103
Injuries and illnesses, 248
  diagnosis of, 249–50
  limitation of harm, 250
  predicted by industry averages versus, 4, 28
  prevention of, 249
  rate goals, problems with, 45–46
Injury/illness trend analysis, 270–71, 356–57
Inspection exemption, 6–8
Inspections
  by line employees, 132
  OSHA, 99–100
  reports, 257
  routine general, 254–57
    frequency of, 255–56
    who should inspect, 256–57
    written documentation, 257
Institute for Safety Through Design, 216
Interviews, employee, 101, 345
Inventory of hazards. *See* Hazard inventory
Investigations. *See* Accident/incident investigations

Job hazard analysis (JHA), 206–7, 220, 221
Job orientation, 308–10
Job safety analysis (JSA), 206–7, 220, 221
Job safety hazard analysis (JSHA), 206–7, 220, 221
Johnston, Jeff, 167
Joint labor management safety committees, 118, 129–30
Judgments, evaluation, 103–5

Kahn, Paul, 145, 146
Keen, Peter, 94, 333
Kincaid, William, 263
Kinney, Joe, 245
Krause, Thomas, 226–30

Labor relations professionals, 183–84
Learning ownership, 279–81, 307–28, 329–30. *See also* Training
Leasing facilities, change analysis of, 202
Lectures, as training method, 290–91
Legal concerns of employee safety involvement, 129–31
Lick, Hank, 216–17

Limitation of harm, 250
Line employee involvement, 117–35
  achieving ownership, 131–34
  benefits of, 119–23
  key points, 134–35
  legal concerns, 129–31
  safety culture, 125–29
    clear expectations, 127–28
    on company time, 127
    part of the job, 127
    resources and authority, 128
    suggestions and recommendations, 128–29
  ways to involve workers, 123–25
Line employees. *See also* Line employee involvement
  inspections, 256
  job orientation, 308–10
  relationship between managers and, 153–55
  requests for maintenance repairs, 260
Line managers, 66, 138, 141, 161, 174–79
  encouragement of, 178–79
  full participation by, 176–77
  leadership role activities, 176–77
  management support of, 177–78
  professional expertise coaching of, 167–70
  resources for, 178
  responsibility for safety of, 64
  systematic accountability, 179
Lippy, Bruce, 284, 288
Livingston, Dennis, 284, 288

McCormack, Adele, 300
McCorquodale, Robert, 226–30
McGehee, W., 283, 286
Maintenance
  assignment of ongoing responsibilities to, 72
  preventive, 239–41
  requests, 260
Management. *See also* Line managers; Middle managers; Supervisors; Top managers
  involvement in worker safety and health. *See* Total involvement concept
  loop, 27–34
    concept of, 27–28
    evaluation step. *See* Evaluation, of program
    as ongoing and continuous, 109–10
    parts of, 31–33, 110

Management (*continued*)
OSHA voluntary guidelines and, 28–29
zero-defect, 29–31, 109
Managing Worker Safety and Health (OSHA manual), 44
Mansdorf, Zack, 198
Manufacturing category, 17
Marriott, Bill, 145, 153
Material safety data sheet (MSDS), 203
Measurability of objectives, 59–60
Medical professionals, 180–81
Medical program, 248–50
Meetings
bypass (split level), 147–48
safety, 38, 323–25
Megan, Graydon, 240
Mentoring program, 20
Merit program, 12–13
Merit sites, 12, 340
approval, 12–13
Middle managers. *See also* Line managers
assignment of ongoing responsibilities to, 68–69
authority and resources for, 140
Milliken, Roger, 93
Minimization of harm, 250
Minter, Stephen, 226
Mobil Chemical Company, 202, 245, 287, 297
Flexible Packaging Plant (Temple, Texas), 37, 125
Mobil Oil Corporation, 19, 47, 92, 155–56
Montante, William, 302, 303

National Labor Relations Act, 184
National Labor Relations Board, 129–30
National Safety Council (NSC), 21, 30, 216, 245
National Safe Workplace Institute, 245
Natural disasters, 242
Near misses, 266
definitions of, 265
New equipment, 202–3
New facilities, 202
New materials, 203
New processes, 204
Non-exempt salaried workers. *See* Hourly and non-exempt employees
Non-union worksites, 17, 114, 115, 130
Numerical goals, 45–46
Nurses, 133, 180, 249–50

Objectives of program, 43, 51–62. *See also* Overall goal of program
communication of, 60–61
ensuring clear, measurable, 58–60, 95
establishing a baseline, 52
evaluation of, 94–97
key points, 61
ongoing, 54–56
evaluation of, 95–97
short-term, 56–60
determining, 56–57
evaluation of, 94–95, 107
examples of formal, 58
quick fixes versus, 57
timelines for, 57
short-term responsibilities and, 72–73
types of, 54–58
Occupational health delivery system (ODS), 248–50
Occupational health professionals, 180–81
Occupational Safety and Health Act (OSHAct), 5
Section 5(a)(1), 10
Section 18(b), 14–15
Occupational Safety and Health Administration (OSHA)
background of, 5–8
Consultation Programs, 163
future of VPP and, 21–22
voluntary guidelines. *See* Voluntary guidelines, OSHA
VPP benefits to, 19
Oklahoma AT&T Network Systems site, 20
Ongoing evaluations, 102–3
Ongoing responsibilities, 65–72
Onsite visits, VPP, 338–40
Open-door policy by top management, 146–47
Operations (unplanned events) drills, 247–48, 315–22
debriefing, 321
guide, 317–20
monitors, 320–21
records, 321–22
scenarios, 315–17
Organizational culture
accountability and, 80–81
employee safety involvement and, 125–29
Orientation to job, 308–10
Outsourcing, 332
Overall goal of program, 43–50
communication of, 47–48

descriptive versus numerical goals, 44–47
developing or revising, 48
key points, 48–49
objectives and, 43, 52
purpose of, 44
Oversight for contracting companies, 152–53

Pantex Plant (Amarillo, Texas), 102, 199–200
Pater, Robert, 269
Pattern analysis, 270–71, 356–57
Peltier, Mike, 245
Performance appraisals, 231
Perry Equipment Company (Texas), 228
Personal protective equipment (PPE), 221–23
Petersen, Dan, 27–28, 36, 230, 264–65, 267, 286
Petrino, Richard, 63
Phase hazard analysis, 210–12
Physicians, 133, 180, 249–50
Pinch point on machinery, 31
Policy statement. *See* Written policy
Positive feedback, 230–31
Positive informal accountability, 83–84
Positive reinforcement, 86–87, 225–31
accountability systems, 231
incentive programs, 225–29
positive feedback, 230–31
Posters, employee, 38
Potential hazards inventory. *See* Hazard inventory
Potlatch plant (Lewiston, Idaho), 99
Power expressions by line employees, 121–22
PPG (Lake Charles, Louisiana), 228–29
Practice
after job orientation, 310
as training method, 295
Pre-bid process, 151–52
Prescribed behavior, enforcement of, 231–33
Prevention
of hazards. *See* Hazard prevention and control
of occupational illness or injury, 249
Preventive maintenance, 239–41
Problem solvers, line employee's as, 120–21
Process hazard analysis (PHA), 207–10
procedures, 209–10
who should perform, 208–9
Process safety standard, 204, 208, 210

Production line employee involvement. *See* Line employee involvement
Professional development courses, 162–63
Professional experts, 133, 141, 159–72, 332
acting as conscience of safety and health program, 170–71
coaching line managers and employees, 167–70
for comprehensive surveys, 200
continuous evaluation by, 169–70
employee access to, 133
employee assistance, 182–83
environmental staff, 181
establishing the vision, 166–67
human resource, 183–84
key points, 171–72
maintenance of expertise, 161–66
benchmarking, 163–65
continuing development, 161–63
tracking regulations, 166
occupational health, 180–81
Professional organizations, 163, 165, 166
Program goal. *See* Overall goal of program
Program objectives. *See* Objectives, program
Program systems, 369
Purchasing, assignment of ongoing responsibilities to, 72

Qualitative risk assessment, 203
Quantitative measurement of safety goals, 45–46

Recommendations by employees, 128–29
Refresher training, 323–24
Regulations, 166
Reinforcement, 86–87, 225–31
accountability systems, 231
incentive programs, 225–29
positive feedback, 230–31
of safety policy, 39
Report of hazard forms, 259
Reprisals, employee protection from, 258, 264
Resources
employee safety culture and, 128
for line managers, 178
for meeting responsibilities, 73–74
for top management, 139–40
Responsibilities, assignment of. *See* Assignment of responsibilities

Rewards, as training technique, 299–300
Richardson, Jim, 233
Role playing, as training method, 292–94
Root causes of hazards, 70, 268, 345–46
Routine general inspections, 254–57
  frequency of, 255–56
  who should inspect, 256–57
  written documentation, 257
Rules, 219–20, 220, 244
Rule violation correction, 149

Safety and health committees, 38
  employees reporting to, 260
  inspection objectives, 55–56
  joint labor-management, 118, 129–30
Safety and health manager, 67–68
Safety and health policy. *See* Written policy
Safety and health professionals. *See* Professional experts
Safety and health program evaluation. *See* Evaluation, of program
Safety and health team, 166–67, 173–86
Safety and health training. *See* Training
Safety culture for employee involvement, 125–29
Safety Day, 104
Safety incentive programs, 225–29
Safety meetings, 38, 323–25
Sandonato, Joe, 182
Schwab, Patt, 298–99
Schweitzer, Albert, 148
Security personnel, 181–82
Sherrill, Leigh, 93
Short-term objectives, 56–60
  determining, 56–57
  evaluation of, 94–95, 107
  examples of formal, 58
  quick fixes versus, 57
  timelines for, 57
Short-term responsibilities, 72–73, 75
Siegel, Robert, 163–64
Simms, Mike, 30
Site lost workday experience, VPP, 3–5, 28
Site manager, communicating safety policy, 38
Sites. *See also* Merit sites; Star sites
  conditions and root causes, 70, 268, 345–47
  evaluation of conditions at, 101–2
  inspection exemption and, 6–8
  makeup of, 17
  medical programs at, 248–50

non-union, 17, 114, 115, 130
  number of, 6, 7
  OSHA inspections, 99–100
  union, 17, 114, 130, 133
  VPP onsite visit, 338–40
Smith, S. L., 227
Society of Human Resource Management, 331
Spencer, Howard, 219
Spigener, Jim, 227
Split level meetings, 147–48
Staff professionals, 180–84
Stalnaker, C. Keith, 315, 321
Standard operating procedures (SOPs), 220–21
  JSAs combined with, 207
Standards setting by OSHA, 5
Star approval, 90–91, 340
Star program, 11–12, 15
Star sites, 8, 11–12, 14, 340
State VPP programs, 14–15, 20
Strain, Roger, 166, 167, 169–70, 239, 267–68
Stress reduction services, 183
Student teaching, 294–95
Subordinate managers
  accountability of, 140
  authority and resources for, 139–40
Suggestion programs, 259
Supervisors
  assignment of ongoing responsibilities to, 69–70
  authority and resources for, 140
  employee reports to, 258–59
  first-line, 175
    assignment of ongoing responsibilities to, 69–70
Surveys. *See* Comprehensive surveys
Suspension, 233
Systems approaches, 191–94, 275–76
  hazard inventory, 195–214
  hazard prevention and control, 215–73
  OSHA guidelines and, 192–94
  VPP and, 191–92

Telephone systems, for reporting hazards, 261
Terrorist acts, 243–44
Texaco Chemical Company (Port Arthur, Texas), 240–41, 242
Thayer, P., 283, 286
Thomen, James, 268
Thompson, Horace, 130
Topf, Michael, 63

Top managers, 174
  responsibilities of
    assignment of, 66–67
    authority and resources for,
      130–40
    demonstration of personal prior-
      ity, 141
    holding subordinate managers
      accountable, 140
    setting priorities for, 139
    use of professional expertise, 141
  support of line managers, 177–78
  visible leadership by. *See* Visible
    leadership of top managers
  walking the fine line, 367–69
Total involvement concept, 113–16,
  187–88
  line employee ownership and,
    117–35
  OSHA guidelines and, 115–16
  safety and health professionals and,
    159–72
  safety and health team and, 173–86
  top manager's visibility and, 137–58
  VPP and, 114–15
Total Quality Management (TQM), 45
Tracking systems
  hazard correction, 237–39
  types of, 239
Trade associations, 163, 165, 166
Trade literature, 163, 165
Training, 5–6, 224–25, 279–81, 283–306,
  307–28
  determining objectives, 284–86
  drills, 247–48, 312–22
  evaluation of, 301–3
  how people learn, 286–88
  job orientation, 308–10
  key points, 303–4, 326–28
  line employees, 131
  methods used, 288, 290–96
    case studies, 292
    conferences, 291–92
    lectures, 290–91
    practice, 295
    role playing, 292–94
    student teaching, 294–95
  ongoing safety and health, 311–12
  role of, in OSHA voluntary guide-
    lines, 280–81
  role of, in VPP requirements, 280
  safety meetings, 38, 323–25
  supplements, 325–26
  techniques, 296–301
    drama, 296–98
    handouts, 300–301

  humor, 298–99
  rewarding contributors, 299–300
  visual and aural interest, 300
Training room, setup of, 301
Trend analyses, 249–50, 254, 269–71
Two-way communication, involving
  employees in, 326
Tye, James, 221

Uncontrolled hazards, short-term objectives for, 56–57
Unionized worksites, 17, 114, 130, 133
Unplanned events, 241–48
  drills for. *See* Operations drills

Ventilation system, 218, 254
Verifiability of objectives, 59–60
Vinson, Jim, 222
Violence, workplace, 182, 244–45
Visible leadership of top managers,
  137–58
  benefits of, 153–56
    improved employee morale, 155
    increased information, 154
    reduced injuries and illness,
      155–56
  key points, 153–54
  methods for, 142–53
    accessibility, 145–48
    active safety and health interven-
      tion, 142–44
    being an example, 148–50
    for contract employees, 150–53
  safety and health responsibilities of,
    138–41
Vision of the goal, 46–47, 48. *See also*
  Overall goal of program
Visitor screenings, 182
Voluntary guidelines, OSHA, 28–29,
  115–16
  accountability and, 79–80, 85
  assignment of safety and health re-
    sponsibilities and, 64–66, 73–74
  authority and resources and, 73–74
  comprehensive surveys and, 197
  employee involvement and, 117–19
  evaluation and, 89–90
  goals of program and, 43, 44, 46–47
  hazard inventory and, 194, 196–97
  objectives of program and, 51, 52,
    53–54
  safety and health policy and, 36, 37
  systems approach concept and,
    192–94
  top management and, 137–38
  training and, 280–81

Voluntary Protection Programs (VPP)
    background of, 5–6
    benefits from, 17, 19
    "command-and-control" regulation
        of, 3
    concepts of, 9–10
    future of, 21–22
    growth of, 6, 7
    participants, 15–17, 18
    process, 337–41
        after approval, 340
        application, 337–38
        approval decisions, 340
        onsite visit, 338–40
        purpose of, 8–9
        site lost workday experience, 3–5, 28
        three programs of, 11–14
VPP Participants' Association
    (VPPPA), 19, 20–21, 164–65

Wainwright Industries (Missouri), 30
Watkins, Conrad, 98
Watson, Paris, 153
Westinghouse's Waste Isolation Pilot
    Plant (New Mexico), 312
What-if analysis, 209–10

Whittier, Diane, 44
Wolf, Ken, 242
Workers. *See* Employees
Workers' compensation costs, 30, 155
Work practices, 218–21
Worksite analysis, 192, 193. *See also*
    Hazard inventory
Worksite responsibilities, as concept of
    VPP, 10
Worksites. *See* Sites
Wortham, Sarah, 183
Written evaluations, 106
Written policy, 35–41
    attitude of, 35–37, 39–40
    communication of, 38–40
    developing or revising, 40
    key points of, 40–41
    length of, 36–37
    purpose of, 35–36
Written reports of general inspec-
    tions, 257
Written statements of responsibilities,
    65–66, 74, 76

Zero-defect management, 29–31, 109
Zero tolerance policy, 244–45